Contrary Investing for the '90s

Contrary Investing
for the '90s

How to Profit
by Going Against
the Crowd

by Richard E. Band

St. Martin's Press
New York

To Clarissa, Georgina and Priscilla,
three independent thinkers

Library of Congress Cataloging-in-Publication Data

Band, Richard E.
     Contrary investing for the '90s : how to profit by
going against the crowd / Richard E. Band.
         p.   cm.
    ISBN 0-312-03804-6
    1. Investments—Handbooks, manuals, etc. 2.
Speculation—Handbooks, manuals, etc. I. Title.
   HG4527.B2328 1990
   332.6'78—dc20   89-24138
                                         CIP

First published in The United States by Alexandria
House Books.

Contents

1.	The Billionaire's Secret	1
2.	The Making of a Mania	17
3.	I Saw It in *The New York Times*	37
4.	Roll Out the Polls	57
5.	Stock Market Timing	75
6.	The Feeling Is Mutual	95
7.	Bargains in the Wall Street Doghouse	111
8.	The Crash and Beyond	129
9.	The Income Investor Fights Back	147
10.	High Yields with a Hedge	171
11.	If Inflation Roars Again	183
12.	More Bang for the Buck	203
13.	Be Your Own Person, Virginia	223
Epilogue	It Pays to Be Contrary	239
	Resources	245
	Notes	249
	Index	253

Graphs

1. *Fortune* Cover 43
2. Bearish Sentiment Index 59
3. Advisory Service Sentiment 61
4. The Gold Bulls 65
5. Bullish Consensus Meter 69
6. Insider Indicator and S&P 500 83
7. *Barron's* Market and Volume Reports 85
8. Member-Short Ratio 86
9. CBOE Put/Call Ratio 89
10. Mutual Funds' Cash Position
   vs. Market Movement 91
11. Wall Street Week Index 100
12. Standard & Poor's 500
   Price/Earnings Ratio 102
13. Standard & Poor's 500
   Price/Dividend Ratio 103
14. P/D Ratio Asset Allocation Gains 106
15. New Horizons P/E Relative
   to S&P 500 113
16. Relative Strength, Value Line vs. Dow 115
17. Total Return, All NYSE Common Stocks 119
18. 90-Day CD Rates 133
19. M1 Growth Rate 134
20. Debt-to-GNP: 1920-1988 136
21. Federal Spending 139
22. 12-Month Growth Rate Total Debt 141
23. Real T-Bond Yield 149
24. Corporate Interest Expense 152
25. Interest Paid on Debt 153
26. Yuppie/Nerd Ratio 155
27. The Social Security Surplus 157
28. Corporate Bond Yields (1789-1987) 158
29. The Quality Ratio 163
30. Relative Yield, S&P Electrics vs. Industrials 174
31. Relative P/E, S&P Electrics vs. Industrials 175
32. Comex Gold Put/Call Ratio 186
33. Central Fund Premium/Discount 191
34. Dollar Cartoon 196
35. Change in the Price of Gold 218
36. Gold: 14-Day Stochastic 220

Acknowledgments

A book is the product of many hands, and I cheerfully acknowledge my debt to those who had a hand in this second edition of *Contrary Investing*. First of all, I wish to thank my former boss at KCI Communications, Allie P. Ash, who encouraged me to undertake the revision, and Leon Rubis, executive editor at KCI, who pressed me to complete it. Bernard Jankowski, my copy editor, patiently smoothed out lumps in the text while Kathy Raines and Robin Croft in the KCI art department painstakingly prepared the charts and graphs. Debbie Miller, my freelance secretary, devoted many hours to typing the rough draft.

Critics, both friendly and unfriendly, of the first edition deserve credit for spurring me to make the current volume more complete and more accurate. You know who you are!

Finally, I must express my gratitude to my family—in particular, my wife Enid and three daughters, Clarissa, Georgina and Priscilla—for their support and understanding throughout the many hours when, chained to my computer, I was, as the French say, *invisible*.

Chapter 1

The Billionaire's Secret

Buy when everyone else is selling, and hold until everyone else is buying. This is more than just a catchy slogan. It is the very essence of successful investment. — J. Paul Getty, *How to Be Rich*

Oil tycoon J. Paul Getty was probably the wealthiest man who ever lived. When he died in 1976 at the age of 83, Getty presided over a business empire that embraced nearly 200 companies, with Getty Oil Co. the crown jewel. He owned an elegant Tudor mansion in southern England and had amassed one of the world's great art collections. His personal fortune was worth an estimated $3 billion.

Was Getty just lucky, or did he know something the rest of us don't? In his autobiography, *How to Be Rich,* he conceded that being in the right place at the right time certainly helped. But, like all great entrepreneurs, Getty also understood the power of contrary thinking. Early on, he discovered what I call "the billionaire's secret": *If you want to make money—the big money—do what nobody else is doing.* Find the niches that nobody else is filling. Look for overlooked opportunities. In baseball parlance, "Hit 'em where they ain't."

J. Paul Getty knew that you can often snare the best profits by putting capital into ventures that most investors either haven't heard of yet or are too afraid to touch. During the 1930s, for example, Getty snapped up choice oil properties in the Middle East for rock-bottom prices while conventional thinkers were wringing their hands over the possibility that the Great Depression might drag on for decades. Where others perceived nothing but headaches, Getty heard cash registers ringing.

The best opportunities, in other words, are often found in places where the prevailing wisdom sees none. Successful business founders grasp this principle almost by instinct. A hundred years ago, railroad financier Russell Sage summed up his formula for accumulating wealth as "buying straw hats in January." Straw hats, of course, are meant to be worn in July, not January. But the far-seeing entrepreneur buys them early, when they're cheap and easy to acquire. Never mind the taunts of those who, while the snowflakes are flying, find it hard to imagine that summer will ever come.

The history of free enterprise brims with examples of mavericks who made names—and fortunes—for themselves by defying the climate of opinion. Take Alexander Graham Bell. Upon inspecting Bell's spanking-new contraption, the telephone, in 1876, President Rutherford B. Hayes is said to have remarked: "That's an amazing invention, but who would ever want to use one of them?" Happily for the world, Bell had a broader and longer vision than his naysayers—and it made him rich.

Or consider a case still fresh in the memories of many readers of this book: in the mid-1970s, observers of the computer industry confidently predicted that it would take a long time—maybe 10 or 15 years—before a mass market would open up for personal computers. The existing machines were too costly for retail merchandising and required college-level training in computer science to operate.

As recently as 1977, the president of a large computer company flatly stated: "There is no reason for any individual to have a computer in their [sic] home." But then, one fledgling outfit, Apple Computer, challenged the consensus. Founded by a 21-year-old engineering whiz kid, Steven Jobs, literally in his garage, Apple turned out a series of low-cost, "user friendly" microcomputers that almost anyone with a grade-school education could learn to operate. In 15 years, the company has grown from nothing to $4 billion in annual sales. Meanwhile, a host of competitors—from IBM to the Japanese electronic giants—have cultivated a burgeoning mass market for personal computers.

Think for Yourself

Contrary thinking is the art of thinking for yourself against the pressures of the crowd. The contrary investor, like J. Paul Getty, buys assets that others are rushing to sell, and sells assets that others are clamoring to buy. He isn't trying to be ornery or eccentric; he merely recognizes that if nobody wants something, it's likely to be cheap. If everybody wants it, it's likely to be dear. Contrary thinking is probably the simplest, sanest and most reliable technique that has ever been devised to buy low and sell high— for maximum profit. In fact, I would argue that every successful investor is a contrarian at heart, whether he recognizes it or not.

You can apply a contrary strategy to any investment market, from stocks and bonds to precious metals, commodities, foreign currencies, real estate, collectibles—you name it. As it turns out, however, most of the existing books on contrary investing (only a handful have been written over the past 30 years) focus narrowly on one market, usually the stock market. I take a slightly different tack. In today's volatile economy, I think it's essential to keep your mind open to all markets, even if as a practical matter you can't (and shouldn't try to) participate in all of them. This book will show you how to profit by "going against the crowd" in any market you choose.

Contrary thinking works in any market because human nature is the same everywhere. Most people are followers, not leaders. In the marketplace, they wait to buy until they see other people buying, and they wait to sell until they see other people selling. As a result, most people buy after prices have already risen, and sell after prices have already fallen.

By chasing the crowd, the typical investor loses profits at both ends: he buys too high and sells too low. On the other hand, if you learn to recognize the extremes of crowd psychology, you can go *against* the crowd when signs of a manic top or a panic bottom appear. Of course, I don't promise that you will always (or ever) hit the exact top or bottom; statistically, such a feat is next to impossible. But with a contrary strategy, you can buy closer to the bottom (or sell closer to the top). In short, you can capture a larger share of the profits to be made from any significant market move.

Some of the techniques I describe in this book will appeal primarily to sophisticated investors—the type who enjoy burrowing through *The Wall Street Journal* with calculator in hand. However, I want to stress at the outset that you don't need an advanced degree in economics or finance to practice the art of contrary thinking. As a matter of fact, you can become a successful contrarian simply by reading between the lines of your daily newspaper.

What you do need is the ability to control your emotions and think calmly when almost everyone else in the marketplace is verging on hysteria. More than brains, contrary investing takes self-discipline and an ounce of courage. But these aren't super-human virtues; anybody with an independent streak can learn to be a contrary thinker. In fact, if you've ever been labeled a maverick or a boat rocker, or simply a lone wolf, you may already be a practicing contrarian without even knowing it!

People Make Markets

The theory of contrary opinion, as it's formally called, is based squarely on the fact that *people make markets*. Even in this age of electronic wizardry and program trading, people—not computers—still make the final decision to buy or sell anything, from stocks and bonds to automobiles, brussels sprouts and teddy bears. A market, after all, is merely a collection of *people* buying and selling.

However, there are two sides to every person. You and I are rational human beings. We think, we plan, we calculate. Reason is what enabled the human race to put a man on the moon, splice genes in the laboratory and build Pac-man video games. But we are also emotional creatures who go through moods of hope and despair, confidence and fear, joy and anger, satisfaction and yearning, pride and shame—and a hundred other feelings that only a professional psychologist could begin to catalog.

When a group of people get together to trade stocks, gold or any other investment asset, we create a market that, like us, has a two-sided character, both rational and emotional. The market is rational in the sense that it "sees" (takes notice of) every scrap of information known to investors great or small. The gold market, for example, knows the rate of inflation in every country, the level of interest rates here and abroad, the supply of newly mined metal coming to market, the dimensions of Third World debt crisis (to the extent that anybody really knows) and many other factors that help determine the price of gold. The market is even aware of all the predictions that all the pundits have made about gold. If a fresh piece of information hits the market—say, that Zimbabwe just dropped an atomic bomb on South Africa's largest gold mine—investors will bid the price of gold up or down (most likely up in this case) to reflect the new reality.

The truly liquid investment markets (stocks, bonds, precious metals and commodities) absorb new information amazingly fast. Within minutes after a company releases a bad earnings report, for instance, the price of its stock can plunge 20 or 30 percent. As academics are fond of saying, the stock market, like the gold market or the commodity markets, is an "efficient" (rational) price-setting mechanism. It adjusts prices almost instantaneously to take account of new developments.

However, while the market knows everything that *has* happened, it doesn't know everything that is *going to happen*. The future is uncertain, risky. No individual this side of eternity knows exactly what the economic future will bring, and neither does any group of individuals (the market). In fact, prices change precisely because things happen that the market didn't expect! Surprises make the market go up and down.

The price you pay for an ounce of gold reflects the market's expectations about the future value of gold, based on historical information. But emotion always colors the market's expectations because economic value depends on the subjective opinions of people. Nobody has a scientific formula that proves conclusively what price gold (or anything else) ought to sell for. Some people think the stuff is worth less than sand at the seashore; others wouldn't part with their hoard for $2,000 an ounce.

To a large extent, the current price of any asset depends on how strongly investors *feel* that current supply-and-demand trends will continue. Analyst X may believe, on the basis of his reading of the monetary statistics, that the Federal Reserve is returning to an inflationary policy that will drive up the price of gold. Analyst Y, reading the same statistics, might come to the opposite conclusion.

The statistics don't lie. But X and Y draw different inferences from the numbers because Y puts greater faith than X does in the integrity of the Federal Reserve Board and the willingness of the American political system to accept a clean break with inflation. Both people are drawing on their experience with human behavior to make personal, subjective, profoundly emotional judgments. And their judgments, along with those of thousands of other market participants, shape the price of gold.

The Myopic Market

In the short term, the market's expectations usually come true. The stock market, for example, is considered a "leading" economic indicator because stock prices generally begin to rise several months before the economy pulls out of a recession and start to fall several (sometimes many) months before the economy peaks.

Think back to the summer of 1982. Stock prices had been falling for almost two years when the Dow Jones Industrial Average tumbled to a low of 777 in August 1982. What did the stock market see on the horizon? Despite the consistently rosy forecasts of many professional economists, slumping stock prices were saying that investors expected the economy to weaken. And the market was correct: the recession that began in the fall of 1981 continued to deepen for four months after the stock market hit bottom.

However, for any investor who had the foresight to look beyond the next few months, the Dow at 777 was ridiculously undervalued. The market was right about the short-term outlook for the economy, but *totally wrong* about the longer-term out-

6

look.What the market couldn't see in the summer of 1982 was that the nation's central bank was embarking on an "easy money" policy that would eventually spark the longest peacetime economic upswing in history. Needless to say, the market quickly changed its mind as the shape of the recovery became apparent to most investors. By June 1983, only ten months after the lows, the Dow had soared 61 percent—one of the steepest advances on record.

Every investment market, no matter how rational, suffers from an incurable case of shortsightedness. The long-term bond market is a classic example. For 35 years (1946 to 1981), bond buyers doggedly loaned out their money at interest rates that turned out to be too low to compensate for inflation over the life of the bonds. Had bondholders been able to foresee the rapid inflation that began in the mid-1960s, they would never have allowed the Treasury to borrow their money in 1946 at 2 percent.

Why were bondholders repeatedly fooled? They made the mistake of assuming that inflation and interest rates would remain indefinitely at (or near) the level that prevailed when the bonds were issued. Bond buyers projected existing trends far into the future.

For a while, perhaps even for four or five years, the supposition looked good. Interest rates stayed above the inflation rate, and bondholders earned a real return. But in the long run, the bond buyers' projections proved disastrously wrong. Investors weren't stupid. They simply fell prey to the all-too-human tendency to believe that good times (in this case, low interest rates) will go on forever. Complacency—a weakness of the heart, not the head—clouded their judgment.

The market has a good record for anticipating short-term economic developments, but not for predicting the long term. In fact, the longer the time horizon, the less likely that the market can foresee what will happen with any degree of accuracy. Too many variables—that is to say, too many unpredictable human actions—can intervene to throw the market's assessment off.

Yet, ironically, even though the long run is inherently unpredictable, the market's *long-term* expectations determine the largest part of the price you pay for any investment asset. When you buy a share of IBM for $125, for instance, you're purchasing a claim on the company's assets, earnings and dividends for as long as IBM is in business. Only a small part of your purchase price reflects the company's near-term prospects; most of the $125 is for a piece of the company's growth into the distant future.

But if nobody has the foggiest idea what IBM will be worth in the distant future, how can the market put a rational price on a share of IBM stock? The obvious answer—the answer that academic theoreticians hate to give—is that it can't. Part of the price you pay for a share of IBM is rational and part is psychological (or emotional). The short-term component of the market price is rational because the market knows pretty much what IBM's earnings will look like for the next quarter or two, perhaps even for the next year or two. But the long-term component, which carries by far the greater weight, depends almost entirely on investor psychology.

If investors feel supremely confident about IBM's long-range future, they may bid the price of the stock up to 40 times the current year's earnings, as they did in early 1973. On the other hand, if investors feel discouraged about the company's long-term prospects, they may trade the stock at only eight times current earnings, as in late 1981. Was IBM a worse company in 1981 than in 1973? Not at all. IBM's earnings, dividends and book value had soared in those eight-odd years. (In fact, IBM's profits grew *faster* during that period than in the late 1960s and early 1970s.) But investor psychology had shifted dramatically. Investors had soured on IBM.

The Mood of the Market

Understanding the psychological climate of the marketplace is the key to contrary investing. Just as individuals go through a spectrum of moods, so does the market. (Remember, the market is composed of people!) The contrary investor is really an amateur psychologist who tries to *identify the mood of the market*—and profit from it.

8

When prices are rising, the market's mood turns increasingly optimistic. Investors who bought earlier feel good about their paper profits. New investors, impressed with the track record, decide to buy, believing that the trend will continue. The opposite happens when prices are falling: the market's mood grows increasingly pessimistic. Investors sitting on losses begin to feel gloomy, even desperate. New investors don't dare to touch an investment that has been faltering (even though, at important market turning points, past performance tends to be exactly the reverse of future performance).

Economists and philosophers may argue endlessly over whether the mood of the market changes prices, or whether price changes alter the mood of the market. For the investor, it doesn't really matter. The important thing is that the mood of the market rises (and falls) more or less in step with prices. As prices change, the mood of the market changes.

Most markets—like the economy as a whole—climb in a jagged pattern for several years at a time (primary bull markets), then fall irregularly for another couple of years (primary bear markets). A primary bull market is characterized by rising prices and growing optimism—not every day or every week, of course, but over a period of many weeks and months. Likewise, falling prices and growing pessimism characterize a primary bear market.

A bull market begins to rise in a climate of *fear*. Later, as the market scores additional gains, fear recedes and an attitude of *caution* takes over in most investors' minds. After prices have climbed substantially, investors start to forget the bad old days of the bear market. *Confidence* reigns. Finally, as prices reach a cyclical peak, *euphoria* sweeps the market. At the top, all but a handful of investors are convinced that the market will keep going up indefinitely.

On the way down, the same emotions predominate, but in reverse order: first euphoria, then confidence, then caution, then fear. At the bottom of the bear market, nearly everyone believes that prices will drop even further.

9

Contrary investors follow the maxim: "Buy into extreme weakness and sell into extreme strength." They seek to buy when the market is enveloped in fear—and prices are low. They aim to sell when the market is gushing with euphoria—and prices are high. In between, they sit still and let the market do its work.

Within a primary bull or bear trend, many secondary reactions take place *against* the trend, lasting for a few days, weeks or even months. In the stock market, for example, prices may fall sharply—even during a strong primary uptrend— for three to five weeks at a time. A rally will then usually ensue, followed by another short-term "correction." If a series of short-term corrections carry prices to successively lower lows, market analysts will often describe the entire period of declining prices as an intermediate-term correction in a bull market.

Corrections are necessary to restore the market's psychological balance when the primary trend pushes prices too far, too fast. In a rapidly climbing bull market, investor sentiment can shift from fear to euphoria in two or three months. By the same token, in a plunging bear market, investor psychology may lurch from euphoria to fear in just a few months. At these short-term or intermediate-term extremes, the market typically undergoes a reaction in the opposite direction, which clears away the excessive optimism or pessimism and sets the stage for the primary trend to continue.

Investors with a long-term perspective can use contrary opinion to spot turning points in the primary trend. However, as I will show in subsequent chapters, contrary thinking is also a helpful tool for identifying intermediate-term and even short-term market peaks and bottoms. Whether you consider yourself a long-term investor or a short-term trader, contrary opinion can sharpen your timing and enhance your profits.

The Madding Crowd

If you consistently buy into fear and sell into euphoria (or greed), you'll make money. It sounds easy. But in practice, people seldom do it. When everyone else is afraid that prices are going to crash, we tend to be afraid too. When everyone else is thrilled with the market, the excitement tends to rub off on us too. Most of us don't like to stand alone, clinging to an opinion that nearly everyone else seems to disagree with.

How many dissenters spoke up at the crucifixion of Christ? How many Michigan football fans dare to boo Notre Dame—from a seat in the enemy grandstands? Our most cherished convictions often melt in the heat of a crowd. Yet it's precisely when the pull of the crowd is strongest that the market makes its most dramatic reversals.

If you've ever attended a sporting event, a political rally or some other mob scene, you've seen the herd mentality in action. *Unanimity* and *hysteria* are the telltale marks of a crowd. Given the first condition, the second is seldom far behind.

A fire breaks out in a crowded theater. One thought instantly races through everyone's mind: "I must get out at all costs." A moment later, unanimity breeds panic as everyone realizes that everyone else is thinking the same thing. People say to themselves: "If I let the others go first, I may not get out alive." Although this fear may be completely irrational, everybody rushes for the exits simultaneously. Some are crushed to death in the stampede and, ironically, the hall empties more slowly than it might have—because of the congestion at the doors.

People do things in a crowd that they wouldn't think of doing if they were acting as isolated individuals. When I was a lad, my father used to regale me with stories about his classmates at Harvard who, as part of their initiation into the Hasty Pudding Club (a prestigious senior society), rolled pancakes through the streets of bustling Harvard Square at five o'clock in the afternoon. Callow youth that I was, I couldn't believe that "big kids" behaved that way. But they did, as far as I know, they still do.

Nobody over 35 years of age can forget the Beatlemania of the 1960s, when teenage girls screamed, fainted and broke into convulsions during the rock-and-roll quartet's concerts. A whole generation of men—some of whom didn't especially care for Beatles music—adopted the mop-headed hairstyle made popular by John, Paul, George and Ringo.

Lest you suppose that crowd following is exclusively a youthful frailty, I should remind you how parents lined up for hours at department stores during the Christmas 1983 shopping season to buy Cabbage Patch dolls for their children. What made this particular mania so curious was that the manufacturer designed the dolls to be ugly. People vying for the limited supply of dolls pushed, scratched and bit each other, and one woman reportedly suffered a broken leg. Men as well as women yielded to the hysteria:

MAILMAN FLIES TO LONDON TO BUY FIVE DOLLS.

London (UPI)—*A Kansas City mailman left for home yesterday after a $900, four-hour stop in London to pick up five Cabbage Patch dolls he could not get at home. Edward Pennington, 44, said he came to Britain because his 5-year-old daughter, Leana, was "almost in tears" when Kansas City stores ran out of the dolls—the current rage of the American Christmas shopping season. Supplies of the British-made versions of the doll were available in major London stores, although Britons were snapping them up as soon as they hit the shelves. Pennington said he took $900 from his savings to spend four hours in London on his quest... "(A) lot of my neighbors thought I was crazy to make the trip and spend all this money," he said at Heathrow. "But I was determined to get Leana a doll for Christmas."*[1]

When people get caught up in a crowd, they stop thinking rationally and allow themselves to be governed almost entirely by emotion. This state of mind prevails at nearly all important market peaks and bottoms. Almost everyone (unanimity) is convinced that the market will keep going up—or down—with no end in sight (hysteria).

During these moments of mass delusion, the crowd extrapolates the current trend too far into the future. The long-term component of market prices becomes grossly (irrationally) exaggerated as investors forget the homely truth that human knowledge has limits, that the future is always uncertain and that there is no "sure thing" in the economy or the investment markets.

Beware the Consensus

Unfortunately, the market never accommodates a crowd for long. It can't. If the market did what virtually everyone expected it to do, making money would be easy. As any bruised and scarred veteran of the "battle for investment survival" will tell you, life doesn't work quite that way. In fact, it's logically *impossible* for the market to follow the path that an overwhelming majority of investors believe it will take.

Investors buy because they expect the market to go up. They sell because they expect the market to go down. But if everyone in the marketplace is looking for prices to go up (a consensus), chances are that everyone who is going to buy has already bought. Who is left to bid prices up?

Likewise, if everyone is counting on the market to go down, everyone who is going to sell has probably already sold. Who is left to knock prices down? A tiny minority of dissenters can turn the market around.

Every uptrend—whether primary, intermediate or short-term—comes to a halt when the last cheerful buyer has emptied his wallet, exhausting the buying pressure in the marketplace. By the same token, every downtrend stops when the last discouraged seller dumps his goods, exhausting the selling pressure. If investors are unanimously cheerful or unanimously discouraged, prices can only go in the other direction, just as a ball thrown high into the air can only come down, or an inner tube held under water can only bob up.

In a free market with millions of participants, you'll never find a true consensus—100 percent agreement—about anything. A contrarian looks for important market reversals when the *overwhelming majority* of investors expect the prevailing trend to continue. Typically, though not always, the size of the majority will be larger at an intermediate turning point than at a short-term peak or bottom. And the majority will usually be biggest, loudest and craziest at a primary turning point—the kind that occurs once every couple of years.

Contrarians do *not* argue that "the majority is always wrong." (This is a common misconception.) The majority is often right, especially about the primary trend, for many months at a time. However, the closer to a consensus, the more likely that the majority opinion is badly mistaken. As the late Humphrey Neill, the "Vermont ruminator" who is considered the father of contrary investing, used to say: "When everybody thinks alike, everybody is likely to be wrong." A virtually unanimous, emotionally charged majority is almost certain to be wrong.

The Limits of Contrary Thinking

Contrary thinking isn't a cure-all or a get-rich-quick scheme. Like any investment technique, it's an art—not a science. Contrarians, too, make their share of mistakes. If you hope to profit from the insights of contrary opinion, you must understand the risks and pitfalls in the method, as well as its strengths. Being contrary doesn't relieve you from the obligation of thinking!

Since a free market never produces a perfect consensus, a contrary investor may sometimes buy or sell too early, at what seems to be a primary turning point, but actually turns out to be an intermediate bottom or top. The primary trend was merely interrupted, not broken. For example, the mood of the gold market was extremely bleak in December 1981 and March 1982. At both points, gold appeared ripe for buying from a contrarian viewpoint. But in each case, the lows turned out to be temporary. After a rally, the market resumed its downtrend and didn't hit a firm bottom until June 1982.

It's also possible for a contrary investor to sell too early, before the frenzy of the crowd reaches its true peak. In fact, since contrary thinkers are so deeply suspicious of fads, a contrarian may be more inclined than other investors to "pull the trigger" and sell out early when the excitement of a bull market becomes psychologically unbearable. Several well-known contrarian advisors and money managers, for instance, disposed of their stocks more than a year—and 1,000 Dow points—before the October 1987 market crash. Similarly, in the 1920s, noted contrarian Roger Babson advised his followers to exit the stock market two years before the Great Crash. The Dow doubled in the meantime.

It may sound like heresy for a dyed-in-the-wool contrarian to say so, but the best way to reduce your chances of making a major blunder is by *not* relying exclusively on any single investment technique, including contrary opinion. Contrary thinking is properly viewed as a *supplement* to—not a *substitute* for—other methods of analyzing the economy and the investment markets.

Before making an investment decision on the basis of a contrarian insight, you should always check out the fundamental dollars-and-cents economics of the situation. Is there a plausible chain of events that would allow this company or this market to turn around, or am I just daydreaming? You should be able to cite a convincing *reason* (better yet, several reasons) why you expect prices to reverse direction. The reasons you come up with will probably be ones that the crowd is neglecting. But make sure they're reasons—not just wishes.

The problem with so-called fundamental analysis, standing alone, is that too often forecasters succumb to the fatal temptation to assume that the future will be just like the recent past. On Wall Street, for example, analysts face powerful emotional pressure to recommend stocks that have been performing strongly, even after prices have been bid up to untenable levels. Invariably, just before a high-flying stock collapses, many of Wall Street's best and brightest analysts will be predicting strong earnings gains for the company into the distant future.

These forecasting lapses don't negate the value of fundamental analysis. Rather, they demonstrate that when you make your forecasts, you need to study the mood of the market *as well as* the economic and financial factors that influence prices. Successful investors can never allow themselves to be married to any widely accepted, pat scenario. They must look for the hidden, potential surprise factors that other forecasters are ignoring. And they must be prepared to change their own forecasts promptly if they see that too many people are adopting their point of view.

Some analysts—the technicians or chartists—maintain that they can predict market movements without any reference to fundamentals. Forget earnings. Forget interest rates, inflation rates and the GNP. Simply study the market action itself, as recorded on the price charts. Strict technicians argue that the market price takes into account all the fundamentals, or as one leading stock market technician puts it: "The tape tells all."

Technicians generally look for certain recurring patterns on their price charts: support and resistance levels, moving averages, head-and-shoulders formations, pennants, double and triple bottoms (or tops), ascending or descending channels, Elliott waves and so on. These patterns are supposed to signal important buying or selling opportunities—and sometimes, I'll grant, they do. Unfortunately, though, the error rate is high. We need only recall the prominent technician several years ago whose coolly "objective" Elliott Wave chart patterns called for the price of gold to sink to $105 an ounce by 1987 and for the Dow Jones Industrial Average to touch 3600 by 1988. You may be committing the financial equivalent of jumping off the Golden Gate Bridge if you base your investment strategy entirely on chart patterns.

Not all technical analysis is voodoo, however. In fact, some of the most reliable technical tools are actually based on contrary thinking, as I demonstrate in Chapter 12. By combining technical analysis with contrary opinion, you can spot trend reversals long before most of the chart readers and thus snap up a much larger share of the profits from any major market move.

The genius of contrary thinking is that it helps you lean the right way at critical market turning points, when emotions drown out reason and other analytical techniques seem to fail. Fundamental analysis and technical analysis tacitly assume that markets are rational. But the markets are *not* rational, at least not always, because people aren't always rational. At the irrational moments, when the lunatics are running the asylum, the contrary investor finds his best opportunities for profit.

16

Chapter 2

The Making of a Mania

*The only thing we learn from history is that we learn
nothing from history.*—Heinrich Heine

*I can calculate the motions of heavenly bodies, but not the
madness of people..*—Sir Isaac Newton

In the spring of 1983, Wall Street was riding a technology boom.
High-tech stocks were "hot." Although there were hundreds of
spectacular gainers, one of the most amazing was Coleco Industries, a toy company that had made its reputation primarily
as a manufacturer of children's plastic swimming pools. Coleco
brought out a couple of low-priced computerized video games and
a home computer called Adam. Almost overnight, the company
was transformed into a high-tech sensation.

Coleco stock had been wallowing around $7 a share in August
1982, before the great 1982-83 market surge began. Ten months
later, in June 1983, Coleco shares were trading at $65 per share,
an incredible 863 percent profit for the handful of investors who
were lucky enough to buy at the bottom and sell at the top.

The ride down was even faster, though perhaps not as
thrilling. Coleco shares plunged more than 50 percent from June
to August 1983 as the company's earnings from its highly touted
computer ventures began to melt away. But the worst was yet to
come. By March 1984, only nine months after the high, Coleco
stock had nosedived to $10.12 per share—a loss of 84 percent.*

*Coleco's slide, as it turned out, had only begun. After a brief rebound in
1985, the company's earnings—along with its stock price—collapsed again. In
July 1988, the creator of the Cabbage Patch Kids filed for Chapter 11 bankruptcy.

Hundreds of other small technology companies (and some not so small) repeated the Coleco story with only slightly less dramatic results. Apple Computer soared five times, then lost 73 percent of its value. Comdisco leaped from a 1982 low of 6 3/4 to a 1983 high of 42 and promptly collapsed all the way back to 9 5/8 by February 1984, a 77 percent loss. The two leading companies in solar-heating technology, A.T. Bliss and American Solar King, both lost approximately 90 percent of their market value between January 1983 and June 1984, after skyrocketing in the first phase of the bull market.

The Boom-Bust Cycle

Was the high-tech mania of 1982-83 an isolated incident—a historical freak? Hardly. The same sequence of boom and bust has occurred over and over again in virtually every investment market throughout the world for centuries. Americans look back nostalgically to the Crash of 1929, which followed an orgy of stock speculation. But at least seven notable, though less severe, panics took place in the United States *before* the Great Crash: in 1819, 1837, 1857, 1873, 1883, 1893 and 1907. A speculative boom in stocks, real estate, gold or railroad building preceded each collapse.

In retrospect, it's easy to fault our grandfathers for buying stocks at the top of the 1929 boom. But how many of us made the same error during the high-tech mania of 1983, or more recently, during the blue chip mania of 1987? How many of us bought gold in 1980 when it soared to $600, $700 or $800 an ounce—or silver at $30, $40 or $50 an ounce? Our ancestors had no thicker skulls than we do.

A runaway market distorts investors' sense of value. People begin to believe that prices can only keep going up, up, up, and that anybody with a buck to spare can get rich quickly by playing the market. Driven by greed, the masses forget risk and think only of reward. Yet, for most people, such hysteria is an aberration, not a normal state of mind. Most of the time, most people are fairly sensible and cautious, skeptical of pie-in-the-sky schemes. It's reasonable, therefore, to ask how thousands, even millions of investors can fail to sense that a crash is coming. Why do only mavericks recognize that the emperor isn't wearing any clothes?

The answer comes from the venerable Austrian school of economics, whose greatest spokesman in this century was Ludwig von Mises (1881-1973). In his masterpiece, *Human Action,*[1] Mises demonstrated that governments and their servants, the commercial banks, cause the unending boom-and-bust cycles in the economy by expanding artificially the supply of money and credit. When the government (in America, the Federal Reserve) pumps new money into the economy, interest rates drop—at first, anyway. Businesses take out bank loans to finance capital projects that weren't economical at the old, higher interest rates set by the free market. As businesses hire workers and buy equipment and raw materials to carry out their investment plans, the economy picks up and the boom phase of the cycle begins.

But the boom is based on an illusion. The government *appeared* to enlarge the pool of savings available for businesses to invest, but it performed this "miracle" by creating money out of thin air. (The government can't create real wealth or real savings, any more than it can turn stones to bread. It can only confiscate wealth through taxation or inflation.) When the government reduces interest rates by inflating the money supply, it in effect steals part of your wealth and lends your money to borrowers at a below-market rate.

This interest subsidy sends a false signal to businesses, encouraging them to invest in projects that the consumer isn't willing to pay for. As the government injects more "funny money" into the economy, the boom heats up. In the business sector, a swelling tide of imprudent investments bids up wages and prices. Finally, to prevent inflation from spinning out of control, the government cuts the flow of credit to businesses and consumers alike, raises interest rates and precipitates a recession or crash. The crash exposes all the mistaken investments that businesses made during the easy-money period.

Politicians love to expand credit because, if they play their cards correctly, the resulting prosperity (though fleeting) will warm the voters' hearts around election time.* Only a killjoy could vote against a man who promised, as Herbert Hoover did in 1928, "a chicken in every pot and a car in every garage." Hoover was swept into office on the strength of one of the greatest credit-induced booms in American history.

Half a century later, Ronald Reagan rode an unprecedented wave of credit expansion to a smashing victory in the 1984 presidential contest. In fact, the "easy money" of the Reagan era continued into early 1987, fueling the longest peacetime business boom in the annals of the republic.

Politicians, though, aren't the only people who benefit from a credit binge. Bankers—who do the government's dirty work by making the loans that puff up the money supply—reap fabulous profits from a credit expansion, at least in the early stages. (Later on, inflation drives up overhead costs and pinches the banks' profit margins.) For a time, investors also make big money from the artificial boom. Typically, the stock market soars in the early phases of a credit expansion. Then, as the inflationary impact of the government's easy-money policy becomes visible, speculation picks up in commodities, real estate and other tangible assets.

In the end, however, everyone gets burned (even the politicians, if they allow inflation to rage unchecked). During the inevitable down phase of the cycle, businesses must liquidate their unwise investments at a loss. Bankers must write off bad loans that seemed solid just a short time before.

Unwary investors, too, must take their lumps. Stocks, real estate, gold, everything that rocketed sky-high during the boom, plunges back to earth. The crash is unavoidable because the boom fostered an *illusion of value*. Deceived by the government's cheap-credit policy, investors paid more for their stocks, their farm-

---

* Government manipulation of the business cycle is as old as paper money. An insightful book about the phenomenon is Prof. Edward Tufte's *Political Control of the Economy,* Princeton University Press, Princeton, N.J., 1978. Tufte quotes Lord Brougham, a British peer, who complained back in 1814: "A Government is not supported a hundredth part so much by the constant, uniform, quiet prosperity of the country as by those damned spurts which [Prime Minister William] Pitt used to have just in the nick of time." (p. 3.)

land, their diamonds, coins and Persian rugs than the long-term prospects for these items justified. When reality caught up, prices came down.

Every speculative mania of the past 300 years (and by extension, every market crash) has resulted from a credit expansion encouraged and, in some cases, directed by the state. When the government injects fiat money into the economy, it upsets the normal balance between savers and borrowers and spurs people to act against their own better judgment, expressed in the market rate of interest before the government began to meddle. If the government rewards people for behaving irrationally, is it any wonder that they accept the invitation?

Charles Mackay, a 19th-century Englishman, analyzed three of the earliest known financial manias—the Dutch tulip mania, the Mississippi Company and the South Sea Bubble—in his classic book, *Extraordinary Popular Delusions and the Madness of Crowds*. Published in 1841, Mackay's book also reviews such non-financial fads and follies as alchemy, astrology, haunted houses, witchcraft hysteria and popular adulation of criminals. This volume belongs on every serious contrarian's bookshelf. After the 1929 stock market crash, financial wizard Bernard Baruch said of Mackay's work: "This book saved me millions of dollars."

Although Mackay was more interested in the psychological symptoms of a mania than its economic causes, each of the booms he discusses began with a credit expansion engineered by the banks, and at least tacitly supported by the government. For a contrarian, these old-time manias followed a script that reads like a page out of today's newspaper.

The Dutch Tulip Mania

The first great financial blowoff of modern times was the Dutch tulip mania of 1634-36. Tulips were introduced into Europe from Turkey in the mid-1500s and soon became a status symbol of the wealthy in Germany and Holland. By 1634, however, Mackay tells us, the rage for possessing them had spread to the middle classes, "and merchants and shopkeepers, even of moderate means, began to vie with each other in the rarity of these flowers and the preposterous prices they paid for them."[2]

As the mania approached its climax in 1636, regular markets for rare tulips were established on the Amsterdam stock exchange and in Rotterdam, Haarlem and other major towns. (When stock-brokers begin hustling investments they barely understand—like tulips or, in recent years, oil-drilling partnerships and variable life insurance—a crash is almost certainly lurking in the wings.) A single tulip bulb fetched the incredible price of 6,000 Dutch florins, or about $22,000 in today's money.

"Many people grew suddenly rich," Mackay relates. "A golden bait hung temptingly out before the people, and one after another, they rushed to the tulip-marts, like flies around a honeypot."[3] The dream of instant riches enticed the hapless public into the speculation—a fateful signal that the market was peaking.

Normally, individual investors who buy for cash and hold for the long term tend to be astute judges of value. But when the public attempts to speculate—to make the fast buck—it nearly always guesses wrong. Mackay reports that "nobles, citizens, farmers, mechanics, seamen, footmen, maid-servants, even chimney sweeps and old clotheswomen, dabbled in tulips."[4] Some people sold their houses and lands, or mortgaged them to the banks, just to acquire a collection of bulbs.

Greed shortened everyone's perspective. "Rich people no longer bought the flowers to keep them in their gardens, but to sell them again at cent (100) percent profit."[5] Like the California real estate speculators of the late 1970s who bought single-family homes, not to live in but to sell at a profit a few months later, the tulip traders told themselves that prices had only one way to go—up. A futures market for tulips developed, with sellers agreeing to deliver, say, 10 tulip bulbs six weeks after the signing of the contract. It was one of the earliest recorded instances of commodity speculation.

Like every speculative mania since, the tulip craze could never have gone as far as it did without the help of the banks (a private monopoly chartered by the Dutch towns). Banking was a fairly new business to 17th century Holland, but bankers had al-

ready discovered how to expand credit—and make big profits—
by lending out money that customers had deposited with them for
safekeeping.

The mechanism was as simple as it was deceitful: since coins
at the time didn't carry uniform weights, the bankers (who were
goldsmiths on the side) sorted out the heavier coins that had been
deposited with them and melted these coins down. If a customer
wanted to redeem his banknote (withdraw his deposit), the banks
would pay him *in the lighter coins.* This trick enabled the bankers to expand the supply of money and credit "out of nothing" by
issuing additional banknotes backed by debased coins.

Inflation—the popular term for a surge in the cost of living—
resulted, as it usually does under fractional-reserve banking systems.* "The prices of the necessaries of life rose again by degrees,"
Mackay recounts. "Houses and lands, horses and carriages, and
luxuries of every sort rose in value with them."[6]

Finally, the whole rotten, credit-crazy structure collapsed.
"The more prudent began to see that this folly could not last
forever," Mackay says. "It was seen that somebody must lose fear-
fully in the end. As this conviction spread, prices fell and never
rose again."[7] The market value of the once-prized *semper augus-
tus* tulip bulb plunged from 6,000 florins to 500 florins—a 91 percent drop. Curiously enough, several of the most famous financial
busts since the 17th century have produced losses on a similar
scale of 85 to 95 percent.

After prices collapsed, lawsuits broke out all over Holland as
sellers tried to enforce their tulip-futures contracts. But judges
decided that the contracts were gambling debts, and hence unen-
forceable at law. Those who owned tulips were stuck with them.
Mackay writes the mournful epitaph: "Many who, for a brief season, had emerged from the humbler walks of life, were cast back
into their original obscurity. Substantial merchants were reduced

*Under a fractional-reserve system, banks are allowed to lend out all but
a small fraction of their deposits. The minuscule "reserve" that the banks
keep on hand is supposed to cover any withdrawals. Prof. Murray N.
Rothbard explains the inflationary impact of fractional-reserve banking in
his book, *The Mystery of Banking,* New York: Richardson & Snyder, 1983.

almost to beggary, and many a representative of a noble line saw the fortunes of his house ruined beyond redemption."[8]

The Mississippi Madness

Nearly a century after the Dutch tulip mania, fiat money sparked a roaring speculative boom in France. The mastermind of the French fiasco was John Law, a flirtatious Scotsman who had fled to the Continent after killing his lady friend's lover in a duel. A compulsive gambler, Law was ideally equipped to launch one of history's most egregious flimflams, the Mississippi Company.

In 1716, Law persuaded the French regent (who was ruling in place of the six-year-old Louis XV) to allow him to set up a bank. At the time, France was deep in debt and the government had just devalued the coinage, reducing its gold and silver content. Law started out on the right foot. His bank issued paper money fully backed by precious metals, and—unlike the government—Law promised never to change the amount of metal standing behind each note. In fact, he declared that a banker deserved death if he issued notes without enough gold and silver on hand to make redemptions.

Inflation-weary Frenchmen beat a path to his door. Within a year, Law's paper money was trading at a 15 percent premium to the government's coinage. Meanwhile, the government's unbacked paper currency, the *billets d'etat* issued during the reign of Louis XIV, had fallen to an 80 percent discount from their nominal value in gold and silver.

Unfortunately, Law's gambling instinct got the better of him. At the regent's urging, he converted his bank into a royal (government) institution. With the blessing of the state, Law began to crank out vast quantities of paper money with no backing whatsoever. Interest rates fell and business picked up. An inflationary boom was under way.

Law quickly hit upon a scheme to exploit the speculative atmosphere he had created. In 1717, the crown granted his Mississippi Company the exclusive right to trade up and down the Mississippi River, including the province of Louisiana, which belonged at the time to France. To attract buyers for the Mississippi Company's stock, Law promised a yearly dividend of 40 percent—an incredible return by the standards of any era.

But Law went a step further. As a favor to his patron, who was trying to reduce the national debt, Law told investors they could pay for their subscriptions with the government's next-to-worthless *billets d'etat*. Since the dividend was to be paid in real money (gold or silver coin), Law was in effect promising that shareholders could earn a 120 percent annual yield from dividends alone.

"The public enthusiasm," Mackay writes, "which had been so long rising, could not resist a vision so splendid."[9] Dukes, marquises and counts—together with their wives—besieged Law with applications to buy shares. Each new issue was a sellout, even after Law upped the price tenfold. The rue de Quincampoix in Paris, where the great man had his office, was jammed with speculators buying and selling Mississippi Company shares.

As the trading reached a fever pitch, share prices sometimes rose 10 to 20 percent in a few hours—a scene reminiscent of the last days of the 1929 stock market boom. Maids and footmen parlayed their meager savings into instant fortunes. Mackay relates that "many persons in the humbler walks of life, who had risen poor in the morning, went to bed in affluence."[10]

Fueled by fiat money, the artificial boom spread from the rue de Quincampoix across Paris and into the hinterlands. Inflation ran wild, with prices spiraling 300 percent in the space of a few months. Luxury goods rose especially fast as successful speculators channeled their profits into hard assets: "The looms of the country worked with unusual activity to supply rich laces, silks, broadcloth and velvets, which being paid for in abundant paper, increased in price fourfold....New houses were built in every direction; an *illusory prosperity* (my emphasis) shone over the land, and so dazzled the eyes of the whole nation, that none could see the dark cloud on the horizon announcing the storm that was too rapidly approaching."[11]

Early in 1720, the first cracks began to appear in Law's magnificent structure. A leading nobleman, the prince de Conti, caused a stir when he brought three wagons full of paper money to Law's bank and demanded payment in specie (metal). The regent browbeat the prince into returning two-thirds of his withdrawal to the bank, but the con game was up. (Fractional-reserve banking is, quite literally, a confidence game. When public confidence evaporates, prompting a rash of withdrawals, the bank fails.) Aware that the banknotes were losing their purchasing power daily, people hurried to cash them in for gold and silver.

However, there wasn't enough specie in Law's bank to satisfy the demand. A run on the bank ensued, together with a disastrous collapse in the price of Mississippi Company stock. Although the government tried to restore confidence in the currency by devaluing gold and silver in terms of paper money, nobody fell for the ruse. The panic only intensified. As a final expedient, the tyrannical regent (like his American counterpart in 1933) forbade private citizens to possess more than a token amount of gold and silver.

In a last-ditch effort to prop up the Mississippi Company's stock, Law asked the government to conscript 6,000 Parisian street urchins to work the supposedly abundant gold mines in Louisiana. Law paraded these derelicts through Paris with picks and shovels, convincing a few naive investors that his scheme still had merit.

The price of the stock took a brief bounce—hope springs eternal—but then, as the effects of Law's public relations stunt wore off, quotations began to slide once more. Mississippi Company shares, which had soared from 500 livres apiece in 1716 to 20,000 livres at the peak in 1720, plunged within a few months to only 200 livres, a staggering 99 percent loss. Law was ruined, and so— very nearly—was the French economy.

The South Sea Bubble

Another famous speculative mania, the South Sea Bubble, took place in 1720 on the other side of the English Channel. Robert Harley, the Earl of Oxford, had founded the South Sea Company in 1711. The new Company invited holders of 9 million pounds

26

worth of British government bonds to exchange their bonds for stock in the South Sea Company. For this patriotic service in retiring part of the national debt, the crown granted the South Sea Company a monopoly on British trade with the South Sea islands and South America.

As it turned out, the monopoly wasn't worth anywhere near as much as the earl had dreamed, because Spain, which ruled most of South America at the time, was unwilling to open its colonies to more than a trivial volume of British trade. But like all skillful corporate con artists before and since, Harley knew how to sell an enticing story to a greedy and gullible public. In 1720, the South Sea Company made Parliament an offer it couldn't refuse: the company would absorb virtually the entire national debt of 31 million pounds by issuing South Sea stock to the bondholders.

Robert Walpole, later Britain's first prime minister, denounced the plan in the House of Commons, saying it was designed "to raise artificially the price of the stock, by exciting and keeping up a general infatuation, and by promising dividends out of funds which could never be adequate to the purpose."[12] But Walpole's eloquence was powerless against the earl of Oxford's rumor mill.

The earl's allies whispered that England and Spain were negotiating treaties that would concede to the English free trade with all the Spanish colonies. Gold and silver from the New World would flood into England, making the South Sea merchants the richest on earth. Every hundred pounds invested would return hundreds annually to the stockholder.

The bill passed, and the speculation began. From a price of 128 1/2 pounds per share in January 1720, South Sea stock zoomed to a dizzying 1,000 pounds in August. Even Robert Walpole, who had spoken out against the scheme, couldn't resist. He, too, purchased a block of shares (and later lost heavily in the crash). People of all sorts and conditions joined the mad rush to get aboard the bull market.

It seemed at that time as if the whole nation had turned stock-jobbers [traders]. Exchange Alley was blocked up everyday by crowds, and Cornhill [a street in London's financial district] was impassable for the number of carriages. Everybody came to purchase stock.[13]

The Bernie Cornfelds of the 18th century sensed an opportunity. Noticing how rapidly South Sea Company shares were running up, swindlers formed hundreds of "bubble companies" that had little or no business purpose other than to peddle their own stock. One company was set up "for trading in hair." Another, which was trying to raise one million pounds when it was outlawed, proposed to manufacture a perpetual-motion machine. A third was established "for the transmutation of quicksilver into malleable fine metal." Since quicksilver, or mercury, is a liquid at any temperature above -38 degrees Fahrenheit, turning it into a solid metal would have been quite an accomplishment for 18th century technology.

Perhaps the most remarkable scam was a company with no stated purpose at all. The prospectus coyly hinted that the company had been organized "for carrying on an undertaking of great advantage, but nobody to know what it is."[14] For every two pounds invested, the promoter declared that subscribers would be entitled to 100 pounds a year in dividends—a 50-to-1 return. Dazzled by this unsubstantiated promise, a throng of people showed up at the entrepreneur's door the morning after the offering circular was published. In six hours, he collected 2,000 pounds.

Having raked in a tidy sum for a day's work, the promoter, Mackay says, "was philosopher enough to be contented with his venture, and set off the same evening for the Continent. He was never heard of again."[15]

Of course, we know that today the Securities and Exchange Commission (SEC) would prevent such shady outfits from selling stock to the public. Right? At the height of the new-issues craze in June 1983, a 20th century bubble company announced on the front page of its prospectus, which was filed with the SEC: "This offering is of securities of a start-up company with no operating history and *no plan of operation*; the company will not engage in

any business whatever until after the completion of this offering."
(Emphasis added.)

On page 5, the prospectus further revealed: "The company
does not know what business it will engage in, has no plan of
operation..."(my emphasis).[16] The wording bears a striking re-
semblance to the advertisement for the bubble company of 1720:
"an undertaking of great advantage, but nobody to know what it
is." Yet amazingly, this modern bubble raised $3 million, at $5
per share. Two-and-a-half centuries later, a sucker is still being
born every minute.

The South Sea Bubble finally burst in August 1720, when
news leaked out that the directors of the company—including the
chairman, Sir John Blunt—had sold their stock. This vote of no
confidence by the corporate insiders triggered a wave of panic selling that eventually drove the price of South Sea shares from
1,000 pounds at the peak to a low of only 135 pounds—an 87 percent decline. Thousands of English families were devastated financially, including many members of Parliament, and a general
commercial depression settled over the land.

Unsound banking practices, the common denominator of all
financial manias, made a scandal like the South Sea Bubble not
only possible but inevitable. In Britain, both the quasi-public
Bank of England and the private London goldsmiths acted as
bankers, making loans to businesses (and later, to stock speculators). In most cases, when a bank made a loan, it issued a note
(banknote) secured by the gold and silver in the bank's vaults.
Supposedly, the bearer could redeem these banknotes, which cir-
culated as money, in precious metal on demand.

However, the Bank of England and the goldsmiths issued far
too many notes for the metal they had in storage. This inflationary expansion of credit sparked a huge burst of deceptive "prosperity" from 1715 onward, culminating in the wild stock market
boom of 1720. When the crash came, the Bank of England shame-
fully reneged on its promise to redeem its notes in specie, and
many of the goldsmiths went bankrupt.

The Crash of '29

The cycle of financial booms and busts has been repeated throughout the 20th century, right up to our own times. For Americans, however, the 1929 crash still stands out as the granddaddy, the *ne plus ultra*—because it ushered in the Great Depression. The memory of stockbrokers jumping out of windows and former corporate executives selling apples on street corners is forever enshrined in our national folklore. More than half a century later, hearts on Wall Street still race and investors' pulses pound whenever a respected analyst draws a parallel to 1929.

Like the early financial manias described by Mackay in his classic book, the frenetic stock market boom of the late 1920s began with an injection of artificially cheap credit into the economy. In the spring of 1927, the Bank of England lowered interest rates in an attempt to stimulate British industry, which had never really recovered from the World War. As a result of the bank's inflationary policy, gold began to flow out of Britain and into the United States and France. To stem the outflow, Montagu Norman, governor of the Bank of England, persuaded the Federal Reserve to lower interest rates in the United States, spreading the inflation across the Atlantic.

As Federal Reserve governor Adolph C. Miller later complained, it was "the greatest and boldest operation ever undertaken by the Federal Reserve System, and...resulted in one of the most costly errors committed by it or any other banking system in the past 75 years."[17] Stock prices exploded in a frenzy of speculation that carried the Dow Jones Industrial Average from a low of 153 in 1927 to the manic peak of 381 in October 1929—a 149 percent gain in two years. Many individual stocks performed even more spectacularly. Radio Corp., ancestor of today's RCA and a "high tech" stock at the time, gained 500 percent in 1928 alone.

The great innovation of the 1927-29 stock market boom was leverage. Margin accounts mushroomed as speculators borrowed money from their brokers at low interest rates to buy common stocks. (Margin is Wall Street jargon for the deposit or down payment you must make when you borrow money from your broker to finance securities purchases.) In early 1928, it was possible to take out a margin loan at only 5 percent interest.

Even after margin rates rose sharply—to 12 percent in late 1928 and a peak of 20 percent in March 1929—speculators eagerly incurred huge debts to buy high-flying stocks. When the crash came, brokers demanded that their customers put up more collateral to support these shaky loans. Rather than meet the broker's "margin call," overextended speculators dumped their shares on the market, forcing prices down even further.

Hundreds of closed-end investment companies were formed during the late 1920s. These companies, whose purpose was to invest in the stocks of other companies, issued their own shares, which traded on the exchanges. Some of these early closed-end funds still survive. Most, however, came to grief during the crash because they had borrowed heavily (usually by issuing bonds or preferred stock) to buy common stocks during the boom. Some 160 funds existed at the beginning of 1927; 140 were formed that year, 186 in 1928, and an astonishing 265 in 1929. The magic of leverage was irresistible.

As the boom approached its zenith, the promise of instant riches sucked thousands of amateurs into the market. Some made fortunes, lending credibility to the myth of wealth without work:

> The rich man's chauffeur drove with his ears laid back to catch the news of an impending move in Bethlehem Steel; he held 50 shares himself on 20-point margin. The window-cleaner at the broker's office paused to watch the ticker, for he was thinking of converting his laborious accumulated savings into a few shares of Simmons. Edwin Lefevre (an articulate reporter on the market at this time who could claim considerable personal experience) told of a broker's valet who made nearly a quarter of a million in the market, of a trained nurse who cleaned up thirty thousand following tips given her by grateful patients; and of a Wyoming cattleman, 30 miles from the nearest railroad, who bought or sold a thousand shares a day.[18]

The market was bursting with extravagant optimism, the epitome being the famous comment by Prof. Irving Fisher of Yale (himself a director of an investment company) several weeks before the crash: "Stock prices have reached what looks like a permanently high plateau."[19]

Not everyone agreed, of course. *Poor's Weekly Business and Investment Letter* warned of "the great common-stock delusion" and William P. Hamilton, editor of *The Wall Street Journal*, had a premonition of the end when he wrote his historic editorial, "A Turn of the Tide," on October 25, 1929. But the great majority of investors and pundits shared ex-President Coolidge's faith, reiterated just before he left office in March 1929, that the economy was "absolutely sound" and that stocks were "cheap at current prices."[20]

From the manic top of October 1929 to the panic bottom of July 1932, the Dow industrials plummeted 89 percent—an across-the-board wipeout of stock market values, the like of which has never been seen, before or since, in American financial history. Excessive credit expansion had ruined the fortunes of millions of Americans from the stock speculator on Wall Street to the shopkeeper on Main Street.

Will It Happen Again?

As long as governments, working hand-in-glove with the private banking system, continue to inflate the supply of money and credit, speculative manias will recur—followed by gut-wrenching busts. Cheap money gives a false stimulus to the economy. Business executives undertake projects that can never pay off, and investors, duped by the same monetary illusion, throw their hard-earned savings into crackpot ventures that are doomed to failure. A credit-based boom spawns a "cluster of errors," in Prof. Murray Rothbard's words. It distorts people's judgments and induces a kind of mass insanity.

At the beginning of this chapter, I cited the speculative boom in technology stocks that came to a head in the spring of 1983. This mania resulted from a record-breaking monetary expansion engineered by the Federal Reserve from roughly June 1982 to July 1983. In the 12 months ending July 1983, the basic M1 money supply (cash plus checking accounts) grew almost 14 percent, up

32

to that time the most rapid expansion in any year since the Federal Reserve was created.

To its credit, the Fed pulled back on the monetary reins from mid-1983 to late 1984. But when the threat of recession came into view at the end of 1984, the nation's central bank panicked again and turned on the printing presses. As I warned in the first edition of this book (1985):

> It is wise to recall that in most [business] cycles, money growth accelerates as the cycle matures. Hence, the worst monetary abuses of the current cycle may yet lie ahead.

Alas, events proved me correct. In 1985 and 1986, the Fed unleashed a dam-bursting torrent of money. By January 1987, the basic money supply had grown 17 percent from its level 12 months previously, another new all-time record. The words of my first edition proved uncomfortably prophetic:

> If Paul Volcker and his colleagues, under pressure from the White House and Congress, open up the monetary spigots in 1985, the U.S. economy could face a once-in-a-lifetime crisis in which the Federal Reserve and the political authorities will have to choose between allowing a crack-up boom (with high inflationary consequences) or forcing the economy through a deflationary wringer to squeeze out the errors and excesses that have built up as a result of 50 years of credit expansion.

Horrified by a rebounding inflation rate and a collapsing dollar, the Volcker Fed drastically tightened credit in the spring and summer of 1987, driving up interest rates. The direct result was the spectacular Crash of '87, which on October 19 produced the most severe one-day decline in equity prices since the New York Stock Exchange opened nearly 200 years ago.

The danger of a crack-up boom was averted in 1987. But does the crash mean that the U.S. economy, in the next few years, is going to be put through a deflationary wringer that will flatten a wide range of investments, just as the deflation of the 1930s did? I'll address that troubling question in detail in Chapter 8. For now, suffice it to say that, toward the end, the 1982-87 bull market in stocks bore numerous resemblances to the ill-fated financial manias of the past. One or more of the following characteristics have signaled the finale of virtually every mania since the Dutch tulip craze of 1636. Ask yourself how many of them were present when the stock market crested in the summer of 1987.

Nine Symptoms of a Dying Boom

• *A breathtaking, parabolic rise in prices,* accompanied by predictions that the advance will go on indefinitely.

• *A widespread rejection of old standards of value.* According to the apologists for the boom, the dawning of a "new era" makes today's high prices reasonable, even cheap, no matter how outrageous they would have seemed only yesterday. Hustlers take advantage of inflated values to promote lower-quality goods as top-grade merchandise.

• *A proliferation of dubious investment schemes* promising huge returns in an inordinately short time.

• *Intense and—for a time—successful speculation by uninformed members of the public,* fostering the belief that making money is easy, a "sure thing."

• *Popular fascination with leveraged investments,* such as futures, options or margin accounts, which enable the speculator to control a large block of assets with a small down payment.

• *Heavy selling by corporate "insiders"* and other conservative investors with a long-term orientation.

• *Extremely high trading volume* that enriches brokers and snarls paperwork as back offices try to keep track of the many transactions.

• *Absurd or even violent behavior* by people who are desperately trying to get their hands on the booming asset. (Remember the "grown-ups" who punched and scratched each other to buy a Cabbage Patch doll.)

Three hundred years of booms and busts demonstrate that human nature changes little, if at all, over the centuries. Many investors dream of a fast, easy track to riches. During a credit-induced economic boom, this illusion takes on a sheen of plausibility. The inescapable lesson of history, however, is that wealth building takes time, work, good saving habits and—perhaps most important—the emotional discipline to steer away from invest-ment fads. When the crowd decides it has found El Dorado, the contrary investor hops aboard the first boat home.

Chapter 3

I Saw It in
The New York Times

All I know is what I read in the newspapers.—Will Rogers

Americans have always stood in awe of the printed word. Perhaps this habit of mind goes back to our ancestors, who were "people of the Book." We couldn't imagine governing ourselves without a written constitution. Whenever we want to make sure someone lives up to a promise, we ask him to "put it in black and white"— a testimony to our faith in the power of print.

Will Rogers was kidding, of course, when he claimed to know nothing except what the newspapers told him. But why do we chuckle at his gag? Partly, at least, because it's a caricature of how many people really think. Many people *do* take the preachments of the media as gospel. Not long ago, a poll singled out TV newscaster Walter Cronkite as the most trusted figure in America, even though studies have repeatedly charged CBS with blatant political bias in its reporting of the news during Cronkite's tenure.[1] Too many people, unfortunately, are willing to let someone else analyze and interpret the news for them, rather than do the hard intellectual labor themselves.

The mass media—newspapers, magazines, radio, and TV— dispense a mixture of fact and opinion (or interpretation). As an investor, you must always distinguish between these two elements when you monitor the financial news. Treat facts with reverence. When the Commerce Department reports that housing starts fell to a six-year low last month, pay attention. (You can be sure the markets are tuning in.) But if the White House press secretary goes on the air to proclaim that the economy is sound

37

and will continue to expand despite any "temporary" weakness in the housing sector—he's simply expressing an opinion, with perhaps little or no factual basis. In matters of opinion, reserve the right to make up your own mind.

Above all, don't march unthinkingly behind the opinions of any supposed expert, including the author of this book. Think critically. Ask yourself: Does this prediction or investment strategy address all the possibilities, or is something missing? What unforeseen events could upset this expert's forecast? The mere fact that *The New York Times* hails Professor Dryasdust as an authority doesn't make his opinions about the future course of the economy or the investment markets any more compelling.

Quite the contrary: the popular financial experts favored by the news media often make their most wildly inaccurate prognostications at or close to important market peaks and bottoms. Even the most learned gurus with their Ph.Ds in economics can—and regularly do—fall into the groupthink trap. (Running with the crowd is an emotional, not an intellectual, failing.) By carefully studying the financial pages of your daily newspaper, you can detect an emerging consensus—when everybody is thinking alike. If you go promptly to the opposite side of the market, chances are good that you'll emerge with a profit.

Because of their frequent publishing schedule, daily newspapers are ideally suited for helping you spot changes in the market's short-term trend, as well as shifts in the intermediate- and long-term trends. Despite the title of this chapter (which was meant to be a spoof of an old *New York Times* advertising slogan), my favorite newspaper for reading the mood of the investment markets is actually *The Wall Street Journal*. The *Times* has the most comprehensive financial section of any general-interest daily in the United States, which makes it invaluable supplementary reading. But *The Journal* covers many more markets, and in greater detail. If you don't already subscribe to the *Journal*, I recommend that you make the investment—if only for the wealth of misguided professional opinion you'll find reported there, dependably, at every significant market peak or bottom.

News magazines like *Time, Newsweek, Business Week* and *Fortune* can also provide useful contrary insights when they quote the opinions of presumed financial authorities. In particular, cover stories in these magazines often signal that a trend of intermediate-term or even long-term importance has gone to an unsustainable extreme.

Several years ago, Paul Macrae Montgomery, analyst with the brokerage firm of Legg Mason Wood Walker in Newport News, Virginia, reviewed over 3,000 *Time* covers going back to 1924—a labor as prodigious and probably as pleasant as cleansing the Augean stables. Montgomery found that in four out of five cases where a financial question was treated on the cover of *Time*, the outcome within a year was just the opposite of what the magazine's editors had foreseen.[2]

All the slick newsweeklies are determined followers of fashion. They know what sells magazines. When they splash a bold, heart-tugging message on the front cover, you can assume that sophisticated Manhattanites—the crowd that always knows what is best for the rest of us—have reached a consensus on the matter. The alert contrarian will run, or at least jog, the other way!

For a long period in the earlier part of the 1980s, *Business Week* stood out as the most slavish trend follower among the major financial news magazines. The result of this mind-set was a string of fractured front-page forecasts, some of them downright amusing in retrospect:

- *May 9, 1983. BW,* reacting to a skyrocketing stock market, hit the streets with a cover story titled "The Rebirth of Equities." No doubt, the roaring bull market was acutely embarrassing to the magazine's editors, who had previously announced "The Death of Equities" in a celebrated 1979 cover. Alas, the "rebirth" came a bit late. Just six weeks later, most stocks touched their peaks for the year.

- *October 3, 1983.* A *BW* cover crowned IBM "The Winner" over Apple in the struggle for dominance in the personal computer market. A week later, IBM stock made its high for the year. Over the next eight months, IBM—the bluest of the blue chips—

plunged 26 percent, while Apple soared 65 percent. Six years later, IBM at 100 or so is *still* trading below that 1983 peak, even though the Dow has doubled in the meantime.

* *May 21, 1984.* In the spring of 1984, a series of hysterical articles in various magazines suggested that nuclear power had, in the immortal words of *Time,* "bombed out." *Financial World* (June 13) chimed in with a cover story that purported to deliver "a post-mortem on the ill-fated nuclear power industry." *Barron's* (June 4), exploiting the gloom of the hour, cast doubt upon not only the nuclear companies but the entire utility industry: "Do Utilities Have a Future?" (In *Barron's* defense, the answer the article gave was a qualified yes.)

BW put in its tuppence with a cover that asked baldly: "Are Utilities Obsolete?" All this one-sided blather was more than a self-respecting contrarian could stand. As I wrote at the time in *Personal Finance,* "Utilities are no more 'obsolete' than light-bulbs." The feverish publicity about the problems of the electric power industry, I said, actually amounted to "the strongest buy signal for utility stocks that you're likely to see in your lifetime."

With apologies to Longfellow, "you know the rest." The Dow Jones Utility Average made its low for 1984 on May 29, just one week after *BW* had pronounced the industry "obsolete." Utility stocks skyrocketed for the rest of the year, paced by the companies with heavy nuclear investment. Some nukes leaped 40, 50 or even 100 percent from their yearly lows.

* *October 8, 1984.* One of the more spectacular boo-boos of *BW*'s long career, this cover depicted "Superdollar" lifting off into space on rocket engines. Inside, the article predicted that the dollar could "soar for the rest of the decade" against the currencies of the leading industrial nations. From its ultimate peak in February 1985, the trade-weighted dollar plunged 48 percent before bottoming in December 1987.

* *December 17, 1984.* To accompany a cover story on "The Death of Mining," *BW*'s artist thoughtfully produced an illustration of a silver ingot shaped into a coffin with golden handles. I replied in *Personal Finance* that "mining shares will rise again." And rise they did! From its cyclical low a month later, the Toronto

Stock Exchange gold mines index (a good proxy for North American precious-metals stocks generally) more than tripled over the following two years.

• *June 9, 1986.* The front cover of *BW* spotlighted "America's Deflation Belt," by which the editors meant the "wide swath of the country" that was suffering from depressed conditions in oil, agriculture and mining. As it turned out, oil prices bottomed the next month at just under $11 a barrel, then doubled within a year. Wheat, oats, soybeans, cotton and other farm products touched their lows at roughly the same time, followed a few months later by corn and rice. Copper, the bellwether of the base metals, bottomed in August.

I could go on, but I think you get the point. Once it hits the cover of *BusinessWeek*, it isn't news anymore. It's a comfortable consensus—and money is rarely to be made by betting on what everybody in the marketplace already knows.

The editors of *BusinessWeek* may have been stung by criticism of the magazine's faddishness. In the past two years or so, I've noticed, *BW* has for the most part steered away from sensational cover stories, even when news events (such as the collapse of the dollar) could have justified a pull-out-all-the-stops approach.

Fortunately for contrarians, however, *Fortune* has stepped into the breach. Under the editorship of Marshall Loeb, who turned *Money* magazine into a kind of Wall Street edition of *People*, *Fortune* has adopted a brassier style of journalism that sounds more than its share of bungled notes. Consider, for instance, *Fortune*'s marvelously timed cover story "Why Greenspan Is Bullish," which appeared just a few days before the October 1987 stock market crash.[3] Scarcely a month later (November 23, 1987), the same magazine headlined its cover story "How to Prevent a New Depression." Had you sold stocks on the first signal and bought on the second, you could have saved—and then made—a king's ransom.

With its December 7, 1987 cover story, *Fortune* proved itself a worthy peer of *Business Week* in forecasting the direction of the U.S. dollar. The headline was "The Dollar and the Deficits" and the cover illustration showed a dollar bill, folded into a paper airplane, zooming downward in front of the twin towers of the World Trade Center in New York. Oh-so-cleverly, the flight path of the dollar bill traced out a dollar sign against the background of the buildings (see Figure 1). Inside, the article asked anent the dollar: "How low can it go?" Not much lower, evidently, for the dollar made a historic bottom three weeks later, on December 31, 1987.

Reading Between the Lines

For precise timing, however, nothing beats your daily newspaper. Newspapers reflect the flow of public opinion almost instantaneously, whereas magazines must often prepare feature articles weeks in advance. Regardless of what newspaper you read, and regardless of the market you're interested in, the signs of an approaching reversal are much the same. When virtually all the seers quoted in your newspaper say the market is headed up—and some affirm that it's about to skyrocket—prices are due to drop. On the other hand, when the vast majority of commentators say the market is going to keep sinking—and some predict a bloodbath—a rally is imminent.

You'll inevitably find unanimity and hysteria, the twin characteristics of a crowd mentality, in the comments of the leading market analysts near important tops and bottoms. In a newspaper roundup of analysts' opinions, however, hysteria is usually easier to detect than unanimity—for a good reason.

Any responsible reporter (and most of the people who work for *The Wall Street Journal*, *The New York Times* and other leading newspapers are conscientious journalists) will try whenever possible to present all sides of a controversial issue. Since predictions about the economy and the investment markets are, like politics and religion, open to controversy, reporters frequently give disproportionate space to dissenting views.

Don't let one or two vaguely hopeful remarks in a deep bear market, or a couple of mildly cautious remarks in a soaring bull market, throw you off track. Ask yourself: Is the overwhelming preponderance of sentiment on the other side? Contrary investing

Figure 1. Fortune Cover

doesn't require you to go against literally everybody else—just against the great majority. Inevitably, a few dissenters (contrarians, whether they know it or not) will correctly call the turn. Don't scorn them, join them!

At an important stock market bottom, for example, it isn't unusual to discover a few technical analysts who argue that the market is "deeply oversold." Other analysts may admit that stocks look like "great values for the longer term." Typically, though, even the few analysts who haven't been shellshocked by the bear market are too timid to say: "The bottom is here, buy with both hands." They cloak their bullishness in rhetoric about the virtues of patience and of a long-term perspective. (All very commendable, of course.) They don't want to be pinned down to a specific timetable for a market recovery.

Likewise, at a peak, a few analysts will wonder aloud how much higher the market can rise without a correction. Some may complain about excessive speculation. But almost nobody says: "Sell now, a crash is coming." In fact, these cautious bears often concede—to be on the safe side—that the market's advance may keep going a while longer.

A Note of Hysteria

Nonetheless, voices of reason are a distinct minority when the market comes under the sway of a strong bullish or bearish consensus. At these critical extremes, a note of hysteria creeps into the thinking of many analysts who normally seem calm and self-possessed. To determine when a crowd has formed, watch for reckless or desperate statements by respected establishment advisors—not the Joe Granvilles or the Doug Caseys, but the mainstream analysts at the old-line investment firms.

You can always find some maverick prophet somewhere who is willing to forecast that almost any market is going to the moon—or through the floor. These predictions may well be hysterical, but *they don't represent the consensus*. A contrarian takes a stand against the overwhelming majority, not against a small fringe element of the investment community.

44

It would be a mistake, for example, to buy gold merely because one prominent technician, Robert R. Prechter, Jr., has been predicting since 1981 that the Midas metal will sink as low as $105 an ounce. This seemingly farfetched forecast doesn't represent the thinking of mainstream metals analysts, technical or fundamental (at least not at present). Few metals investors are basing their day-to-day decisions on the belief that gold will drop to $105—a circumstance that actually weighs in Prechter's favor.

On the other hand, Prechter's prediction that the Dow Jones Industrial Average would reach 3600 by 1988 attracted a great deal of attention and a lengthy coterie of believers during the last bull market for stocks. In January 1987, *Barron's* acknowledged the popularity of the "3600 by 1988" thesis by devoting a cover story to Prechter.[4] (A few weeks later, my own newsletter, *Personal Finance*, carried an article sardonically titled, "Dow 3600: A Lot of Bull-oney?") When an extreme point of view is accepted widely enough not to be laughed out of court, it's generally because investors have reached a state of near-hysteria. The market is setting up for an about-face.

A maverick's opinion may also carry significance when he reverses himself after waging a long, lonely, losing battle against the market's primary trend. James Dines, the self-proclaimed "original goldbug" (and a first-rate stock picker, by the way), promised his subscribers way back in 1962 that he would instruct them just once to sell their precious metals—his "Much Vaunted All-Out One And Only Gold And Silver Sell Signal." He chose to flash the signal on June 17, 1982—two trading days before gold made an important cyclical bottom. For Dines, the psychological pressure of gold's two-year bear market (the price dropped from $850 in January 1980 to less than $300 in June 1982) had simply grown unbearable.

But his capitulation was a ringing buy signal because it indicated that the last person in the marketplace who could have sold had finally decided to do so. The market had nowhere to go but up—and go up it did, with gold soaring 72 percent over the next eight months. (To give a generous and genial man his due, Dines also counseled his subscribers in that famous bulletin to switch

45

from gold into common stocks, a strategic coup that put him into the market with the Dow below 800.)

At the next primary low for gold, which took the yellow metal to $282 during the last week of February 1985, the celebrated Aden sisters of Costa Rica trumped James Dines' ace. The Adens, you may recall, made a name for themselves in the early 1980s by predicting that the price of gold would rise to $3,000 an ounce by 1986. (Well, it did reach $440.) In the March 1985 issue of their newsletter, the Adens proclaimed that "a major gold reversal has occurred" and urged their followers to sell gold. From the 1985 low to the 1987 peak, gold soared 78 percent—a worthwhile gain in anybody's book.

As colorful as some of the fringe analysts may be, the people whose views reveal the most about the real mood of the marketplace are the analysts and traders at the major banks, brokerage firms and other financial institutions. These people control (or influence) the deployment of literally trillions of dollars' worth of assets. They wield far more power than James Dines or even Robert Prechter. *They* represent the mainstream. When these respected blue chip advisors throw caution to the breezes, run—don't walk—to the other side of the market!

Most of the time, people who hold responsible positions in the investment establishment shy away from making extravagant forecasts (at least in public). It isn't good for business. People don't generally entrust their money to crackpots. As a result, most investment advisors with prestigious credentials tend to be careful when talking to the press—if they give interviews at all.

At major market turning points, though, a few respected establishment advisors invariably get caught up in the emotions of the mob and "let it all hang out." For a contrarian, the emotionally charged statements of these advisors virtually leap off the newspaper page, shouting "Buy!" (when fear grips the market) and "Sell!" (when euphoria carries the day).

If you suffer from an inferiority complex, you can boost your ego (and enjoy a good belly laugh in the process) by keeping a file of fractured forecasts, all of them issued, of course, by sensible, well-regarded investment advisors. For even the best and the brightest investment professionals with years of academic training and on-the-job experience can lose their emotional equilibrium when the crowd stampedes. Let's take a look at some of the kinds of comments they make when the market is about to reverse field.

Stock Market Bloopers

The 1973-74 bear market on Wall Street brought the worst collapse of stock prices since the 1929 crash. The Dow Jones Industrial Average skidded 45 percent and hundreds of other stocks took a still worse pounding. Avon Products, one of the "Nifty Fifty" stocks that every bank, mutual fund and insurance company wanted to own during the previous bull market, plummeted 87 percent. Polaroid, another favorite of the smart set, nosedived an incredible 91 percent.

Most stocks, and most of the major averages (except the Dow industrials) hit bottom in early October 1974. The morning after the market reached its nadir, a battle-hardened veteran analyst with the brokerage firm of Laidlaw-Coggeshall Inc., was quoted in the *Journal*: "I've been in this business since 1937, and *I don't think I've seen a market this bad*. I'd like to see some stabilization...but I've almost given up on resistance points" (emphasis added).[5]

Worst market in 37 years? Giving up hope for a stabilization (to say nothing of a rally)? This is the mood of despair (or fear) that always envelops the marketplace when it is at a major bottom.

The week before, the investment chief at Marine Midland Bank had suggested that the bottom was near when he opined that the market "looks like a screaming buy" but that *"nobody wants to be the first in the water."*[6]* At the bottom, the timid bull sees bargains all around but is too afraid to buy. This type of remark is common at both primary and intermediate market lows. A variant is the statement that "there are no buyers to be found" or "the buyers are on strike." A contrarian who sees such comments can almost hear the ghost of J. Paul Getty thundering, "Buy when everyone else is selling."

In December 1974, the same day the Dow Jones industrials touched their bear market low, a distinguished analyst with Reynolds Securities, who still appears on TV's *Wall Street Week*, told the *Journal*: "Stock market participants are *giving up hope* that the October lows will hold."[7] This gentleman was merely articulating the despair that millions of investors felt—at the exact bottom of the bear market. Similar comments by other pundits appear at the bottom of every bear market, regardless of the type of investment.

More recently, the same mood of fear and despair was rampant in August 1982, just before the stock market launched into its historic ascent. (The Dow industrials gained 61 percent in the following 10 months, the steepest rise in the shortest time since 1932-33.) According to a Tulsa money manager who was quoted in the *Journal* the morning after the Dow bottomed at 777, the fact that the market had "demonstrated no ability to rally on good news [of lower interest rates] probably indicates that a *selling climax* will be required to end the bear market."[8]

A selling climax, also known as a *waterfall decline*, is probably the most dreaded phenomenon in any market. Prices go straight down without interruption. As disheartened investors dump their holdings at any price, trading volume soars.

Simply talking about the possibility of a selling climax is enough to send chills up the typical investor's spine. When prices are making an important low, however, frightened bears will often *predict* a climax—not recognizing that one has just taken place under their noses!

Many analysts seem to think that markets customarily form a bottom after a climactic burst of heavy trading. Just the opposite is true. Bear markets usually end, as T.S. Eliot might have said,

*In the following pages, the emphases added have been my own.

"not with a bang but a whimper." The climax that occurs at the end of most declines is really an anticlimax: trading volume drops, selling pressure dries up and the bear market fades away.

By contrast, heavy volume at the end of a market rise usually indicates a climactic blowoff, a last burst of euphoria that exhausts the buying pressure in the marketplace. Oddly enough, few analysts are willing to acknowledge a buying climax when they see one, usually because the market seems to be going straight up. Instead, they predict that the heavy trading will push prices even higher. The activity and excitement blind them to the fact that the market is tracing out an important top.

The same day our Tulsa money manager was warning of a selling climax, a vice president of E.F. Hutton & Co. told the *Journal* that investors were witnessing "the most emotional period [of the bear market] with *outright capitulation and panic selling* by both large and small investors."[9] He was right, of course. However, he failed to draw the proper inference: if most investors were capitulating and selling in a panic, it was time to mortgage the farm and buy.

The Sunday before the powerful 1982-87 bull market roared off the launching pad, *The New York Times* financial section proclaimed, "Even the Bulls Are Bearish."[10] Could a contrarian ask for a better reason to buy? But the nicest part of the story is that the respectable news media don't leave you hanging after they've rendered a buy signal. (It wouldn't be respectable.) They also tip you off when it's time to sell.

At the top of the 1978-80 bull market for stocks in November 1980, the *Journal* interviewed an analyst who confidently predicted that the Dow industrials would range for the *rest of the decade* between 1000 and 2000.[11] A 10-year bull market! Great expectations, wouldn't you say? Remember that the Dow at the time had barely edged over 1000 (on the strength of the Reagan landslide). While the market eventually did reach 2000 and beyond, this analyst's hopes ran far ahead of reality.

The same week, as it turned out, most stocks on the Big Board slipped into a severe 21-month bear market that shaved 25 percent off the Dow and 31 percent off the broader-based New York

Stock Exchange composite index. The starry-eyed bulls who thought the Dow wouldn't go below 1000 for the rest of the decade were ground into hamburger.

At the top of the huge speculative boom in the spring of 1983, the chairman of a $10 billion investment management firm in Los Angeles told the *Journal*, "I have *never felt more confident* in maintaining a fairly fully invested equity position."[12] Another money manager talked about "the *exciting gains* in store for corporate profits."[13] Those happy-go-lucky opinions were published the morning after most stocks peaked for the year. A few days later, the same analyst who had given up hope in October 1974 (when stocks were cheap) called for "a continuation of the *irrepressible bull market.*" He added: "We're in a *new era* of investor confidence."[14] Experience may be a great teacher, but some people, it seems, never learn.

In the weeks leading up to the manic stock market peak in August 1987, the news media brimmed with euphoric assessments of the market's potential. But the Crash of 1987 is still a controversial event and deserves a chapter all by itself. I'll treat it in detail in Chapter 8.

Gold Market Follies

Almost unfailingly, when the stock market is about to make a dramatic turnaround, several esteemed gurus will jump off the deep end—publicly—in your newspaper. But contrary thinking is a valid approach to any market, not simply the stock market. In the gold and silver markets, the "experts" regularly serve up delectable morsels for a contrarian to feast on.

In mid-January 1980, with gold changing hands at the stratospheric price of $744 an ounce (up from $475 a month earlier), a trader for Drexel Burnham Lambert told the *Journal* that "the potential to see $1,000 gold in the next week is easy," and that he wouldn't be surprised if gold reached $1,500 within the next month.[15] When normally cautious establishment types project a 33 percent gain in *one week* and a 100 percent gain in a month, you can safely deduce that the market has lost its senses. The roof is ready to cave in.

In the same issue of the *Journal*, a London dealer "at a large firm" said he wouldn't be "at all surprised" to see gold at $1,000 an ounce. "It's good business," this thoughtful gentleman confided, "but looked at objectively, it's pretty horrifying. We're all booking our beds in the looney bin."[16] As this comment shows, it's not unusual for sober analysts to recognize, at a speculative peak, that the market has gone mad. Nonetheless, like moths attracted to a flame, they can't bear to take their profits and fly away. Instead, greedy for the last penny of gain, they continue to believe that the market will go up.

The next day's *Journal* (January 18) printed the ultimate hysterical view of the market. Gold had closed on New York's Commodity Exchange the previous afternoon at $802 an ounce. A trader, again from Drexel Burnham as it happens, said: "We're in a runaway market. It's almost like going to a strip show knowing the place is about to be raided. *No one wants to leave* until they're sure the party's over."[17]

That comment appeared in Friday's newspaper. On Monday, the party was over. The price of gold touched an all-time high of $875 on the Comex, then plunged to $825 at the close. A bone-crunching two-and-a-half-year bear market had begun.

Precious metals seem to excite violent emotions at the bottom of the market as well as at the top. A treasured clipping in my file is a Commodity News Service story that appeared in *Western Mining News* a few days after gold made a primary bottom in June 1982. Headlined "$190 Gold? Analysts Disagree," the article reported that an analyst with ContiCommodity envisioned a "long-term downside objective" of $191 an ounce for gold.[18]

Most of the time, responsible analysts (of gold or any other market) tend to predict that prices will fluctuate in a narrow range. Conventional thinkers prefer to assume that patterns of the recent past will carry into the future, because that usually appears to be the "safe" position. Conformists know that if they forecast a sharp move up or down, they run the risk of not only being proved wrong, but being remembered for it as well. They might acquire the reputation of a crank or an oddball—deadly for anyone with ambitions in a big organization.

When the market is trending strongly in one direction, however, the bolder types within the investment community will often throw off the shackles of professional decorum and predict that the market will take off like a runaway railroad car *in the direction of the existing trend*. Beware of a respectable mainstream advisor who says the price of gold is going to plunge another 30 percent, after it has already plunged 60 percent in the past two years! This person is emoting, not thinking.

Interestingly enough, our analyst from ContiCommodity who was looking for $191 gold based his bearishness on a familiar argument: "There is nothing to indicate the selling has climaxed," he said. The climax, of course, was taking place as he spoke. But he couldn't see it, because he had worked himself into a mood of exaggerated pessimism. "I am waiting for the public to start selling its gold," the Conti analyst maintained. "When John Q. Public decides his Krugerrand is worthless and sells it, that's when I will buy."

This man obviously *thought* he was acting contrary to the majority. But he was waiting for the impossible: John Q. Public will never decide that his Krugerrand is worthless. (In fact, the small investor has a good record for buying physical metals near the bottom of the market and selling them near the top.) By refusing to change his mind unless some impossible condition was met, the analyst from ContiCommodity showed that he was really endorsing the prevalent bearish consensus. He wasn't thinking independently at all.

The contrary investor must guard against the fatal temptation to become gloomier and gloomier as prices fall. Instead, train yourself to become increasingly cheerful as prices decline, because you know that the market is drawing closer to its ultimate bottom! Likewise, you should feel more and more nervous as prices rise, because the market is approaching its ultimate top. When the risk in the market seems highest (at the bottom), it's really lowest because there's no room left for prices to fall. On the other hand, when the risk seems lowest (at the top), it's really highest because there's no room left for prices to rise.

Telling the Trends Apart

Perhaps the most difficult task facing any investor—but especially those investors who rely on their newspapers for buy and sell signals—is to distinguish the primary from the intermediate trend, and the intermediate from the short-term trend. Investors with a long-term perspective (six months to two years) want to buy as close as possible to a primary bottom and sell as close as possible to a primary top. If they miss the primary turning point, they try to buy at the bottom of an intermediate reaction or sell at an intermediate peak.

Investors with an intermediate time horizon (six weeks to six months) seek to buy at an intermediate low and sell at an intermediate high. But if the intermediate turning point slips by them, they look for the next short-term low at which to buy (or a short-term high at which to sell).

Traders with a short-term viewpoint (less than six weeks) have the hardest job of all. If they miss the turning point, they either must make their move as quickly as possible (taking the risk that the market may reverse on them), or they can stand aside and wait until the next short-term peak or bottom provides another opportunity to trade.

In general, newspaper commentary isn't especially helpful to the short-term trader, because respected investment analysts usually don't lose their nerve at minor turning points. (For the short-term speculator, I describe a number of more sophisticated contrarian trading techniques in later chapters.) However, the more extreme the statements by establishment pundits, the more likely that the market has reached a turning point of longer-term significance.

Near intermediate or primary tops and bottoms, newspapers and magazines often begin to run emotionally tinged feature (background) articles about the market, in addition to the usual daily commentary. For instance, when the gold market was forming an intermediate bottom around $335 an ounce in July and August of 1984, *The Wall Street Journal* and *Barron's* published a flurry of full-length articles pooh-poohing gold.

Barron's carried an interview with investment advisor John Dessauer, titled "Crash in Gold: Analyst Sees Only Short Respite"[19] and another with Harry Schultz, headlined "The Greening of a Gold Bug."[20] On July 9, the same day gold made an important (though not its final primary) low, the *Journal* ran an interesting feature noting that while most professionals were expecting gold prices to slide further, the average person was buying gold coins heavily. Coin dealers were swamped with retail orders to buy Krugerrands and other bullion coins—a recurring phenomenon at market bottoms. (Within three weeks, gold jumped more than $20.) Small investors who pay cash and buy for the long term typically have a much better sense of value than the professional analysts at the giant brokerage houses. If only the pros had the humility to listen to them!

Of course, there's no guarantee that hysterical newspaper or magazine articles will always coincide precisely with a significant market turning point. Even though contrary opinion is a powerful timing tool, it isn't perfect—no investment technique is. Sometimes contrary thinking will put you into a market a bit early (as it might have with gold in 1984) and take you out a bit early, since extremes of crowd psychology don't always coincide precisely with the highest or the lowest price. Over the long pull, though, the connection is amazingly close, as I'll explain in Chapter 4.

Catching the Big One

Fortunately for long-term investors who don't like to trade frequently, primary turning points are usually the easiest to recognize. The dispensers of investment wisdom become irrepressibly enthusiastic or unrelentingly gloomy. Dramatic predictions abound. Feature articles in newspapers and magazines report on the blessings or disasters that the market has wrought. *Time* or *Newsweek* may even devote a cover story to the market.

At a major cyclical turning point, it isn't uncommon for a book touting or condemning the market to reach the best-seller list. In 1979-80, for example, a spate of books predicting runaway inflation and economic collapse rose to the top of the charts. Howard J. Ruff's *How to Survive and Prosper During the Coming Bad Years* became the best-selling financial book in history. A close runner-up was Douglas Casey's book, *Crisis Investing*, which hit the best-seller list in September 1980. John A. Pugsley's best-selling *Alpha Strategy* recommended stockpiling food, fuel and other necessities to combat inflation. Jerome Smith, in another bestseller, *The Coming Currency Collapse*, prophesied the demise of the dollar—again due to inflation—just before the dollar exploded upward into a five-year bull market, one of its greatest rallies in history.

In fairness to Casey and Ruff, I should note that neither is a bigoted goldbug and both have urged their followers on various occasions to sell (as well as buy) precious metals. Furthermore, Ruff's book in particular reached the best-seller list early enough to give many of his readers an opportunity to profit from the surge in metals prices during 1979. Nonetheless, it was hardly an accident that all four of these books captured the mass imagination just when inflation and metals prices were cresting—before a devastating collapse. In retrospect, the success of the inflation-doomsday books should have warned the contrary investor that precious metals and other inflation hedges were nearing a primary peak.

Naturally, a book isn't published at every primary turning point to warn you that the market is about to shift gears. Often, you must rely on an accumulation of signals from newspapers, magazines, TV and other media to know when a change in the primary trend is at hand. Interpreting these signals is an art, not a science. As a rule, though, the more frightened you feel when you decide to go against the crowd, the more likely that the market is presenting you with a major buying or selling opportunity.

In addition, as you'll see in the next few chapters, there are many statistical indicators you can track to confirm the message from the media. These indicators give you objective evidence of what investors in the marketplace are thinking (and, more important, doing). But since even the best of statistical indicators can occasionally go haywire, you should never overlook the indicator that is sitting on your doorstep every morning. All you really need to know is right there, in black and white.

Chapter 4

Roll Out the Polls

If 40 million people say a foolish thing, it does not become a wise one.—W. Somerset Maugham

Newspapers, magazines and books will usually give you a pretty good idea of the market's mood. But sophisticated contrarians also rely on a bevy of statistical indicators to help read the mind of the crowd more precisely. One of the easiest—and most accurate— ways to determine whether the market is approaching unanimous agreement (hence, a reversal) is by taking a poll.

Ideally, a pollster who wanted to gauge the mood of the market could collect a scientific sampling of several thousand investors nationwide (or worldwide) and ask them whether they thought prices were headed up or down. However, since markets fluctuate so quickly, altering the lineup of bulls and bears, it would be necessary to take a poll weekly, or even more frequently, to keep the data fresh. So far, nobody has attempted such a costly project, although the Sindlinger organization comes closest with its weekly poll asking a cross-section of U.S. households about their immediate and long-range plans to buy stock. Someday, perhaps, some shrewd entrepreneur will set up a phone-in polling system that would make it possible for thousands, or even millions, of investors to register their opinions of the market at regular intervals on a central computer.

The next best thing to polling the investors themselves is a survey of investment advisors. In fact, since investment advisors tend to shape the thinking of their clients, this elite group may provide an even better insight into the market's likely direction. Certainly, it isn't difficult to find out what investment advisors are thinking. They publish hundreds of newsletters laying out their opinions for all to see. Despite the verbal smoke screens that some advisors send out, careful readers who have subscribed to a newsletter for a while can readily judge whether the author is bullish, bearish or on the fence.

Abe Cohen's Brainchild

Investor's Intelligence (P.O. Box 2046, New Rochelle, NY 10801, $124 per year) is the oldest investment "newsletter on newsletters," having been founded in 1959. The late Abraham W. Cohen, who edited the letter for many years, inaugurated its most famous feature in the early 1960s: the "sentiment index" of investment advisors. Focusing primarily on the stock market, *Investor's Intelligence* currently monitors 123 investment services. Each week, the newsletter's editors report the percentage of advisors who are bullish, bearish or looking for a "correction" (a temporary pullback within a primary upward trend).

The more-than-20-year history of the *Investors Intelligence* poll confirms what a contrarian would expect. Typically, the largest percentage of advisors are bullish (optimistic) on the stock market at the top, when prices are about to come down. The bearish (pessimistic) contingent is generally largest at the bottom, when prices are about to turn up. In short, most advisors— like their followers—lean the wrong way at important market turning points.

Historically, a reading above 60 percent on the bearish scale has nearly always marked the bottom of a primary bear market. As you can see from Figure 2, the Dow Jones Industrial Average made a triple bottom at the end of the 1981-82 bear market—once in March 1982, again in June and again in August. Bearish sentiment was strongest at the March low (61 percent), slightly less intense at the June low (58 percent), and least intense (54 percent) at the final August low. Any of these low points would have presented a good opportunity to buy stocks.

By contrast, only 17 percent of the advisors were bearish in August 1987, just before the market crashed. Bulls outnumbered

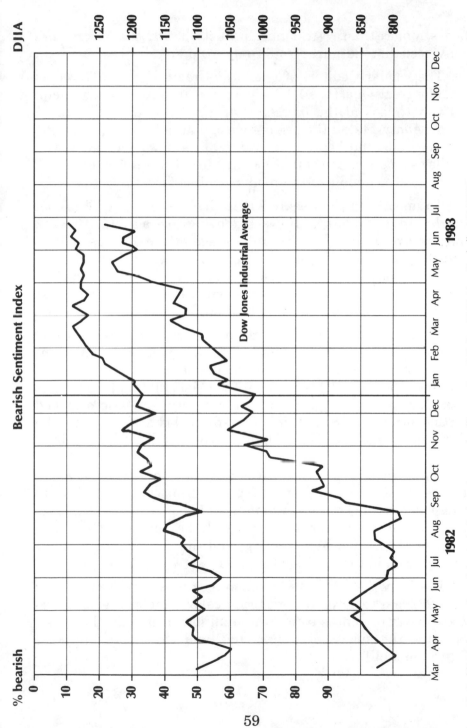

Fig. 2. Bearish sentiment index

Vertical lines represent 5-week intervals. **Source:** Investors Intelligence, Inc., P.O. Box 2046, New Rochelle, NY 10801.

bears by more than a 3-to-1 margin. Just when most advisors were convinced that the market could only go up, stock prices collapsed.

The scholarly editors of *The Bank Credit Analyst* (3463 Peel St., Montreal, Que. H3A 1W7, $545 per year) have devised a helpful way to look at the *Investors Intelligence* figures. *The Bank Credit Analyst* takes the percentage of bulls and divides it by the sum of bulls and bears. Essentially, this maneuver gives you "bulls as a percentage of those willing to express a firm opinion." It ignores the middle-of-the-roaders calling for a correction.

To smooth out the weekly fluctuations in the data, *The Bank Credit Analyst* plots a 10-week moving average. (A 10-week moving average starts with an average of the 10 most recent weekly readings; each week, you drop the oldest 11th week back and add the newest weekly reading.) Figure 3, which depicts this 10-week average of advisory sentiment, shows how far off base the majority usually is at important market turning points.

Note, however, that the peak in advisory bullishness sometimes occurs *before* the peak in the market, just as the low point in advisory sentiment sometimes occurs before the bottom of the market (as in 1982). This was one of the "foolers" that threw many a good contrarian off guard in 1987: advisory bullishness peaked in the spring of 1987 and had already cooled somewhat by the time the Dow hit 2722 in August. When analyzing sentiment figures, you should keep in mind that technical analysis has found favor with a growing circle of investment advisors in recent years. Before the 1987 stock market top, as I'll discuss more fully in Chapter 8, many key technical indicators had already been deteriorating for several months. As a result, the technicians' enthusiasm for stocks had been waning, and this growing caution reflected itself in the sentiment figures.

Precisely the same phenomenon took place, in reverse, near the 1982 market lows: various technical barometers began to improve several months before the final low in August that year, boosting the spirits of technicians (and thus, the sentiment figures as well).

With the caveat that turns in sentiment sometimes lead the market by a few weeks or a few months, here are several broad conclusions you can draw from *The Bank Credit Analyst* chart:

• *A reading above 75 percent is likely to accompany a primary top* in a powerful bull market. This was the case in early 1973; at three points in 1976; and in the spring of 1987. Long-term investors would have been wise to dispose of most or all of their stocks at these junctures. Such lofty readings can also signal an intermediate peak in a strong bull market, as in 1971, 1983 and 1986.

• *A reading below 35 percent is likely to indicate a primary bottom*, as in 1974, 1978 and 1982. Stocks were a screaming buy at these points. In late 1979, the spring of 1980 and the fall of 1981, such extremely low readings marked an intermediate bottom with excellent opportunities for the nimble investor to earn profits over a three- to six-month period.

• *A drop from 75 percent to 60 percent in a strong bull market represents a normal correction.* In a dynamic primary bull market, it isn't necessary for the bullish percentage to shrink drastically before the market can go on to new highs.

In 1971, 1975, 1985 and 1986, for example, serious pullbacks occurred within powerful primary bull markets. All four times,

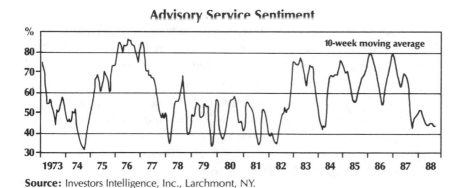

Source: Investors Intelligence, Inc., Larchmont, NY.

Fig. 3. Advisory service sentiment

the bullish consensus tumbled from over 75 percent to about 60 percent on a 10-week basis. A sizable group of nervous advisors threw in the towel and concluded that a major downturn had begun. At that point, the market resumed its advance and promptly climbed to new high ground.

Statistical tools like the *Investors Intelligence* poll provide you with an objective yardstick for measuring the market's mood. But no index or formula can eliminate human judgment. You must still exercise discretion when you *interpret* the figures, as you'll see if you take another glance at Figure 3. From early 1979 to early 1983—a four-year period—the percentage of bulls never rose above 60. If you had hung on to your stocks in the belief that the bullish consensus would rise to 75 percent or more before the market peaked, you would have been obliged to sit through the mini-crashes of late 1979 and early 1980, as well as the destructive primary bear market of 1981-82.

Rapid inflation and high interest rates in the late 1970s and early 1980s subdued Wall Street's natural optimism. As a result, the "bullpen" never expanded to its traditional limit. The contrary investor must always watch for longer-lasting shifts in the climate of opinion that might push the upper limit for the sentiment index either higher or lower.

A nagging problem with opinion polls of all types is that different pollsters come up with different results. However, if the same person conducts a poll over many years, you should at least be able to compare the results at different points in time. Michael Burke, who took over as editor of *Investors Intelligence* when Abe Cohen died in 1983, was the old master's longtime assistant. Thus, the *Investors Intelligence* poll offers a quarter-century of continuity—a remarkable record in the advisory business, which is known for its high mortality rate. For the contrarian who plans to commit serious money to the stock market, *Investors Intelligence* is an indispensable timing aid.

Tracking the Commodity Bulls

Like *Investors Intelligence* in the stock market, Earl Hadady's weekly *Bullish Consensus* newsletter (P.O. Box 90490, Pasadena, CA 91109, $345 per year) tracks the opinions of commodity advisors. *The Bullish Consensus* scans approximately 100 sources of professional commodity-trading recommendations, including about 30 market letters published by the leading commission houses (Merrill Lynch, Shearson Lehman Hutton, Drexel Burnham and so on).

Hadady, who has been running *The Bullish Consensus* (formerly known as *Market Vane*) since 1974, has made several notable refinements in the polling techniques pioneered by *Investors Intelligence*. For one thing, *The Bullish Consensus* weights each advisor according to his estimated audience. "Obviously, more traders follow the recommendations of the analysts of large brokerage firms than those of smaller firms," Hadady explains.[1] For independent market analysts who publish their own advisory letters, Hadady uses the size of each analyst's subscriber list to estimate how many traders the advisor influences.

By weighting the advisors in proportion to their influence, Hadady ensures that an opinion held by a large number of relatively small (uninfluential) advisory services won't distort his figures. He also grades each advisor on a nine-point scale from 0 (extremely bearish) to 8 (extremely bullish). No other poll in either the stock or the commodity markets attempts to measure advisory sentiment so precisely.

This weighted index or "bullish consensus" is calculated on a scale of 0 to 100 percent. A reading of 0 means that everyone is unequivocally bearish and expecting prices to move lower. Fifty percent is a neutral reading, while 100 percent means that everyone is unreservedly bullish and expecting prices to move higher.

Most of the time, the bullish consensus fluctuates between 30 and 70 percent. "At 30 percent," Hadady notes, "an oversold condition is beginning to develop, whereas at 70 percent an overbought condition is developing."[2] In this context, *oversold* means that there are too many underfinanced bears in the marketplace, hoping to make a killing if prices drop. *Overbought* means that there are too many thinly margined bulls who are hoping to make a fortune if prices rise. (Hadady argues that the well-financed "big money" always wins, over the long haul, in the commodity pits.)

As the consensus approaches the extremes of 0 or 100 percent, an imminent price reversal becomes more and more likely. Once prices have turned around, the bullish consensus will follow suit. The percentage of bulls will rise as the market bounces back from an oversold extreme, and will fall as the market retreats from an overbought extreme.

Waves of Sentiment

No market goes straight up or down. Prices rise or fall in waves. In a primary bull market, the waves tend to form a pattern of higher peaks (and higher troughs, or low points). Likewise, in a primary bear market, the waves tend to peak at successively lower levels while the troughs tend to bottom at successively lower levels. In fact, you can also observe a pattern of ascending or descending waves when the market undergoes a significant intermediate correction against the primary trend, lasting from a few months to a year.

Figure 4 illustrates this wave phenomenon. The primary bull market for gold that began in 1976 reached a climactic peak at $850 in January 1980. From that point onward, gold entered a declining phase that carried the price down to $297 in June 1982. During this 29-month primary bear market, the price of gold formed a series of lower peaks and lower troughs.

After gold made a primary bear market low in June 1982, the price climbed steeply to $510 in February 1983. During this powerful but short-lived bull market, gold traced out a series of higher peaks and troughs. Then a new primary bear market set in, taking the gold price all the way down to $282 an ounce in February 1985. Starting in February 1985, gold rose in another primary bull market, 33 months in length, that peaked at $502 in December 1987.

64

The Gold Bulls

Source: Commodity Trend Service, *The Bullish Consensus.*

Fig. 4. The gold bulls

Some analysts would argue that the 1982-83 and 1985-87 up-swings in gold were merely "corrections" in a giant bear market dating back to 1980. I prefer to adhere to the more common terminology, which defines a primary bull market as any period stretching six months or more in which prices rise at least 20 percent. (In a primary bear market, prices *fall* 20 percent or more over a period of at least six months.)

But regardless of the labels you assign to gold's behavior during the 1980s, the wave pattern is clear. Advisory sentiment follows the same wavelike pattern as the market. Since most investment advisors are trend followers, their outlook typically grows more cheerful as prices rise and more gloomy as prices fall. Figure 4, which is based on data from *The Bullish Consensus*, shows how the percentage of advisors who were bullish on gold gradually declined between 1980 and 1982 as the primary bear market wore on.

After gold prices started to rally from the primary bottom in June 1982, the bullish consensus rose—in a series of waves—from 17 percent in June 1982 to 88 percent in January 1983. At that point, both the bullish consensus and the price of gold declined in waves until the bottom of the next primary bear market was reached in February 1985.

Then the process repeated itself. From a low of 16 percent the same week bullion hit bottom, the bullish consensus steadily worked its way higher over the next two years, peaking at 85 percent in August 1987 with London gold at $477 an ounce.

The correlation between prices and advisory sentiment isn't always perfect. For example, the percentage of gold bulls was higher in June 1982 than in March 1982, even though the price of gold had sunk to a lower low. Again, in 1987, the consensus peaked in August, whereas the price of gold touched its final high for the cycle four months later, in December, accompanied by a lower reading on the consensus. In both of these cases, 1982 and 1987, the extreme in advisory sentiment was reached at the same time as an extreme in the market's upward (1987) or downward (1982) rate of change or "momentum"—a concept I explain more fully in Chapter 12.

As we saw with the stock market illustration earlier in this chapter, sentiment sometimes turns *before* prices. But the link is remarkably close. If you trade commodities, you can greatly improve your odds of success by adopting a contrarian strategy based on the *Bullish Consensus* index.

Contrarian Trading Rules

The same basic rules apply to any commodity from gold and silver to pork bellies and Treasury bonds:

• *If the bullish consensus goes above 80 percent or below 20 percent, you should immediately position yourself against the prevailing trend.* A sharp price reversal is imminent. For example, if the consensus on Treasury bonds climbs to 84 percent (as it did in May 1983, when the bond market was forming a major peak), you should sell the bonds short. An 81 percent consensus also greeted the major top for bonds in April 1986. If the consensus drops to 20 (as it did twice when the bond market became deeply oversold in May-June 1984 and again the week before the famous Black Monday low in October 1987), you should buy with both hands.

Readings above 80 or below 20 are rare. Sifting through six years of *Bullish Consensus* data (1977-82), which represented over 7,500 consensus readings on 31 commodities, I discovered that only 5 percent of the weekly figures were above 80 and less than 4 percent fell below 20. In other words, the typical commodity achieves a bullish consensus above 80 percent or below 20 percent about twice a year.

• *Until the consensus reaches the 80/20 extremes, you should trade with the prevailing trend.* As Humphrey Noill, the "Vermont ruminator," used to say, "The public is right about the trends, but wrong at both ends." For illustration, let's assume that the bullish consensus for hogs was 15 percent last week and 23 percent this week. Under the 80/20 rule, you should have bought a hog contract last week when the consensus reached an oversold extreme. You should now hold the contract until the consensus stops rising.

Of course, the consensus may not get all the way down to 20 percent or all the way up to 80 percent. Sometimes the market bottoms with a 25 or 30 percent consensus and peaks with a 70 or 75 percent consensus. In such cases, you can still buy on any reading below 30 or sell on any reading above 70, but you should recognize that the odds aren't running quite so strongly in your favor. If, after you enter your trade, the consensus stalls for a couple of weeks at mid-range (40 to 60 percent), you should pull out and wait for the next genuine overbought or oversold extreme. Never play the commodity market when your chances of making a profitable trade appear to be only about 50-50. Those are losers' odds. If you take a 50-50 bet, the professional floor traders, who have access to information that you don't and can react faster than you, will edge you out more often than not.

• *In a strong primary bull or bear market, a short-term correction usually won't carry the consensus down to 20 percent or up to 80 percent.* Look back at Figure 4. During 1981, a bearish year for gold, the consensus never rose above 71 percent (the September peak). In fact, the March, May and December peaks for the consensus were all in the 40 to 50 percent range. By the same token, when gold was rising sharply in the second half of 1982, the lowest point that the consensus attained was 35 percent (at the August trough).

The October and November lows were around 50 percent. In general, a short-term reaction in a strong bull or bear market will reverse itself and the primary trend will resume when the consensus moves into the 40 to 60 percent range. In a powerful bull market, you should buy (go along) when the consensus retreats from the overbought area to mid-range. Likewise, in a powerful bear market, you should sell short when the consensus bounces up from an oversold area to mid-range. Figure 5 illustrates this principle.

In most cases, you shouldn't try to trade against the primary trend in a vigorous bull or bear market. The dips in a bull market are usually too brief and too shallow for short selling, just as most rallies in a bear market are too ephemeral and too weak for snatching profits on the long side.

However, every primary bull or bear market eventually comes to an end. In addition, many primary markets undergo severe intermediate reactions or corrections that bring the consensus down to 20 (or below) on the low side or up to 80 (or above) on the high side. You can tell that the primary trend is about to change, or that a severe intermediate reaction is about to set in, when the

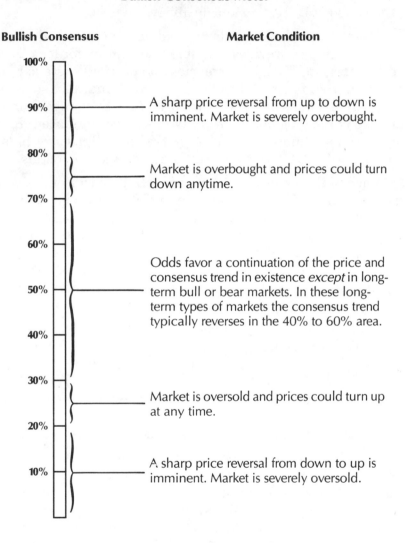

Bullish Consensus Meter

| Bullish Consensus | Market Condition |

A sharp price reversal from up to down is imminent. Market is severely overbought.

Market is overbought and prices could turn down anytime.

Odds favor a continuation of the price and consensus trend in existence *except* in long-term bull or bear markets. In these long-term types of markets the consensus trend typically reverses in the 40% to 60% area.

Market is oversold and prices could turn up at any time.

A sharp price reversal from down to up is imminent. Market is severely oversold.

Fig. 5. Bullish consensus meter

bullish consensus goes to an 80/20 extreme *and stays there for three to five weeks in a row*. Markets simply can't sustain an extreme degree of optimism or pessimism for long. A sharp swing in the opposite direction nearly always ensues.

Even if you don't regularly trade commodities, the *Bullish Consensus* index provides valuable information for long-term investors in stocks, bonds, currencies and precious metals. Futures contracts tied to several well-known stock indexes (such as the Standard & Poor's 500, the New York Stock Exchange Composite and the Value Line Composite) have been trading since 1982, joining the older financial-futures contracts on Treasury bills and bonds, bank CDs, foreign currencies and precious metals.

Each of these major markets has a bullish consensus you can track for signs of an important buying or selling opportunity. For example, the string of low readings for gold in February 1985 sent out a buy signal for all forms of gold, not merely futures contracts but also physical bullion and mining shares. Similarly, the sky-high readings for Treasury bonds in April and May 1983 (averaging almost 80 percent over a four-week period) provided a timely sell signal for *all* bonds: Treasurys, corporates and municipals.

My rule for long-term investors is fairly simple. If the bullish consensus averages 80 percent or more over a four-week period, it's usually a good time to sell. The market is probably making a peak that won't be seen again for many months, perhaps years. If the consensus averages 25 percent or less over a four-week period, the market is virtually begging you to buy. (*Barron's* now carries the bullish consensus on stocks and bonds every week.)

Finally, a caution to keep in mind when you're trying to interpret the bullish consensus—or indeed, any measure of investor sentiment: beware of any sharp swing in the consensus that isn't accompanied by an equally large movement in prices. If bullish sentiment climbs rapidly but prices don't, chances are that the prevailing downtrend is still intact. To be genuine, a new trend must usually meet with skepticism and disbelief—at least at the outset.

The same principle applies on the downside, too. If investor sentiment cools noticeably but prices don't drop, it's generally a sign that the existing uptrend is still alive. As an old Wall Street saw has it, "a bull market must climb a wall of worry." For the contrarian, worry is to be welcomed in a market trending up-ward—*as long as the worry isn't well founded*. If, however, investors feel uneasy because, say, the market's technical health is deteriorating or because some macroeconomic force is threatening to smash market values, there may be good reason for worry. In such cases, worry can breed panic selling in a kind of self-fulfilling prophecy. Meltdown Monday in 1987 was an extreme example of this phenomenon.

Informal Polls

The *Investors Intelligence* and *Bullish Consensus* polls are two of the most reliable guides to what investment professionals and, by extension, their clients are thinking. You can also devise your own informal poll of investment advisors by subscribing to a representative sampling of financial newsletters. While many newsletter writers acknowledge the power of contrary thinking (at least in theory), few attempt to practice it consistently. Most simply follow the prevailing market trend. If the market is going up, they advise their subscribers to buy; if the market is going down, they recommend selling.

This strategy has at least one virtue. Because the advisor changes his tune at every twist and turn of the market, he never appears to be drastically wrong. (As the old saying goes: If you can't predict, predict often.) To be sure, the trend-following advisor seldom helps his subscribers make big profits. But he reinforces their emotional penchant to buy after prices have risen, and to sell after the market has fallen—to buy high and sell low. Since he's a kindred spirit and massages their psyches, they renew their subscriptions.

Fortunately, you can conduct your own private, thoroughly unscientific poll without wading through 70 or 80 investment newsletters. Select four or five publications, preferably written by advisors with a fondness for brash or flamboyant statements, or by "pure" technicians who believe that trendlines and chart patterns tell all. These advisors (who shall remain nameless to protect the guilty!) are most likely to get swept up in the emotions of the crowd when a powerful market trend is approaching a climactic reversal. Here are some of the signals letter writers will send you at important market turning points:

• *Longtime bulls will suddenly turn bearish* at the bottom. Bears will predict a further price collapse of 20, 30 or 40 percent. The few bulls who don't turn bearish will sharply lower their forecasts.

• *Diehard bears will turn bullish* at the top, while bulls will make outrageously optimistic projections. The few timid bears who remain won't dare to advise short selling (when the risk is all but nil).

• *Normally cautious bears will recommend short selling* and other aggressive tactics at the bottom. At the top, normally cautious bulls will urge you to speculate (with low-priced stocks, futures contracts, options, margin accounts, etc.).

• *Technicians will cite heavy trading volume* at the top as evidence that the market is headed higher. "Over 160 million shares can't be wrong!" was a typical advisor's misguided comment on the stock market in early January 1984, just before the Dow industrials plunged 15 percent. The same technicians will poohpooh low trading volume at the bottom because they will be looking for a "selling climax."

• *Chartists will worry about broken trendlines*, violated moving averages and "downside confirmation" at the bottom. The same analysts will blithely reassure you at the top that all is well because the Dow or pork bellies or gold (you name it) is trading above its trendlines and moving averages, and indeed has just climbed to a new high.

• *Advisors will wax eloquent on the virtues of a buy-and-hold strategy* at the top, urging you to "sit tight." At the bottom, they'll point out all the benefits of timing the market, in-and-out trading, telephone switching and so on.

Whether you make your own informal survey of advisory opinion or subscribe to one of the polling services, the stark fact remains that *most investment advisors are wrong precisely when it pays the most to be right*—at primary and important intermediate turning points for the market. How can "professionals" with such dismal records stay in business? As an investment advisor myself, I'm tempted to plead the Fifth.

But the answer to this paradox, it seems to me, is that the better advisors don't stay wrong for long. Because they're flexible enough to recognize a mistake, they reverse themselves before their clients suffer irrecoverable losses (or miss out completely on a good upswing). As a result, *most* of the time, *most* advisors are *more or less* right about the market—at least about the primary trend. If you want to rise above this mediocrity, you must buy and sell when market sentiment reaches its greatest extremes: when most advisors are too afraid (at the bottom) or too greedy (at the top) to join you.

Chapter 5

Stock Market Timing

Ripeness is all.—Shakespeare

In selecting the soundest financial investments, the question of when to buy is far more important than what to buy.—Roger W. Babson

Happiness is a stock that goes up when the rest of the market is going down. Nothing makes you feel more intelligent, more self-satisfied, more disdainful of the millions who are wringing their hands while the Dow Jones averages plummet day after day.

On the other hand, nothing is quite so infuriating as a stock that refuses to budge when the rest of the board is racing ahead. It makes you feel like a fool, an incompetent—an amateur. "You could have picked better stocks by throwing darts at the newspaper," you ruefully remind yourself.

Anyone who plays the market for long will occasionally experience the delight, or the disappointment, of a stock that scoots off in the opposite direction from the market. Just as Republican renegades on Capitol Hill sometimes vote for Democrat-sponsored measures (and vice versa), every stock is to some extent a free agent, marching to its own drumbeat.

Gold shares, for example, rose during the 1929-32 crash, while the Dow Jones Industrial Average plunged 89 percent. Or, to take a more recent contrasting case: at the Dow's August 1987 high, after the venerable average had skyrocketed 44 percent in eight months, 16 stocks listed on the Big Board reached new lows for the year.

My intent, however, isn't to show how perverse the stock market can be. Quite the contrary. These are the exceptions that prove the rule: *Most of the time, most stocks go up or down together.* Of course, not every stock, every day, follows the same path as the major market averages (the Dow industrials, the Standard & Poor's 500, the Value Line Composite, etc.). In fact, it isn't unusual, even on a day when the major averages move strongly in one direction, to find that a quarter to a third of all issues with price changes went the opposite way.

But if the market averages follow a sustained trend for many weeks or months, the great majority of stocks will do likewise. Looking for stocks that will go up in a bear market is as thankless a task as looking for stocks that will go down in a bull market. Unless you consider yourself a genius at stock picking, I don't suggest that you attempt it.

During the 1980-82 primary downswing, for instance, about 80 percent of the industrial shares on the New York Stock Exchange (NYSE) were worth less at the August 1982 lows than at the November 1980 highs. Thus, your chances of selecting a winner that would have bucked this downtrend were approximately one in five, and the 1980-82 bear market was remarkably less severe than most. In the famous smash of 1973-74, over 95 percent of the stocks on the NYSE declined.

Market Timing or Stock Selection?

Some Wall Street sages maintain that it's impossible to detect major bull or bear markets in advance. Therefore, the argument runs, you should always remain fully invested in stocks that appear to be good long-term values. "Don't try to time the market," such folk advise. "Just select the right stocks and you'll come out ahead in the long run."

Most brokers, securities analysts, *Forbes* columnists and others who tout stocks for a living display a fondness for this point of view. It isn't difficult to see why. What would your broker do to stay busy during the long months of a primary bear market if he didn't think that *some* stock *somewhere* is always a good buy? An aggressive broker could, I suppose, urge you to profit from falling prices by selling short, but most brokers shy away from short selling. They firmly believe this type of investing is "too risky." *

Market timing is probably an inappropriate strategy for big institutions, which require weeks, even months, to build up or liquidate their massive stock portfolios. Even for individuals, moreover, a couple of good reasons argue for keeping at least a portion of your wealth in common stocks most of the time:

• *The longer you hold your stocks, the lower the risk that you'll lose money,* regardless of how badly you may have timed your purchases. Over the past century, an investor who bought and held a diversified basket of stocks for at least 10 years, reinvesting his dividends throughout, would have lost money only if he had bought in 1928 or 1929—the peak years before the Great Depression. Stock prices can drop fast and far, and can remain depressed for long periods. However, dividend income will usually bail you out from losses on your stock if you hang on for a decade or more. Small consolation? True. But it's worth something, especially in light of the next item.

• *Over the long pull, stocks have generated a better return than any other major type of asset.* Consider how the following popular investments have performed over the most recent 25-year period (year-end 1962 to year-end 1987). Despite the enormous inflation of these years, so-called "inflation hedges" like real estate and precious metals actually lagged behind common stocks when you count the value of reinvested dividends:

*In a short sale, you borrow stock from your broker and sell it. Naturally, you must eventually return the borrowed stock. But if the market price of the stock drops after the short sale, you can buy the stock back (cover the short) for less than the price you received when you sold it short. A short seller profits from a *decline* in the price of a stock. However, since the stock could theoretically rise to infinity, saddling you with an infinite loss, brokers generally steer clients away from short selling.

Investment	1987 value of $10,000 invested in 1962	Compounded annual return
Common stocks	$105,569	9.9%
Residential property	84,275	8.9
U.S. $20 gold piece	82,000	8.8
Commercial property	78,658	8.6
Platinum	60,679	7.5
Silver	54,754	7.0
Treasury bills	50,918	6.7
Corporate bonds	46,319	6.3

Standard & Poor's 500, with dividends reinvested. Stock, bond and bill data from Ibbotson Associates Inc., Chicago. Real estate data from Morgan Stanley & Co. Coins and metals data from market sources.

• *A buy-and-hold strategy will save you a shiny penny (perhaps even two) in brokerage commissions and capital-gains taxes.* Whenever you make a profitable trade, Uncle Sam wants part of the bounty. At the moment, the top rate on capital gains is 28 percent, with any state taxes added on from there.

Furthermore, your broker will take his cut regardless of whether you make money—a powerful incentive to sit still and let others do the trading.

The Virtues of Timing

If these arguments for buying and holding common stocks are starting to convince you, let me add that a good case can be made for market timing, too. Investors try to "time the market" mainly in order to sidestep deep declines. Avoiding losses in a bear market puts you on a higher platform when a new bull market begins.

Let's say the stock market drops 20 percent. If you bought at the top and ride the market all the way down, your $100 share of Whizbang Corp. will fall to $80. You'll require a 25 percent gain just to break even. The steeper the decline, the greater the rebound you'll need to recover your losses, as the following table makes clear:

If prices drop...	You'll need this gain to break even
10%	11.1%
15	17.6
20	25.0
25	33.3
30	42.8
40	66.7
50	100.0

Going back to our example, let's say you bought Whizbang from a market timer. After selling to you at 100, he stashes the cash proceeds under his mattress. If the market timer now buys back into the stock at 85 (not even at the absolute bottom), he'll show a 17.6 percent profit by the time you're just breaking into the black.

This example isn't merely a chalkboard exercise. Millions of investors worldwide stampeded into stocks during the first eight months of 1987, when a sense of market timing would have told them to tread lightly because the risks were high. It will probably take several years, and perhaps a good deal longer, for these disillusioned masses to recoup all their losses. Meanwhile, the market timers who forehandedly reduced their exposure to stocks and thus preserved capital in the crash will enjoy a performance edge over those who bought in 1987 and held.

In Chapter 7, I'll discuss in detail several contrarian strategies for choosing your own stocks to buy and hold irrespective of the overall market. Contrary thinking, however, can also give you an edge when you're trying to spot important turning points for the market as a whole. If you can correctly identify the market's primary trend, almost any diversified portfolio of 15 to 25 stocks will ring up profits for you, even if you make your selections by lobbing darts at the stock tables in your newspaper!

As a matter of fact, if you master the art of market timing, you can dispense with selecting individual stocks. A mutual fund, which represents a diversified portfolio, will do the job for you. All you need to know is when to buy shares of the fund, and when to sell them.

In previous chapters, I explained how to spot important reversals in the stock market by analyzing the comments of market gurus quoted in your daily newspaper. I also described the *Investors Intelligence* poll and how to interpret it. Now let's focus on some of the less-well-known, and often more precise, contrary indicators that can point you to major buying and selling opportunities.

Year in and year out, certain groups of investors consistently do well while others, with equal regularity, fare poorly. For convenience, we might call these groups the *smart money* and the *dumb money*. The smart money buys low and sells high, while the dumb money does just the opposite.

Smart-money investors tend to be successful Wall Street professionals who trade stock for a living, or well-heeled private investors who buy stocks and hold them for the long term. These people typically possess a keen sense of value—the mark of a true contrarian. The dumb money, on the other hand, generally consists of amateur short-term speculators—in-and-out traders—who are looking for a quick profit. They go where the action is, and usually hop on the trolley right at the end of the line.

The only requirement to join the winner's circle in the stock market is that you follow a simple axiom: Do what the smart money is doing, and do exactly the opposite of what the dumb money is doing. When the smart money is buying, you buy; but when the dumb money is buying, you sell. Likewise, when the smart money is selling, you sell; but when the dumb money is selling, you buy. At significant turning points, these two groups are nearly always poles apart in their thinking. But who is the smart money and who is the dumb money?

America's Most Knowledgeable Investors

When it comes to recognizing the primary trend, the shrewdest group of stock market investors in America is probably the *corporate insiders*—officers and directors of publicly traded companies. Nobody has ever investigated whether these corporate bigwigs are more adept than other investors at managing their entire portfolios. But the insiders certainly do much better than the public at trading *shares of their own companies*—partly because the insiders know more about their companies than the best-informed securities analysts, and partly because federal law requires insiders to take a long-term view of the markets.

Insiders aren't allowed to sell their company's stock until six months have elapsed since their last purchase (vice versa if they wish to buy). In addition, if insiders acquire their stock at bargain prices through a company stock-option plan, they're required to hang on to the stock for at least two years. These provisions of the law discourage short-term trading and encourage insiders to focus on long-term values.

Federal securities law also prohibits insiders from buying or selling their company's stock on the basis of *material* information not known to the public. (Supposedly, any piece of news that might significantly affect the price of the stock is material.) Hence, if you were the president of XYZ company, it would be illegal to buy XYZ stock if you knew that another firm was about to make a takeover offer for XYZ. In the same vein, it would be illegal to sell your shares if you knew that XYZ was about to announce a huge loss.

However, a lot of *nonmaterial* but valuable information passes through the hands of insiders day after day, week after week. The chairman or president of a corporation, who usually sees his firm's daily or weekly sales reports and knows when the company is working on a new product or negotiating a big contract, can form a fairly accurate picture of the company's earnings prospects long before an official announcement is made.

Furthermore, members of the board of directors, even though they may not work full time for the corporation, often pick up useful tidbits from conversations with management. Studies have shown that of all insiders, the chairman, president and directors typically make the most profitable judgments about buying or selling a company's stock.[1]

As a rule of thumb, stocks heavily purchased by insiders outperform the market averages by about 2-to-1 in a bull market, and fall half as fast in a bear market. Stocks with heavy insider selling, on the other hand, tend to rise only half as much as the market averages when the primary trend is up, and fall twice as hard when the primary trend is down. In Chapter 7, I discuss insider trading as a tool for selecting individual stocks to buy or sell.

However, insider trading is also a revealing indicator of the market's general direction. When the market averages are close to an important bottom, insiders as a group usually swing to the buy side; when the averages are approaching a significant top, the insiders tend to sell heavily. Figure 6 documents this remarkable correlation.

Over the past 15 years, whenever insider purchases, as a percentage of total insider trades, exceeded 50 percent (i.e., there were more purchases than sales), the market was forming a good bottom. At the 1974 lows, which presented the best buying opportunity in 25 years, insider purchases soared to 73 percent of all trades. Likewise, after the 1987 crash, insider buying rocketed to 76 percent of all trades—an all-time record.

By contrast, insider sales outnumbered purchases by a 4-to-1 margin—the insiders index dipped to 20 percent—at the important market peaks in 1976, 1978 and 1980. During the orgy of speculation that marked the June 1983 top, insider selling reached epidemic proportions. One week, sales outweighed purchases by a 9-to-1 count. Small wonder that the most overheated sectors of the market—the high-tech stocks and the glamorous over-the-counter growth stocks—nosedived soon afterward.

You'll note, if you study the chart, that the insiders often begin to sell heavily weeks or even many months before an important market peak. The most notorious recent case was in 1986-87, when the insiders completed most of their selling in the spring of 1986 and became uncharacteristically more reluctant to sell as the Dow forged higher. Thus, it's wise to give greater weight to insider buying than selling in your market-timing deliberations. Remember: an insider can sell for many reasons (tax bill coming due, estate-planning needs, building a new home, etc.). But a corporate officer or director buys stock on the open market for one reason only—to make a profit.

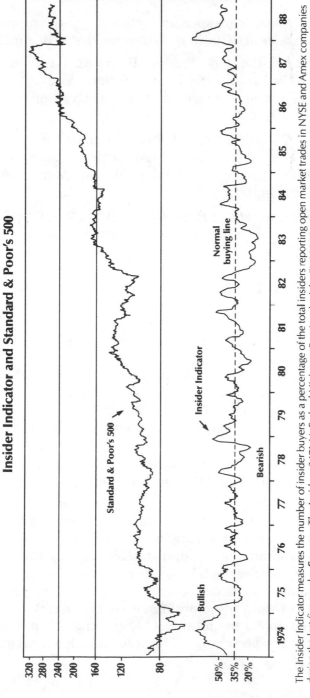

Fig. 6. Insider Indicator and Standard & Poor's 500

The Insider Indicator measures the number of insider buyers as a percentage of the total insiders reporting open market trades in NYSE and Amex companies during the last five weeks. **Source:** *The Insiders*, 3471 N. Federal Highway, Fort Lauderdale, FL 33306.

Several newsletters are specifically devoted to monitoring and interpreting insider activity in the stock market. They include:

• *The Insiders* (3471 N. Federal Hwy., Ft. Lauderdale, FL 33306; fortnightly, $100 a year). Ranks stocks according to insider ratings and keeps tabs on marketwide insider trading for timing purposes.

• *Insiders Chronicle* (P.O. 272977, Boca Raton, FL 33427; weekly, $350 a year). Lists all significant insider trades on NYSE, AMEX and OTC. In-depth articles analyzing companies with heavy insider buying.

• *Insider Transactions Report* (P.O. Box 1145, Costa Mesa, CA 92628, monthly, $190 a year). Recommends stocks to sell short as well as buy, based on insider activity.

The Members' Club

Besides the corporate insiders, some Wall Street professionals belong to the elite fraternity of smart money. Member firms of the stock exchanges make good profits, on balance, when trading for their own account—although too often they seem to lose the knack when trading for your account! To read the minds of the members, you can turn each week to the "Market Laboratory" section of *Barron's*, a daunting eight-page spread of statistics that probably carries a greater quantity of useful information than the rest of the newspaper combined. Figure 7 shows a portion of the "Market Laboratory" page with the data you need.

Under the heading "Market and Volume Reports," you'll notice that *Barron's* prints the total number of shares traded on the New York Stock Exchange during the most recent reporting week, together with the number of shares sold short by the member firms. (The NYSE releases the numbers with a two-week delay, but the information is usually current enough to give you an accurate picture of what these professionals are thinking.) Divide the member shorts by the total weekly trading volume, and express the result as a percentage. This figure is known as the *member-short ratio*.

Barron's Market and Volume Reports

All numbers in thousands save percentages and ratios

New York Stock Exchange

	Week Sept. 9	Previous Week	Year-Ago Week
Total Volume			
Weekly	554,721.1	544,099.8	769,320.6
Average Daily	138,680.3	128,820.0	192,330.1
Member Activity			
Specialists Buys (#†)	52,021.8	57,724.6	87,022.9
Specialists Sales (#†)	50,427.2	61,604.7	92,386.1
Floor Traders Buys	0	21.7	27.5
Floor Traders Sales	7.9	16.0	29.0
Other Member Buys (#)	80,536.5	89,398.8	138,588.7
Other Member Sales (#)	75,059.0	89,566.1	133,265.2
Total Member Buys	132,558.3	147,145.2	225,639.1
Total Member Sales	125,494.1	151,186.7	225,680.3
Net Member Buy/Sell	+7,064.2	−4,041.5	−41.2
Member volume as % of total	23.26	23.16	29.33
Short Sales			
Total	41,312.7	51,744.8	59,716.4
Public	13,211.6	15,655.6	12,424.0
Members Total	28,101.1	36,089.2	47,292.4
Specialists	18,047.5	20,040.4	24,590.7
Floor Traders	0	0.5	5.5
Other Members	10,053.6	16,048.3	22,696.2
Specialists/Public Short Ratio	1.4	1.3	2.0
Members/Public Short Ratio	2.1	2.3	3.8

Customers Odd-Lot Activity

NYSE	Week Sept. 9	Previous Week	Year-Ago Week
Purchases, shares	1,494.2	1,589.9	1,961.4
Purchases $	52,663.0	54,776.6	99,257.8
Sales, shares	2,881.0	3,364.8	3,155.1
Sales $	97,868.4	11,025.5	146,999.0
Short Sales, shares	71.3	77.9	4.2
Short Sales $	2,493.6	3,008.6	259.3

American Stock Exchange

	Week Sept. 9	Previous Week	Year-Ago Week
Total Volume			
Weekly	34,894.4	49,522.2	58,200.5
Average Daily	8,723.6	9,904.4	14,550.1
Member Activity			
Specialists Buys (#†)	3,416.2	4,117.6	7,233.2
Specialists Sales (#†)	3,784.0	4,424.7	6,877.6
Floor Traders Buys	42.5	24.1	81.9
Floor Traders Sales	26.9	32.4	84.8
Other Member Buys (#)	2,651.2	4,451.1	6,138.2
Other Member Sales (#)	2,533.5	6,355.7	5,601.1
Total Member Buys	6,109.9	8,592.9	13,453.4
Total Member Sales	6,344.4	10,812.9	12,563.5
Net Member Buy/Sell	−234.4	−2,220.0	+889.9
Member volume as % of total	17.85	19.59	22.35
Short Sales			
Total	693.1	760.0	1,479.6
Public	455.6	550.9	783.2
Members Total	237.5	209.1	696.4
Specialists	22.1	34.6	86.9
Floor Traders	5.5		26.2
Other Members	209.9	169.5	583.3
Specialists/Public Short Ratio	0.0	0.1	0.1
Members/Public Short Ratio	0.5	0.4	0.9

Customers Odd-Lot Activity

AMEX	Week Sept. 9	Previous Week	Year-Ago Week
Purchases, shares	53.2	56.3	97.0
Sales, shares	117.8	133.3	161.6

Includes transactions effected by members acting as Registered Competitive Market-Makers. † Including offsetting round-lot transactions arising from odd-lot dealer activity by specialists and other members. w-Shares and warrants.

Fig. 7. Barron's market and volume reports

The members are usually right about the direction the market is going to take over the intermediate to long term. When these savvy operators are selling short at a breakneck pace (betting that prices will fall), you would be well advised to sell with them. Contrariwise, when the members cut back on their short selling, you can infer that they're expecting stock quotes to rise. Step up to the counter and buy!

A reading above 7.5 percent on the member-short ratio (see Figure 8) flashes a warning for the intermediate term and often signals that the primary trend is turning down as well. At the famous stock market peak of August 1987, the member-short

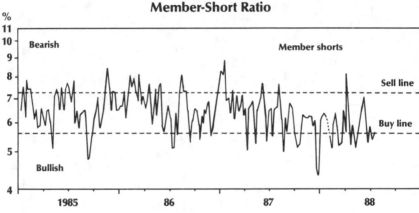

Member-Short Ratio

Member short sales as a percent of total NYSE volume. **Source:** *Technical Trends,* P.O. Box 792, Wilton, CT 06897.

Fig. 8. Member-short ratio

ratio surged to 7.6 percent, one of its highest readings (although not *the* highest by any means) in recent years. After the big summer rally in 1984, this barometer soared to 10.6 percent, its high for the decade—and the Dow was stopped in its tracks for the next four months.

Normally, a reading below 5.5 percent on the member-short ratio signals an upturn in the market's intermediate trend. A dramatic drop in member-short selling can also coincide with the beginning of a primary bull market, as in August 1982 and (perhaps) again in December 1987, when the ratio plummeted to 4.2 percent, its lowest level in almost eight years.

Since no indicator is infallible, you should never make an investment decision solely on the basis of the member-short ratio. Consider it one of many arrows in your quiver. If it's sending the same message as the other contrary indicators, treat it with respect. If, on the other hand, it's out of sync with the other gauges, don't be too alarmed. Investing is a game of probabilities, not certainties. Seldom will all your indicators be pointing in the same direction at the same time. Go with the preponderance of the evidence and tune out the statistical "noise."

Wall Street's Wrong-Way Corrigans

When the insiders take a strong stand on the stock market, bullish or bearish, time usually proves them right. Ditto with the stock exchange's members. Unfortunately, though, many other groups of investors aren't nearly so successful. In fact, I can state categorically: *When the public engages in fast-buck speculation, it nearly always loses money in the end.*

The hapless options trader is a case in point. This unlucky lad provides what is probably the most dependable market-timing indicator in the whole contrarian galaxy. By nature, people who play the options market tend to be gamblers, dreamers who hope to parlay a couple of thousand dollars into a fortune. (*Value Line* lately has been exploiting this yearning by advertising its options advisory service under the provocative headline, "Is It Still Possible to Amass Great Wealth?") There are many individual exceptions, but options traders *as a group* represent the dumb money at its dumbest.

Two types of options exist. A *call* gives the buyer the right to purchase (call away) 100 shares of a specified stock at a fixed price (the strike price) during the life of the option (never more than nine months). A *put* gives the buyer the right to sell (put) 100 shares of a given stock at the strike price up to the expiration date. Speculators buy calls when they expect a stock to go up; they buy puts when they expect a stock to go down.

87

Although it's possible to devise a conservative strategy for trading these highly volatile instruments (see Chapter 12), most options speculators take a "go for broke" approach and end up broke as a result. Nonetheless, the rest of us can learn from these losers' mistakes. Their biggest error, which makes them such an interesting study from a contrarian point of view, is that they usually become more and more bullish as prices rise, and more and more bearish as prices fall. Call buying increases when the market is tracing out a top, while put buying surges when the market is forming a bottom.

Figure 9 gives you an idea of how the options traders have behaved over the past couple of years. At the primary market bottom in August 1982, speculators were betting their bottom dollar that prices would drop further. The number of puts purchased on the Chicago Board Options Exchange climbed to within 80 percent of the number of calls. In perfect contrary style, the market exploded upward. Similar readings occurred near intermediate bottoms in the spring of 1984 and the autumn of 1985.

At the other extreme, euphoric speculators were buying three calls for every put in June 1983. Result: most stocks backpedaled for the next 13 months, and hundreds of issues collapsed. Too much call buying also signaled intermediate correction phases for the market in the spring of 1985 and at the end of that year.

To calculate the put/call ratio for yourself, you can refer to the options pages of *The Wall Street Journal*. Although options are traded on several exchanges, the most important market, and the only one you really need to track, is the Chicago Board. Just divide the put volume for the day by the call volume.

Since daily readings can swing up or down quite sharply, I suggest that you keep a 10-day moving average to smooth out the fluctuations. (The graph in Figure 9 plots a 10-day average.) Or, if it's too much trouble for you to consult the *Journal* every day, you can find a summary of the past week's options trading in *Barron's*. By adding together the figures from two issues of *Barron's*, you can quickly compute a 10-day average.

In general, a reading above 0.7 on the 10-day put/call ratio indicates that an intermediate bottom is at hand, and a reading

CBOE Put/Call Ratio

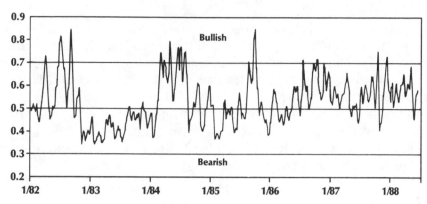

IU-day moving average. **Source:** Shearson Lehman Hutton.

Fig. 9. Put/call ratio

above 0.8 suggests a spectacular buying opportunity. But when the ratio plunges below 0.4, you should watch out for a drop in the market. A reading below 0.4, sustained over several weeks, is likely to mean that a sharp downswing lies immediately ahead.

Typically, the put/call ratio, like most sentiment indicators, lingers in overbought territory for stretches of several weeks in the early stages of a bull market. It also wallows deeply in oversold territory for weeks at a time in the late phases of a bear market. Thus, when the trend of the market has been running strongly in one direction for a few months, the cautious investor should wait for several extreme readings, each a few weeks apart, before going contrary to the options traders. Let them empty their wallets completely before you bet against them! The put/call ratio did its followers a disservice in 1987, when it failed to warn of the approaching crash. However, very few (if any) market indicators—technical, fundamental or contrarian—hinted that a debacle of the magnitude of Meltdown Monday was in the offing. Should you jettison a tool that has served well for many years merely because it failed to anticipate what may turn out to be the shortest and strangest market panic in history? I wouldn't. For a fuller analysis of the crash, see Chapter 8.

Our Mutual Friends

It may seem unfair to lump megabuck institutions under the heading of dumb money. As I noted earlier in this chapter, banks, pension funds and other institutional investors are, for the most part, simply too big to practice market timing successfully over the long term. Nonetheless, many of them try their hand at it. Managers of common-stock mutual funds are notorious for building up their cash holdings just as the market is nearing a significant low. Likewise, mutual funds tend to be fully invested, with minimal cash, near the market's highs.

For a graphic depiction of this phenomenon, take a glance at Figure 10. Since 1966, the mutual funds' cash holdings have regularly peaked at 10 to 12 percent of their assets—right at the bottom of every primary bear market, when calm, rational *contrary* investors should have owned stocks up to their ears!

However, this indicator has been somewhat less helpful in calling market tops. Interest rates have risen sharply since the beginning of the Vietnam era, encouraging fund managers to hold more cash throughout the market cycle than they would have thought advisable during the "go-go" years of the early 1960s. (With today's high rates, Treasury bills and other risk-free, interest-bearing cash equivalents present formidable competition for common stocks.) In addition, the growing popularity of "telephone switch" mutual fund trading has forced many fund managers to keep larger than normal cash reserves on hand to make redemptions.

Thus, in the months leading up to the Dow's manic peak in August 1987, the mutual fund cash ratio never dropped below 9.3 percent. Back in the early 1960s, readings as low as 4 percent accompanied major market tops. But Treasury bills paid only 3 to 4 percent in those days. Until short-term interest rates fall back to the levels that prevailed 25 or 30 years ago, the market is likely to make primary tops with the funds' cash holdings in the 8 to 9 percent range. Primary market bottoms will probably occur with the funds' cash in the area of 11 to 12 percent. (*Barron's* publishes the figure each week under "Mutual Fund Monthly Indicators.")

Mutual Funds' Cash Position vs. Market Movement

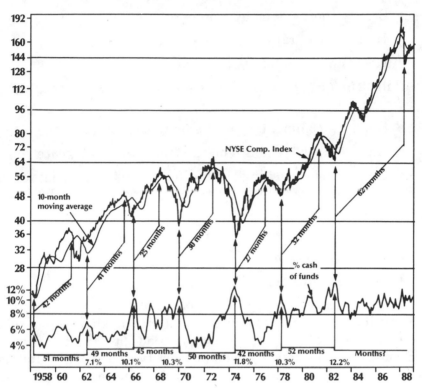

Source: *Growth Fund Guide*, P.O. Box 6600, Rapid City, SD 57709.

Fig. 10. Mutual funds' cash position

Let's distill the market-timing principles I've discussed so far into three basic rules.

Rule 1. *Buy when the stock market is displaying the classic signs of a primary bottom.* You'll know a primary bottom is at hand when you see the following:

- Panicky commentary in the news media
- High "bearish" readings on the *Investors Intelligence* poll

- Heavy insider buying (including major programs by corporations to buy back their own shares)
- Scanty short selling by members
- High put/call ratio
- Hefty mutual fund cash reserves

Rule 2. *Sell when the market is showing the characteristics of a primary top*:

- Euphoric commentary in the news media
- High "bullish" readings on the *Investors Intelligence* poll
- Heavy insider selling (including a flood of new issues of stock by corporations and public secondary offerings by large shareholders)
- Heavy short selling by members
- Low put/call ratio
- Depleted mutual fund cash reserves

Rule 3. *If you miss the primary bottom or top, wait* for the next intermediate bottom to buy, or the next intermediate top to sell. Most bull markets give you at least two good opportunities to buy, and most bear markets give you at least two good opportunities to sell, typically one to five months after the primary turning point.

Many older investors can tell charming stories about how well a long-term buy-and-hold strategy worked in the 1950s and 1960s. If you had bought almost any blue chip stock in the late 1940s—IBM, General Electric, General Motors, U.S. Steel—and held it for the next 20 years, you would have racked up fabulous profits.

But the success of a buy-and-hold strategy can depend on the time frame you're looking at. Had you bought a portfolio of blue chip stocks in September 1929, for example, it would have taken you 25 years to show a gain on the price of your stocks, although dividend income would have enabled you to break even on your cost as early as 1944! Investors who bought such well-known high-tech stocks as Advanced Micro Devices, Control Data, Tandy

Corp. and Wang Laboratories in the spring of 1983 are still waiting to get their money back. And I suspect that many of the stocks people bought in the summer of 1987 at Dow 2500, 2600 and 2700 won't bring a profit for five to 10 years—if then.

Most investors either don't care to or can't afford to wait a decade or more to recoup their losses. To avoid such disasters, it's critical that you sharpen your sense of timing. In these days of roller-coaster volatility for all markets, "ripeness is all."

Good timing, as we'll see in the next chapter, doesn't necessarily mean that you've got to be constantly trading in and out of the market or that you must take an all-or-nothing approach— always 100 percent in stocks or 100 percent in cash.

But if you plan to invest in the stock market, it pays to heed the "signs of the times." Buy individual stocks and mutual funds when the odds are with you, when the sentiment indicators proclaim that the market as a whole is cheap. Sell when the odds of picking a winner are stacked against you, when the indicators warn that most of the bargains are gone.

Imitating the smart money (and going contrary to the market's perennial losers) may not sound like a heroic investment strategy. But it's common sense—and it works.

Chapter 6

The Feeling Is Mutual

No-load mutual funds are as close to the perfect investment ve-hicle as you can find.—Sheldon Jacobs

Actually, as I write in the cold, gray dawn of the post-crash era, the feeling is *anything but* mutual. Mutual funds have fallen on hard times in the wake of Black Monday. Before the 1987 stock market crash, equity funds were sucking in new cash like your mother-in-law's Electrolux. For a while, net sales were running a rate of more than $4 billion a month.

Then October 19 lowered the boom. For the next year, money flowed out of stock-oriented mutual funds as more and more investors, embittered, gave up hope of recovering their losses from the crash. Yesterday's favorite financial vehicle is now unmentionable in polite cocktail party conversation. *Sic transit gloria mundi.*

More's the pity, because mutual funds do offer some outstanding advantages for the stock market investor. Here are just a few:

• *Diversification.* By pooling your stake with that of thousands of other investors, a mutual fund can put together a portfolio of 50, 100 or more stocks—easily a broad enough selection to protect you from a freakish catastrophe affecting any single company (a plane crash killing the entire executive management, for example). Studies have shown that an investor generally needs to own at least 15-20 stocks in different industries to achieve adequate diversification in a portfolio.

• *Cost savings.* Because mutual funds buy and sell stocks in large quantities, they incur far smaller brokerage commissions (as a percentage of the total value of the transaction) than you

95

would as an individual investor. Large institutions can trade stocks for 5 cents or less per share. Try to get that rate at Merrill Lynch, or even at Charles Schwab!

• *Flexibility.* Many mutual funds belong to "families" that allow you to switch from one fund to another within the same family via toll-free telephone call. If you decide that you want to go from stocks to bonds, for example, or from cash equivalents (money market funds) back to stocks, you can transfer your fund balance instantly, with no letter writing or signature guarantees necessary.

• *Low initial investment.* True, you can theoretically buy as little as one share of a $5 or even a $1 stock through any broker. However, the commissions attached to small deals are so high as to make it impractical to buy stock that way. Most mutual funds, on the other hand, will let you open an account for $1,000 or less—and a few funds impose no minimum at all. In addition, most funds allow you to build your stake with subsequent payments of $100 or less.

• *Professional management.* I left this benefit for last because it's probably less important than some mutual fund boosters would like you to believe. Granted, a certain select group of fund managers with a clearly defined, highly disciplined investment strategy have been able to outperform the market averages over a period of many years. (I'll name a few of them shortly.) Most funds, though, are lucky to keep up with the market—because they *are* the market. Institutions such as mutual funds, pension funds and insurance companies now account for the bulk of the trading volume on the New York Stock Exchange. Small wonder, then, that the typical mutual fund is hard put to beat the market averages after you deduct the manager's fees and the fund's administrative expenses.

Selecting a fund with low overhead—known in the business as a low *expense ratio*—will generally produce far better investment results than chasing after the fund manager who has the hottest hand during the current calendar quarter. As a rule, total expenses for a well-managed equity mutual fund shouldn't amount to more than 1.5 percent of the fund's assets per year, and

I prefer funds with an expense ratio closer to 1 percent. *Exception:* a few special-purpose funds with unique management philosophies run up annual expenses of 2 percent or more, usually because the fund pays stockbrokers a small recurring fee (called a 12b-1 charge) for having sold the fund's shares. Before you pay 2 percent a year, however, make sure you're getting something special in return. Over a 10-year period, an annual difference of just 1 percent in the expense ratio can make a huge difference in your wallet.

Suppose, for example, that two fund managers rack up a compounded return (before expenses) of 10 percent a year for 10 years. Pinchpenny has an expense ratio of 1 percent; Prodigal lays out 2 percent a year for overhead. After 10 years, $10,000 invested with Pinchpenny will grow to $23,674. The same amount entrusted to Prodigal will increase to only $21,589. By choosing Prodigal, you've thrown away more than $2,000—a year's worth of heat, light and telephone at my house, or a week's rent in Manhattan.

I strongly recommend *no-load* mutual funds, which impose no up-front sales charge. Taken as a group, funds without a sales load perform just as well as the "load" funds that stockbrokers love to hawk. That's *before* you deduct the sales charge. Net of the sales charge, your results are unmistakably better with the typical no-load. For every top-performing load fund your stockbroker can rattle off, there's generally a no-load with similar objectives that has done equally well (or better) over the long pull. It astonishes me that old-line load funds, with their sales charges ranging up to 8.5 percent, can survive in today's cost-conscious investment world. Who buys these dinosaurs? Probably the same kind of people who got fast-talked into buying Florida swampland 60 years ago.

Slightly less obnoxious, though still worth detouring where possible, are funds that charge a redemption fee. Some funds sponsored by the major brokerage houses mug you for as much as 5 or 6 percent of the value of your investment if you redeem your shares during the first year after purchase. In most cases, thankfully, these redemption charges—which the brokerage firms prefer to call a "deferred sales charge"—decline each year and eventually vanish after the fifth or sixth year. My counsel is to avoid funds with redemption fees unless they offer some valuable feature you can't find anywhere else.

Timing Your Moves in Mutual Funds

Many clever strategies have been developed for trading mutual funds. In most cases, these programs are designed simply to "follow the trend." For example, one system tells you to buy stock funds after the Dow Jones Industrial Average and a composite index of mutual funds rise above their respective 39-week moving averages.* You're supposed to get out when both of these indicators fall below their moving averages.

Mechanical programs of this sort can provide a degree of emotional discipline for investors too easily swayed by the hurly-burly of the marketplace. As I've pointed out before, though, a major weakness in trend-following systems is that they often signal you to buy after prices have already risen substantially and to sell after prices have already fallen substantially. For instance, the system I just described didn't sell out of the market until the Friday before the 1987 stock market crash, *after* the Dow had already shed almost 500 points (18 percent). When the system switched back into the market in May 1988, the Dow was already up more than 300 points from its lows (again, 18 percent).

Most trend-following systems also generate a fair number of whipsaws—rapid in-and-out moves that saddle you with a string of small but irksome losses. Over the years, these whipsaws can wipe out any advantage you might have gained over a buy-and-hold strategy applied to the same mutual funds.

For mutual fund investors who demand an ultra-simple trading system that takes only five minutes a week to monitor and re-

---

*To compute a 39-week average, you add up the Friday closing prices for 39 weeks and divide by 39. Each week thereafter, you drop the oldest number in your list and replace it with that Friday's latest figure.

98

quires no calculations, the Technical Market Index featured on the television show "Wall Street Week" is a helpful contrarian market-timing tool. The index is normally flashed on the screen during the first five minutes of the show. While most viewers seem to watch "Wall Street Week" primarily for the good-natured banter of host Louis Rukeyser and for the stock tips purveyed by his guests, the WSW Index—also known as "Rukeyser's elves"— is easily the most valuable information you'll find on the program.

Originated by Robert Nurock, editor of *The Astute Investor* (P.O. Box 988, Paoli, PA 19301, $247 per year), the WSW Index actually consists of 10 separate indicators rolled into one. Insider activity is one of the components, options trading is another and advisory-service sentiment a third. In fact, the only indicator of the bunch that isn't at all based on contrary opinion is a cost-of-money gauge designed to show whether the Federal Reserve's monetary policy is "tight" or "easy."

Normally, the WSW Index fluctuates within a range of +5 (very bullish; buy) to -5 (very bearish; sell). Over the past 15 years, every +5 reading has resulted in gains of at least 20 percent for the stock market in less than a year. Similarly, every -5 reading has led to a serious decline (10 to 25 percent). See Figure 11 for the record. To take a recent case, the WSW Index registered an extremely bearish -5 in June 1983, foreshadowing the painful market swoon that followed over the next 13 months. Then, in May and June 1984, the index shot up to a bullish +5. The market exploded in late July, soaring two-and-a-half times over the next three years with nary a 10 percent pullback.

In 1987, the WSW Index never registered a fully bearish -5 before the Dow topped at 2722 in August. (The worst reading was a series of -4s in the spring.) This was the first major miscue the elves have ever committed. The elves, however, weren't alone: most of the nation's top market analysts, including not a few practicing contrarians, fell into the same trap as well. Many of the best analysts were worried, troubled and bothered by the market for several months before the crash—but not sufficiently to issue a clear-cut "everybody out of the water" sell signal. I'll talk a bit more about this failure in Chapter 8.

Wall Street Week Index

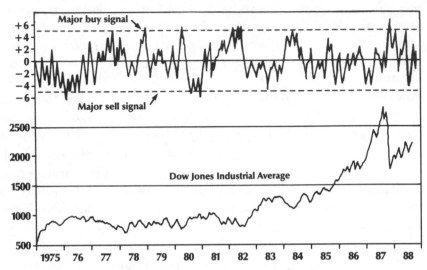

Source: *InvesTech Market Analyst,* 2472 Birch Glen, Whitefish, MT 59937.

Fig. 11. Wall Street Week Index

Dusting themselves off after their humiliating slip, the elves came back in November 1987 with their strongest buy signal ever—a +8 reading. Four weeks later, the broad-based stock indices (all, in other words, except the Dow Industrials) made their lows for the year and a solid rally was under way. From the December 1987 low to the October 1989 high, the Standard & Poor's 500 jumped more than 60 percent.

The easiest (and probably most effective) strategy with the WSW Index is to buy mutual funds when the index hits +5 and hold them until the index falls to -5. This procedure, which is ideally suited to long-term investors who like to hold their funds several years at a time, should allow you to capture the lion's share of the profit to be made from a primary bull market.

Active traders can buy and sell the intermediate swings in the WSW Index. A reasonable set of rules might run as follows:

• Switch to 100 percent invested in stock funds whenever the elves give an all-out bullish reading of +5 or higher.

• After receiving a buy signal, reduce the stock sector of your total fund portfolio by 20 percent each time the WSW Index drops to -3 or -4. Ignore "duplicate" -3 or -4 readings that occur less than two months apart.

• While still operating on a buy signal, increase the stock sector of your total fund portfolio by 40 percent each time the WSW rebounds from -3 or -4 to +3 or +4. Again, ignore duplicate readings that occur within two months of each other.

• Switch to 100 percent cash whenever the elves give an all-out bearish reading of -5 or lower.

• After receiving a sell signal, increase the stock sector of your total fund portfolio by 20 percent each time the WSW Index jumps to +3 or +4. Ignore duplicate +3 or +4 readings that fall inside a two-month period.

• While still operating on a sell signal, reduce the stock sector of your total fund portfolio by 40 percent each time the WSW sinks from +3 or +4 to -3 or -4. Again, ignore duplicate readings that occur within two months of each other.

This method would have allowed you to buy all the major stock market bottoms since 1974 and would also have insulated you with a sizable cash cushion during each of the nasty intermediate "corrections" that have hit the market in the past 15 years. Equally important, it would have gradually taken you out of equity funds in the months preceding the 1987 stock market debacle, leaving you 100 percent in cash by April 1987.

Fully Invested Switching

Some investors, wary of market-timing schemes, prefer to remain fully invested in stock funds at all times. As I noted in Chapter 5, there are good arguments for maintaining a position in common stocks through thick and thin. However, it doesn't take a genius to recognize that the level of risk in the stock market fluctuates widely as prices rise and fall. The investor who wants to keep at least some of his money at work in the market at all times can limit his risk and enhance his return by shifting to a more aggressive strategy when the market is cheap by historical value standards, and to a more conservative strategy when the market is dear.

Figures 12 and 13 portray two of the most significant yardsticks of stock market value. Both are based on the Standard & Poor's 500 Index, although the Dow Jones Industrial Average would provide similar results. You can check these indicators every week in the "Market Laboratory" section of *Barron's*.

The *price-earnings* ratio, charted in Figure 12, is the price of the Standard & Poor's 500 divided by the aggregate earnings per share, for the most recent 12 months, of the companies that make up the index. In the post-World War II era, stocks have traded above a P/E of 18 only about 10 percent of the time. Thus, a P/E of 18 or higher on the S&P 500 has signaled a high-risk zone for

Standard & Poor's 500 Price/Earnings Ratio

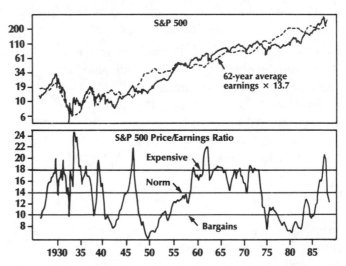

Source: Ned Davis Research, 7600 Glenridge Dr., Suite 210, Atlanta, GA 30342

Fig. 12. Standard & Poor's 500 price/earnings ratio

the stock market. By the same token, the market has traded below a P/E of 8 only about 10 percent of the time. Hence, a P/E of 8 or lower has found the stock market in a low-risk zone.

The *price-dividend ratio* of the S&P 500 is pictured in Figure 13. To calculate this ratio, the current price of the S&P index is

Standard & Poor's 500 Price/Dividend Ratio

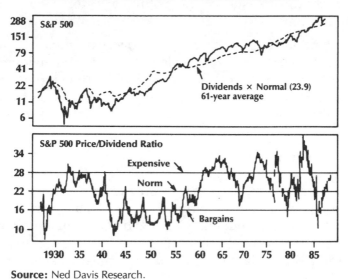

Source: Ned Davis Research.

Fig. 13. Standard & Poor's 500 price/dividend ratio

divided by the aggregate dividend per share paid by the 500 companies in the index over the past 12 months. Mathematically, the P/D ratio is the reciprocal of the dividend yield. (Yield is dividend over share price; you flip the numerator and denominator to get the P/D ratio.)

Since 1948, the P/D ratio on the S&P 500 has risen above 32 only about one-tenth of the time. At such low dividend yields (3 percent or less), the market has always been overpriced and risky. At the other end of the spectrum, the P/D has dropped below 16 only about one-tenth of the time since 1948. With dividend yields at that lofty height (6 percent or more), the market has always been undervalued and "safe" to buy for almost any holding period—a year, three years, five years or 10 years.

How can you make use of this intelligence in your mutual fund investment program? First of all, if you *do* consider yourself a market timer, you can add these value benchmarks to your tool kit. When P/E ratios are in the highest decile and dividend yields in the lowest (a situation that occurred in the summer of 1987), the market timer should cut his holdings of stocks and stock funds to a minimum.

Cash is king in a dangerously overextended market. Contrariwise, when P/Es are in the lowest decile and dividends in the highest (a circumstance that prevailed in the summer of 1982), the market timer should freight his portfolio with common stocks and equity-type mutual funds. Cash is trash when the market is brimming with cheap stocks.

These value benchmarks are well-nigh infallible, having proven themselves repeatedly over many decades of experience. The problem with them, however, is that they usually give a strong signal no more than two or three times in a decade—if then. For example, P/Es and dividend yields warned of three major market tops in the 1960s, but didn't pinpoint any major bottoms between 1953 and 1974. While these long-term indicators speak with great authority, they don't speak often.

As a result, value yardsticks usually aren't too helpful for market timers—only once in a blue moon. However, they do convey vital information about risk for the investor who wants to keep a finger in the market at all times. In fact, Walter Rouleau, editor of the respected mutual fund advisory, *Growth Fund Guide* (P.O. Box 6600, Rapid City, SD 57709, $85 per year), has developed a system, based on the dividend yield of the Standard & Poor's 500, that enables you to switch mutual funds for minimum risk and maximum performance while remaining fully invested in the market all the time.

When the dividend yield on the S&P is high (market risk is low), Rouleau suggests that you emphasize aggressive stock funds in your portfolio. When the yield is low (market risk is high), you should switch to conservative stock funds. Aggressive funds typically invest in small, fast-growing companies that pay minimal dividends. Conservative funds generally focus on established firms with liberal dividend yields. The contrarian aspect of the strategy is that when the market cares most about dividends (yields are high), you care most about growth. And when the market is obsessed with growth (dividends are low), you opt for stocks that pay above-average dividends.

Rouleau's system doesn't take an all-or-nothing approach. Rather, he suggests that you move gradually from aggressive funds to conservative funds as the market rises from the depths of undervaluation to the heights of overvaluation. On the way back, the same principle applies: you gradually increase your holdings of aggressive funds as the market's dividend yield goes up.

Dividends, Rouleau points out, are the most solid evidence of a corporation's earning power, since they're paid in cash. Corporations can fudge their earnings reports through dubious accounting methods, but it's hard to fake a dividend. I might add that dishonest managements who "cook the books" to produce phantom earnings seldom take the next step—paying those earnings out to shareholders in the form of cold, hard cash dividends.

Here's how Rouleau advises you to allocate your money between aggressive and conservative funds as the market's P/D ratio rises and falls:

Table 6.1 Asset-Allocation Formula

P/D ratio	Conservative %	Aggressive %
34 and up	100	0
30-33.99	87.5	12.5
23-29.99	62.5	37.5
20-22.99	37.5	62.5
below 20	0	100

History shows that a common-sense system of this sort really works. Rouleau back-tested his theory from December 31, 1966 to June 30, 1988, using two funds that his service has frequently recommended over the past two decades: *Mutual Shares* (conservative) and *Twentieth Century Growth* (aggressive). During the test period of 21 years and six months, an investor who simply placed half of his assets in each of the funds would have racked up a total return of 2,499 percent.

As shown by Figure 14, however, an investor who used the P/D plan would have accumulated far more wealth—a return of

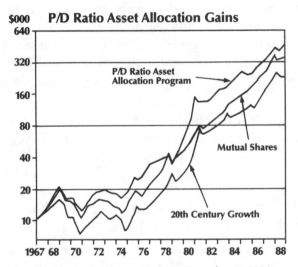

Fig. 14. P/D ratio asset allocation gains

4,951 percent, to be exact. Every $1 invested in 1966 would have grown to $50.51 by 1988. The switching portfolio performed better than buy-and-hold because the more conservative fund gave up less ground than the more aggressive fund in bear markets.

As this book goes to press, the dividend yield on the Standard & Poor's 500 is hovering around 3.4 percent. Thus, the price-dividend ratio is about 29. According to Rouleau's formula, a long-term mutual fund investor should be placing approximately five-eighths of his stock market assets into conservative funds and three-eighths into growth funds.

Selecting a Fund

Which funds to buy? For market timers, aggressive funds are best because they tend to be more volatile than the market as a whole: they gain faster, and they lose faster, too. From 1983 to 1987, many—indeed, most—aggressive funds lagged behind the S&P 500. But this was an anomaly, caused by the poor performance of small-company stocks during the latter phases of the Reagan bull market. Historically, small stocks have run rings around the big-name Blue Gyps. Furthermore, as I explain in the next chapter, it appears that "small cap" issues have begun to take back the mantle of market leadership in the wake of the 1987 crash. If so, aggressive growth funds are likely to outperform conservative funds *during periods of market strength* over the next few years.

For market timers, therefore, and for the aggressive segment of a fully invested "permanent" portfolio (a la Rouleau), I recommend the following no-load funds. All of these funds either concentrate in small-company stocks or maintain a hefty weighting in such stocks:

Table 6.2 Aggressive Growth Funds

Fund	Minimum investment (initial/ subsequent)	Telephone switch?	Change in fund value 12/31/87 to 12/31/88
Babson Enterprise Suite G-15 2440 Pershing Rd. Kansas City, MO 64108 800-422-2766, 816-471-5200	$1,000/$100	Yes	32.5%
Columbia Special P.O. Box 1350 Portland, OR 97207 800-547-1037, 503-222-3600	$2,000/$100	Yes	42.5%
Dreyfus New Leaders 666 Old Country Rd. Garden City, NY 11530 800-645-6561, 718-895-1206	$2,500/$100	Yes	23.3%

Legg Mason Special $1,000/$500   Yes   19.7%
P.O. Box 1476
Baltimore, MD 21203
800-822-5544, 301-539-3400

Vanguard Explorer II $3,000/$100   Yes   22.0%
P.O. Box 2600
Valley Forge, PA 19482
800-662-7447, 215-648-6000

For the conservative segment of a "permanent" mutual fund portfolio, I suggest the following low-volatility funds:

Table 6.3 Conservative Growth Funds

Fund	Minimum investment (initial/ subsequent)	Telephone switch?	Change in fund value 12/31/87 to 12/31/88
Evergreen Total Return 550 Mamaroneck Ave. Harrison, NY 10528 800-235-0064, 914-698-5711	$2,000/none	Yes	15.8%
Guardian Mutual 342 Madison Ave. New York, NY 10173 800-367-0770, 212-850-8300	$1,000/$100	Yes	28.0%
Mutual Shares 51 John F. Kennedy Pkwy. Short Hills, NJ 07078 800-457-0211, 201-912-2100	$5,000/none	No	30.9%
T. Rowe Price Equity Income 100 E. Pratt St. Baltimore, MD 21202 800-638-5660, 301-547-2308	$1,000/$100	Yes	27.7%
Windsor II P.O. Box 2600 Valley Forge, PA 19482 800-662-7447, 215-648-6000	$1,500/$100	Yes	24.4%

If you intend to follow a long-term asset-allocation strategy like Rouleau's, a good way to accumulate fund shares is through regular monthly investments. Most of the funds listed above offer, as an option, automatic monthly investment programs. Each month, on the day you designate, the fund will automatically debit your checking account to buy additional shares of the fund. Some funds allow you to make these automatic monthly purchases in amounts as small as $50.

Not only do such programs discipline you to save regularly, but they also smooth out your purchase cost—an additional safeguard against the all-too-human tendency to buy heavily when the market is high and to shy away from investing when the market is low. Dollar-cost averaging *forces* you to buy more shares at lower prices and fewer shares at higher prices.

For investors who prefer to "let George do it," several asset-allocation funds have sprung up in the past few years to do the switching for you. Typically, these funds work with a mix of stocks, bonds and cash, although some include foreign currencies and gold-related assets. The fund's manager adjusts the weightings of the different asset classes as market conditions change.

In my experience, the main drawback to these funds is that most base their allocation decisions on the hunches of the manager, rather than on any rigorous economic model. Most money managers come to the task with a bias in favor of one or more asset classes—stocks, bonds, gold, foreign securities, etc. Such bias can hurt the performance of an asset-allocation fund if the manager doesn't recognize it and correct it.

One fund that bases its decisions strictly on a mathematical model is *Paine Webber Asset Allocation Fund*, available through any office of Paine Webber, the old-line brokerage firm. Paine Webber's model, which calculates an ideal mix of stocks, bonds and cash, has performed superbly in real time over the past 15 years—and scored a coup on Black Monday. In the weeks immediately preceding the crash, the Paine Webber model called for a huge weighting in bonds and almost no exposure to stocks—a stance that flew in the face of the conventional wisdom at the time. (Paine Webber's model, designed by the firm's two ace investment strategists, Edward Kerschner and Charles Pradilla, often emits contrarian noises at important market turning points.) Bond prices exploded on the heels of the stock market debacle, making Paine Webber's asset-allocation fund one of the better-performing mutual funds in the nation for the two years ended September 30, 1989.

The Paine Webber fund does incur rather hefty expenses, amounting on an annual basis to more than 2 percent of the fund's assets. And the fund imposes a redemption fee, scaling down from 5 percent in the first year after you buy to zero after six years. However, there's no initial sales charge. Minimum to open an account: $1,000.

Mutual funds provide a host of benefits for stock market investors, including instant diversification, cost savings (if you go the no-load route), telephone-switch flexibility, low minimums for the small investor and—for what it may be worth—professional management. As with the stock market itself, however, there's a time to buy and a time to sell. The Wall Street Week Index, together with the other indicators I discussed in Chapter 5, will help you know when.

Even if you decide to keep some of your money working in the stock market all the time, you can reduce your risks dramatically by heeding the message of a simple value indicator, the market's price-dividend ratio. This trusty guidepost will tell you to be aggressive when the crowd is fearful, and cautious when the mob is aggressive. Whether you fancy yourself a short-term trader or a long-term investor, a contrarian approach to mutual funds can put you on the road to bigger, more consistent gains.

Chapter 7

Bargains in
the Wall Street Doghouse

But many that are first shall be last; and the last shall be first.—Matt. 19:30

If Wall Street hates a stock, buy it.—Martin Sosnoff

So you've decided that the market looks inviting. Stocks in general are cheap, or at least not overvalued. What's your next step? A contrarian can take any of several approaches to stock selection, all of them equally valid and potentially profitable. In essence, you should buy stocks that are out of favor—that nobody else wants. You should sell stocks that the Wall Street crowd has fallen in love with. But from that starting point, the road forks off in at least four directions. Let's explore the different routes.

The 'Small Cap' Strategy

One of the recurring themes of stock market history is that small-company stocks, like the old song Jackie Gleason used to croon about, "come into style and then go out again." Over the years, small companies have grown much more rapidly than large companies, for the obvious reason that a small company starts from a small base. It's easier for a company with $1 of sales to double in size than it is for IBM.

Because of their superior growth characteristics, small-company stocks have outperformed the big, lumbering Blue Gyps by a wide margin over the long pull. Ibbotson Associates of Chicago has analyzed the total return (capital gains plus reinvested dividends) of small and large stocks all the way back to 1926. Defining "small" stocks as the 10 percent of New York Stock Exchange issues with the smallest market capitalization (shares outstanding times share price), Ibbotson reports that small stocks have easily beaten the blue chip Standard & Poor's 500 index over the past 10, 20, 30, 40 or 50 years!

| | $1,000 invested in— | |
| | Small stocks | Blue chips |
Holding period	grew to:	grew to:
1978-87 (10 years)	$5,688	$4,139
1968-87 (20 years)	9,711	5,887
1958-87 (30 years)	77,466	19,719
1948-87 (40 years)	225,469	90,312
1938-87 (50 years)	1,680,120	226,259

Source: *Stocks, Bonds, Bills and Inflation: 1988 Yearbook*, Ibbotson Associates.

In the short term, however (and here I'm defining *short term* to mean periods of less than five years or so), small stocks have frequently lagged behind the blue chips. It seems that investors fall in love with the small-stock concept, bid up the prices of these issues for several years, then recognize that small stocks have run too far ahead of their fundamental value. A reaction ensues, driving the Pee Wees down relative to their blue chip brethren for several years, until the small stocks again offer compelling value. Then the cycle starts all over again.

Figure 15 depicts this cycle in action. This graph plots the price-earnings ratio of the T. Rowe Price New Horizons Fund, a no-load mutual fund that specializes in junior growth companies, versus the P/E of the Standard & Poor's 500. Since the early 1960s, small stocks have enjoyed two furious bull markets: 1965-68 and 1977-83. In each case, at the peak of the small-stock mania, the New Horizons Fund boasted an average P/E twice as high as that of the S&P 500.

After both of these huge runups, a period of disillusionment set in. The New Horizons P/E sank relative to the S&P 500 until the two stood virtually at parity. Most recently, in December 1987, the New Horizons P/E fell slightly below the market P/E for the first time in 10 years. Appropriately, this historic moment was

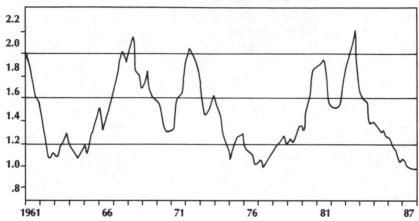

New Horizons P/E Relative to S&P 500

Ratio of average P/E of T. Rowe Price New Horizons Fund portfolio companies to average P/E ratio of S&P 500. **Source:** T. Rowe Price Associates.

Fig. 15. T. Rowe Price New Horizons P/E

accompanied by a *Wall Street Journal* article panning small stocks.[1] Titled "Many Gloomy Returns from Small Stocks Prompt Big Investors to Rethink This Fad *[sic]*," the article quoted noted growth stock pioneer John Westergaard, who had just dissolved his emerging-companies mutual fund the month before. Westergaard, the story said, "doubts small companies *will ever again* be able to put together consecutive years of earnings growth [my emphasis]." Never again? Never say never in the investment business! The same week the *Journal* trumpeted Westergaard's capitulation (vividly reminiscent of Jimmy Dines' "one and only" sell signal for gold in 1982), small stocks began to outperform big stocks again.

When I wrote the first edition of *Contrary Investing* in 1984, small stocks were coming off their most overvalued levels ever, as measured by the New Horizons barometer. As a result, I warned of "the mounting risks in emerging growth companies" and opined that the "carnage" of 1983-84 in that sector was "probably just a hint of what is coming." I suggested that investors follow a conservative strategy with secondary growth issues, using

113

them principally as short-term trading vehicles. The advice turned out to be sound. During the last two years of the Reagan bull market, small stocks lagged badly, except for a couple of brief pops. Moreover, the crash decimated small stocks. By December 1987 (after Meltdown Monday), the smallest decile of NYSE stocks sold for *less* than it had at the June 1983 market peak.

The silver lining in this cloud is that small stocks are now certifiably cheap. When you can buy above-average growth for a market (or even below-market) P/E multiple, it makes sense to include small companies—or mutual funds that invest in such equities—in the long-term segment of your stock portfolio. To be sure, an adept trader can also make money with these stocks by switching in and out according to the market-timing guidelines I proposed in the last two chapters. But given the superb *relative* value that now exists in the secondary stocks, it isn't necessary to do a lot of trading. Even if the stock market puts on a lackluster showing over the next few years, small companies should forge ahead, just as they did in the late 1970s. From December 1976 to December 1979, for example, the typical blue chip stock registered zero gain, while the average low-cap stock racked up a stunning total return of 122 percent.

As Figure 16 indicates, small stocks reached their most recent low ebb in relative performance in December 1987. This chart shows the ratio between Value Line Composite Index and the Dow Jones Industrial Average. The Value Line is a geometric average of the prices of more than 1,600 common stocks. Thus, each stock in the Value Line carries equal mathematical weight. IBM has the same clout as hundreds of little companies you've never heard of. The Dow Jones Industrial Average, of course, is an index of 30 large, well-established companies. When the Value Line is *declining* versus the DJIA, small stocks in general are faring poorly. When the VLCI is *gaining* on the DJIA, small stocks are acting well.

As you can see, the Value Line has now been outperforming the Dow since the end of 1987—its longest period of relative strength since the second-tier stocks dropped the leadership baton in June 1983. Assuming history repeats, I suspect that

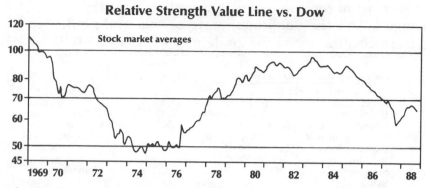

Value Line Composite vs. Dow Jones Industrial Average (12/31/67 = 100). **Source:** Value Line.

Fig. 16. Relative strength Value Line vs. Dow

small companies will continue to outperform the blue chips into the 1990s.

Building a Portfolio of Small Stocks

It isn't as hard as you might think to decide which second-tier stocks to buy. For starters, you can buy shares of the aggressive growth funds that I recommended in Chapter 6. If you prefer to select your own stocks, I suggest that you consult a statistical service like the *Value Line Investment Survey* (available in many public libraries) and ferret out stocks with the following qualities:

• *High return on equity* (over 15 percent a year);

• *Earnings projected to grow 15 percent or more annually for the next five years;*

• *P/E ratio no higher than return on equity;*

• *Little or no debt.* Long-term debt should total less than one-quarter of stockholders' equity; and

• *Strong cash position.* In most industries, current assets should exceed current liabilities by at least a 2-to-1 margin, and preferably 3-to-1.

115

Any list of companies with these characteristics is bound to change before the publication date of this book, but here are some stocks that make the grade as I write in the fall of 1989:

Company and ticker symbol	Price 9/29/88	Industry
Bandag Inc. (NYSE: BDG)	86 3/4	Tread rubber
Great Lakes Chemical (NYSE: GLK)	58 1/4	Specialty chemicals
Hillenbrand Industries (NYSE: HB)	39 7/8	Funeral caskets
Interpublic Group (NYSE: IPG)	36 3/4	Advertising
Kelly Services (OTC: KELYA)	37	Temporary help
Oshkosh B'Gosh (OTC: GOSHA)	36	Apparel
Premier Industrial (NYSE: PRE)	33 3/8	Industrial products
Stryker Corp. (OTC: STRY)	18 3/4	Medical supplies
Sysco Corp. (NYSE: SYY)	38 1/2	Food wholesaler
Wausau Papers (OTC: WSAU)	41 1/4	Specialty papers
Worthington Industries (OTC: WTHG)	22 3/4	Steel processor

The best time to buy these or other volatile growth stocks is after a sharp sell-off in the broad market, when investors are afraid to buy anything that seems risky. Once the speculative sap rises and your timing indicators warn that the market is entering a high-risk area, you can begin to take profits. Regardless of the overall market, sell any individual stock if the company's year-to-year rate of earnings growth slows to less than 10 percent for two consecutive quarters. Growth stocks can be savagely unforgiving if you buy them too high or fail to sell them high enough. Altogether too often, they can fall even faster than they rose, a cruel but not unusual form of "capital punishment" for the investor whose timing was slightly off.

Accordingly, I recommend that you invest in growth stocks only if:

• *You don't mind watching the market on a daily or at least weekly basis.*

• *You can accept sharp short-term fluctuations in the value of your shares.* It's much easier to be patient with volatile stocks if you restrict them to a fairly small percentage of your portfolio.

• *You're willing to buy at least 10 and preferably 15-20 different companies* to assure adequate diversification.

For investors who prefer not to wade through the 2,000-odd pages of *Value Line*, several outstanding publications focus specifically on smaller high-growth companies:

• *Growth Stock Outlook* (P.O. Box 9911, Chevy Chase, MD 20815, fortnightly, $175 per year). Editor Charles Allmon is as crusty and contrary a character as you'll find. He has a superb record, stretching back over two decades, for selecting acorns that later grew into oaks. His commentary on the broad market is also well worth studying: in the summer of 1987, Allmon stood virtually alone in predicting that the Dow would soon plunge 1,000 points.

• *Personal Portfolio Manager* (P.O. Box 439, Purdys, NY 10578, $325 per year). This weekly computer-generated letter, edited by William T. Chidester, screens thousands of stocks, searching for companies with specific growth and risk characteristics. Commentary on the market is also included in each issue. Unique feature: this service allows you to submit a list of up to 20 stocks of your choice to be monitored continuously by the service's computer. The computer cranks out a report on your stocks each week as part of the newsletter.

• *The Prudent Speculator* (P.O. Box 1767, Santa Monica, CA 90406, monthly, $200 per year). Editor Al Frank has one of the best long-term records of anybody in the investment newsletter business. According to the independent *Hulbert Financial Digest*, his letter's model portfolio appreciated 461 percent in the nine years ended June 30, 1989. While Frank doesn't always select small-cap stocks (he made a fortune on Chrysler in the early 1980s), most of the shares he has recommended over the years are from the second tier.

The Last Train to Dullsville

The second contrarian approach to investing in common stocks is to buy neglected, *dull* companies that the market has overlooked. Ironically, some of the most boring stocks in the market—the pariahs of Wall Street—pack the heftiest profit potential. While offering far less risk than their better-liked brethren.

Identifying dull companies is child's play. You simply turn to the stock pages of your local newspaper and look for companies with price-earnings ratios well below the market average. A stock trades at a low price in relation to the company's current earnings per share because most investors expect the company's earnings growth to be sluggish. By contrast, if investors feel confident that a company's profits will soar, they'll bid up the price of the stock to a large multiple of the company's current earnings.

David Dreman's classic book, *Contrarian Investment Strategy*,[2] presented a barrage of evidence that, over the long pull, stocks with low price-earnings ratios dramatically outperform stocks with high multiples. The graph in Figure 17 adds further weight to his thesis. It shows the total return (dividends plus capital appreciation) provided by all stocks on the New York exchange over a 26-year period from 1959 to 1984.

This graph breaks the NYSE down into quintiles (each quintile is one-fifth of the market), ranked according to their price-earnings ratios. Stocks in the lowest quintile generated the highest return (15.8 percent a year), while stocks in the three highest quintiles trailed the low P/E stocks by a country mile.

In late 1989, the price-earnings ratio for the Standard & Poor's 500, the most broadly based of the blue chip stock indices, was about 14. Thus, any stock with a P/E 20 percent or more below the market (i.e., below 11) would qualify as a bargain, assuming—as Dreman does—that the company's finances are reasonably solid (Dreman doesn't like distressed companies) and its accounting truthfully reflects current earnings.

Dreman recommends that you limit yourself to large, well-known companies that pay above-average dividend yields. (The yield on the S&P 500 in late 1989 was 3.4 percent.) In addition, he favors companies that boast a higher rate of earnings growth than the S&P 500, both in the past few years and projected into the near future. For simplicity, he suggests that you hold each stock in your portfolio until its P/E ratio approaches that of the market, then replace it with a new low P/E selection.

It isn't necessary to buy stocks on the absolute bottom rung of the P/E ladder. In most studies, stocks in the second-lowest quin-

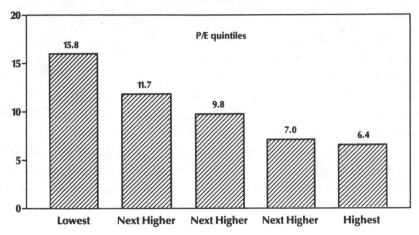

Total Return, All NYSE Common Stocks 1959-1984

Source: Provident Capital Mangement.

Fig. 17. Total return, all NYSE common stocks

tile have performed nearly as well as those in the bottom quintile, and have sometimes even beaten the bottom fifth. But if you're determined to buy the cheapest of the cheap, you can find a weekly listing of the 100 stocks with the lowest price-earnings ratios in the *Value Line Investment Survey* (711 Third Ave., New York, NY 10017, $495 a year).

Gaps in the Theory

Before you rush out and buy a Dullsville portfolio of low P/E stocks, however, let me offer a few caveats about the Dreman method:

• *Stocks in some industries can languish with low P/Es for years, or even decades.* A striking example is the international oil companies (Exxon, Mobil, Chevron, Texaco, etc.). These stocks as a group have traded below the P/E of the market *without interruption* since 1950! Even during the oil boom of the late 1970s, the international oils never came closer than a 10 percent discount to the price-earnings ratio of the Standard & Poor's 500.

119

Bank stocks, too, have sold below the market P/E for many years. Yet neither group has outperformed the S&P 500 over the long pull.

Stocks in these laggard industries do run ahead of the market from time to time, but only after they've fallen to a *deeper-than-normal discount* to the market P/E. Thus, if an oil stock, for example, has sold for an average of 80 percent of the market P/E over the past five years, a value-driven investor might consider buying it at 60 percent—but not at 80 percent or higher.

• *Price-earnings ratios for cyclical stocks are often deceptive.* Certain industries like autos, steels, savings and loans, homebuilders and stockbrokers make hay while the economic sun shines. In times of prosperity, they report gigantic profits that push the P/E ratios of their stocks down to tantalizing levels. (If earnings rise much faster than the stock price, the price-earnings ratio drops.) As soon as business turns sour, however, their profits plunge—along with their stock prices.

Take a case in point: Ford Motor Co., a stock that Mr. Dreman recommended in the 1979 edition of his book.[3] At the time, Ford was trading at only three times earnings—a seemingly irresistible bargain. But the company and the auto industry were at a cyclical peak in their sales and earnings. By September 1981, a little over two years after Dreman's book was published, Ford stock had plunged 63 percent. Ironically, when Ford was a truly great buy (at the September 1981 lows), it had no earnings at all.

A more recent example may still ring a bell with thousands of unhappy investors. In August 1987, Merrill Lynch—not a Dreman recommendation, as far as I know—was selling for a P/E of 9, less than half the market P/E. The crash proceeded to slice Merrill's share value by more than 50 percent. As I write, more than two years after Black Monday, Merrill is still languishing more than 30 percent below its August 1987 high, a far worse showing than the major market averages over the same period.

With cyclical stocks, it's best to buy when P/Es are high—50-100 or more. This circumstance usually occurs during a recession, when the earnings component of the P/E equation is low or nonexistent. It's wisest to sell cyclicals when their P/Es are low—because P/Es of such stocks tend to compress as earnings approach a cyclical peak, usually near the top of an economic boom. Thus, the low P/E strategy is exactly the wrong approach to investing in cyclical stocks.

Please don't misunderstand me. I'm not citing these unfortunate cases to discredit low P/E investing—far from it. Rather, I'm bringing up this evidence to rebut the suggestion (by Dreman and others) that you can ignore the general state of the market when you select low P/E stocks. Market timing is a vital discipline, especially when you combine value yardsticks like the market price-dividend ratio or the market price-earnings ratio (see Chapter 6) with the traditional barometers of investor sentiment.

Both Ford and Merrill Lynch registered low P/Es *close to important market peaks.* Had you been analyzing the broad market from a contrarian point of view, using the tools described in Chapters 5 and 6, you would have hesitated to buy *any* stocks—high P/E or low P/E—at those treacherous junctures. I might add that Dreman himself seems to recognize, at least tacitly, the force of this argument. In the weeks immediately prior to the 1987 crash, he advised readers of his *Forbes* column to boost their cash reserves. Market timing is alive and well, even in quarters that officially spurn it.

The time to buy stocks, whether they sport high or low price-earnings ratios, is after the market has fallen—near the bottom of either a primary bear market or an intermediate pullback in a bull market. Don't attempt to pick out bargains in a dangerously steamed-up, runaway market. There simply aren't any! Wait until prices have dropped and the contrary indicators are once again giving off bullish signals. Then, if you don't mind taking a businessman's risk, purchase growth stocks (and aggressive funds). If you want less risk with a better-than-average long-term reward, buy the low P/E issues (and conservative mutual funds that invest in these types of stocks).

Low P/E stocks will generally make money for you over the long haul even if your market timing isn't the sharpest. But there's no excuse for a contrary investor to chase stocks—even low P/E stocks—that have run up dramatically in a bull market. Wait for a good, hair-raising decline before you buy. Given a little time, the market will nearly always accommodate you. As Charles Allmon has often observed, "In this business, patience is worth more than money."

Distressed Companies: Up from the Swamp

The third contrarian path to stock market profits leads through jungle and swampland—the habitat of distressed companies. Distressed doesn't necessarily mean *bankrupt,* although it can. Many fine companies with impressive long-term growth records go through troubled periods because of technological change, weak management, intransigent unions, regulatory harassment and other factors.

Some of these unlucky firms drop into the dustbin of history, like W.T. Grant. Others pass through the purgatory of Chapter 11 and emerge in better health than ever, like Penn Central. Still others—the most numerous group—manage, after a brush with disaster, to bounce back under a tough-minded chief executive (often a newcomer to the company). Chrysler is probably the most spectacular example of corporate back-from-the-brinkmanship in recent years.

The one feature that all distressed companies share is that their stocks crash—60, 70, 80, 90 percent or more. Investing in such companies *after* their stocks have crashed can bring astonishing gains. Toys "R" Us shares leaped 30 times in five years after the company emerged from bankruptcy in 1978. Penn Central, a more modest success, saw its stock quadruple in four years. However, each bankruptcy is unique, and it's often difficult to form an intelligent judgment about whether a bankrupt company will survive.[4]

Because bankruptcy presents so many legal and other complications, I suggest that you get professional advice before speculating in this area. A carefully researched newsletter that specializes in troubled companies is the monthly *Turnaround Letter* (225 Friend St., Suite 801, Boston, MA 02114, $195 per year). Founded in 1986 by George Putnam III, an attorney with considerable experience in bankruptcy cases, this publication has had a remarkably good batting average in its short career. Mutual Shares, a fund recommended in Chapter 6, has invested in bankrupt firms for more than 35 years, with outstanding results.

Perhaps the simplest formula for selecting troubled (not bankrupt) companies with strong recovery potential was outlined several years ago by Lowell Miller in his book, *The Perfect Investment.*[5] Miller's first requirement is that the company's shares must have dropped to 20 percent or less of their previous five-year high. He imposes a somewhat less stringent standard for big companies and for stocks that have crashed despite an increase in earnings. If a stock was formerly valued in the market at more than $2 billion, for example, he advises buying when the stock drops to 35 percent of the former high.

Utility stocks also qualify for the 35 percent cutoff, while banks must meet a 30 percent standard. If a company's earnings or dividends have increased from the former five-year high to the crash-point low, or if the company was valued in the market at over $1 billion and earnings have declined less than 25 percent from the high, the 30 percent benchmark is acceptable.

To screen out the dogs, Miller suggests a few other criteria:

- Generally, the stock, after its crash, should sell below book value per share.

- There must be apparent "signs of life," such as dividends or earnings.

- Fad companies with obsolescent products should be avoided.

- The stock's price chart must show solid evidence of an uptrend.

Miller also looks for *plus factors*, kickers that might indicate that the company is on the mend: a dividend reinstatement or increase, a low price-earnings ratio, insider purchases of stock, a monopoly market for the company's products and so on.

I can testify that this method works. In August 1982 (before Miller's book appeared), I recommended Chrysler common stock and warrants to readers of *Personal Finance*. (A *warrant*, like an option, gives you the right to buy a stock at a fixed price for a specified time. But a warrant typically has a longer life than an option, ranging in some cases up to 10 years.) Although I hadn't heard of Miller at the time, my criteria were virtually identical to his: the stock had crashed, its book value was triple the market price, Lee Iacocca was putting on the hard sell and the stock was moving up despite a powerful downdraft in the broad market. Chrysler turned out to be the best-performing stock I've ever selected (so far, anyway!), soaring 400 percent in 10 months. The warrants jumped nearly 10 times over the same period.

To get the full benefit of speculating in troubled stocks, you should take care to spread your risks among at least half a dozen (and preferably more) industries. A crash in oil prices, or copper prices, or computer-chip prices may spawn a whole school of bargain stocks in the affected industry. But it's a mistake to lay all your money on the turnaround prospects of just one or two industries. Industries, like individual corporations, can take a maddeningly long time to recover their health. If you're going to buy a depressed bank, buy a depressed computer maker, too—and a department store, a truck manufacturer, a building-products supplier and an electric utility. Each industry will follow a different timetable on the road to recovery, sparing you (ideally, anyway) the agony of an endless wait for a single industry to turn its fortunes around.

The Inside Scoop

One of Lowell Miller's plus factors for a stock, you'll recall, was insider buying. Some successful contrary investors have stopped right there. It's possible, they've found, to build a winning portfolio simply by purchasing stocks the insiders are buying, and selling stocks the insiders are selling—without doing any further research! This is the fourth contrarian method of stock selection.

Of course, I don't suggest that you should ignore the other factors that might draw your attention to a stock—a low P/E ratio, for example, or a Lowell Miller-style "crash." But if you lack the time or the expertise to research stocks thoroughly, you'll generally stay on the right track by following the lead of the corporate insiders—America's most knowledgeable contrary investors.

In Chapter 5, I mentioned the rule of thumb that stocks favored by insiders typically go up twice as fast as the market during a general rise, and that stocks dumped by the insiders go down twice as fast as the market during a general slide. Tables 7.1 and 7.2 show how this principle has worked on two occasions in recent years, during the huge first leg of the Reagan bull market from August 1982 to June 1983 and during the drawn-out market decline from June 1983 to July 1984.

Each table is composed of the 10 stocks on the Big Board with the greatest amount of insider buying and selling, respectively, before the major market turning points in August 1982 and June 1983. As you can see, the insiders knew what they were doing: the stocks they liked best outperformed the Dow Jones Industrial Average by nearly a 2-to-1 spread, while the stocks they deserted fell more than twice as far as the Dow when the market weakened.

Table 7.1 Insider Buy Signals

Stock	Insider purchases/ sales in preceding 12 months	Price 8/12/82	Price 6/16/83	Gain %
Pacific Lumber	9/0	15 3/8	28 1/4	83.7
Emery Air Freight	8/1	8 1/2	20 5/8	142.6
Planning Research	8/1	5 3/4	21 1/8	267.4
Baker International	7/0	19	18 3/8	(3.3)
Bay Financial	7/0	8 5/8	15 3/4	82.6
Royal Crown Cos.	7/0	15 5/8	26 1/2	69.6
United Merchants	7/1	4 7/8	12 1/4	151.3
Handy & Harman	6/0	12 7/8	21 1/4	65.0
Tri-South Investments	6/1	3 3/4	6 3/4	80.0
Macmillan Inc.	5/0	13	33 3/4	159.6
Average gain				109.8
Gain for DJIA				60.7

Table 7.2. Insider Sell Signals

Stock	Insider purchases/ sales in preceding 12 months	Price 6/16/83	Price 7/24/84	Loss %
A.G. Edwards	4/35	38 7/8	19 7/8	(50.2)
Motorola	1/40	44.33*	32 1/2	(27.3)
Digital Equipment	0/31	113 1/2	78 5/8	(30.7)
Control Data	0/27	60 1/2	24 5/8	(59.3)
Hilton Hotels	0/23	56	46 3/4	(16.5)
Humana	1/22	32.81	25 7/8	(21.2)
National Med. Enter.	0/21	30 3/8	18 3/8	(39.5)
American Med. Intern.	2/21	34 3/4	22 7/8	(34.2)
Wal/Mart Stores	2/19	41 1/8	39	(5.2)
Lear Siegler	1/18	46	40	(13.0)
Average Loss				(29.7)
Loss for DJIA				(13.0)

*Adjusted to reflect stock split.
Source: *The Insiders* (3471 N. Federal Hwy., Ft. Lauderdale, FL 33306, $100 per year).

The same pattern was repeated during the 1987 stock market crash, although it would have been nearly impossible for the stocks with heavy insider selling to fall twice as far as the market averages in that famous debacle. From the August 1987 peak to December 4, 1987, when most of the broad-based market indices touched their crash lows, the New York Stock Exchange Composite index fell 33 percent. Over the same period, the 10 NYSE stocks with the heaviest insider selling dropped 39.9 percent. Interestingly, most of these stocks were well-known blue chips (such as Citicorp, Digital Equipment, DuPont, General Motors, Lockheed and Westinghouse), which you would ordinarily expect to fare somewhat better than the average stock in a market downdraft.

Here are some basic rules for trading stocks with heavy insider activity:

• *Buy* when, marketwide, more insiders are buying than sel-ling. Sell when insider sales exceed purchases by a 3-to-1 margin (higher in an extremely strong bull market).

• *Buy* an individual stock if three or more insiders buy the stock within a three-month period, or if the chairman (or presi-dent) and any other insider buy the stock within a three-month period.

• *Sell* a stock if four or more insiders sell within a three-month period. For technology companies and brokerage firms, raise the sell signal to six. But sell regardless of whether any other insiders are selling, if the chairman, president or an outside direc-tor dumps a big block of stock (worth at least $500,000). In general, insiders sell more often than they buy, for reasons I dis-cussed in Chapter 5.

Thus, it takes more insider sales to generate a sell signal than buys to generate a buy signal.

• If you get a mixture of buys and sells, go with the pre-ponderance of insider transactions. Buy if buyers outnumber sellers by 3-to-1, and sell if sellers outnumber buyers 4-to-1. (See previous rules.) A transaction by the chairman or president counts as two votes on the buy side and three votes on the sell side.

Choose Your Weapons

Despite what some advocates for the theory of contrary opinion may say, there's no single, true-blue contrarian method for pick-ing stocks. Some investors may prefer to buy small-company growth stocks after these "cats and dogs" have lagged the market averages for several years. Others may favor stocks with low price-earnings ratios, while still others may dabble in distressed companies whose stocks have plummeted 70 or 80 percent. All in-vestors can benefit from studying insider trading—and indeed, you can build a contrarian strategy on insider trading alone, if you wish.

Which method you follow depends largely on your own tastes and temperment. If you're the patient, methodical sort, David

Dreman's low P/E strategy will probably appeal to you. On the other hand, if you enjoy a good horse race, you might want to take a flyer in depressed growth stocks or turnaround candidates. Follow a strategy that makes you comfortable, or even several strategies if you want to experiment. For the contrarian, there's only one hard-and-fast rule of stock selection: *Don't buy what everybody else is buying.* If a stock is riding the crest of popularity, the best profits are probably already sitting in someone else's pocket.

Chapter 8

The Crash and Beyond

A crash is a financial shout for the hard of hearing.
—Robert C. Beckman

For millions of investors, October 19, 1987—Black Monday—will live on forever as a day of infamy, a financial Pearl Harbor. Worldwide, more than a trillion dollars of stock market wealth was wiped out in the space of a few hours. In the United States, the Dow Jones Industrial Average plunged 508 points, or 22 percent—by far the worst daily percentage drop since the New York Stock Exchange was set up under the buttonwood tree in 1792.*

More than a year after Meltdown Monday, many investors and their advisors, eager to get back to business as usual, are trying to put the crash out of mind. Yet difficult questions remain about this momentous event: Why did it happen? Will the crash turn out to be the harbinger of a depression worse than that of the 1930s? Or, at the opposite extreme, was it merely an aberration caused by computerized program trading? Why did so many normally reliable indicators fail to signal that a debacle of historic proportions was in the offing?

Satisfactory answers to these questions are only beginning to take shape, and scholars will probably tussle over them for decades. Nonetheless, it's important for an investor operating in the post-crash environment to develop some working hypotheses for himself about that famous incident—if only to help understand

*The Dow suffered a larger one-day percentage decline on December 12, 1914—the first day of trading after the market had been closed for nearly five months at the beginning of World War I. However, prices were merely adjusting for the many economic developments that had accumulated during the shutdown. In this sense, the decline wasn't sudden or precipitous at all.

129

whether, and to what extent, the rules of the investing game have changed.

Don't Blame the Computers

Almost from the closing bell on Black Monday, some pundits have attempted to dismiss the crash as a fluke triggered by gremlins inside a bunch of big financial institutions' computers. This argument, in my opinion, is seriously flawed. No doubt, program trading exaggerated the market's plunge. But once the programmed selling subsided and the market reversed to the upside, programmed buying proved insufficient to lift stock prices back to anywhere near their old highs.

A year after the crash, the Dow stood more than 500 points below its August 1987 high of 2722. If program traders with all their supposed muscle were unable to boost stocks after the crash, it seems unreasonable to blame them for causing the collapse in the first place. To slash the market value of America's publicly traded corporations and keep it down, something fundamental in the economic picture must have changed.

Had investors been willing to step up and buy stocks on Meltdown Monday, all the program traders in the world couldn't have knocked 508 points off the Dow. Let me explain. Program traders take advantage of price disparities between stock-index futures and the actual shares traded on the New York Stock Exchange. (A computer is used to keep track of these misalignments.) When the futures are trading below their theoretical fair value* in relation to the shares, it makes sense for arbitragers to buy the futures and simultaneously sell the shares—for a guaranteed profit. Such selling in the cash market puts downward pressure on stock prices until the two markets come back into line with each other.

*The theoretical fair value of an index future consists of three parts: (1) the price of the cash index, plus (2) the interest charge an investor would have to pay on a loan to buy and hold the stocks in the index until the expiration date of the futures contract, minus (3) the dividends due on the stock in the index up to the expiration date.

But wait a minute. Amid all the huffing and puffing about program trading, nobody seems to have asked the obvious question: Why were the futures trading at a discount to their fair value in the first place? The simple answer is that big institutional investors were stampeding to sell stocks on October 19 (and indeed, in the week or so leading up to the crash). The quickest and cheapest way to sell stocks is through the futures market.

As it turned out, so many institutions were clamoring to sell futures that the futures began to trade at a discount to fair value. That discrepancy caught the attention of the "arbs," who proceeded to equalize the futures and cash markets by selling stocks.

If this program-trading drama has a villain, it ought to be the megabuck institutions like the General Motors pension fund who sold futures in a frenzy to "insure" their stock portfolios against loss. (As we'll see, however, the institutions had good reason to sell.) The arbitragers deserve no more blame for speeding the market's fall than kudos for accelerating the previous rise.

Program trading, then, did *not* "cause" the Crash of '87 in any sense of the word. You can put that red herring back into the can. In fact, if you're looking for the real causes of the crash, Wall Street—despite its many sins—is the wrong place to start your search. For this panic, like its illustrious predecessor in 1929, was manufactured not in New York or Chicago, but in Washington, D.C.

Not Baker, Not Bork, But the Fed

When I say that the crash originated in Washington, I don't mean—as some commentators have suggested—that Treasury secretary James Baker triggered the sell-off with his threat to drive the dollar down if the Germans didn't lower their interest rates. Nor do I mean to imply that the defeat of the Bork nomination in the Senate touched off the worst financial debacle in history.

To attribute such a momentous event to such trivial causes is self-evidently absurd. Treasury secretaries from Alexander

Hamilton onward have made countless dumb remarks before, and Ronald Reagan himself uttered many more fatuities during his two terms in office than Baker could spit out in a lifetime. Furthermore, the Senate has rejected approximately one-quarter of the Supreme Court nominees that have been sent up to it since 1789. Did the stock market crash when two of Nixon's choices, Haynsworth and Carswell, went down in flames?

No, the Crash of '87 had much deeper, more fundamental causes—two, in fact. As lawyers like to say, there was a proximate (or immediate) cause and an ultimate cause. Let's take a careful look at each in succession.

The proximate cause of the crash—the straw that broke the camel's back—was the same in 1987 as it was 58 years before: the Federal Reserve tightened monetary policy, driving up interest rates. For two years (from the fall of 1984 to the fall of 1986), the Fed had aggressively eased credit and pushed interest rates down. The money supply soared and stock prices followed. At the peak for the major market averages in August 1987, stocks were trading at some of their highest valuations in history as measured by price-earnings ratios and price-to-book-value ratios. Dividend yields had sunk to an all-time low.

But in the spring of 1987, the Fed—spooked by rising inflation and by the dollar's nosedive in the foreign-exchange markets—started to tug the credit reins. In the six months ending with the crash, yields on 90-day jumbo bank certificates of deposit leaped from 6.4 to 8.8 percent—a 36 percent increase (see Figure 18). It was the steepest jump in short-term interest rates over a comparable period since 1981.

As interest rates rose, astute investors began to sense that the economy was headed for a slowdown—or perhaps something worse. In a slowing economy, it would be difficult or impossible for corporate earnings to fulfill the lofty expectations that had been built into stock prices when the Dow reached 2722 in August 1987. If companies couldn't deliver the profits that investors were anticipating, not only for 1988 but far into the future, stocks had to drop.

90-Day CD Rates

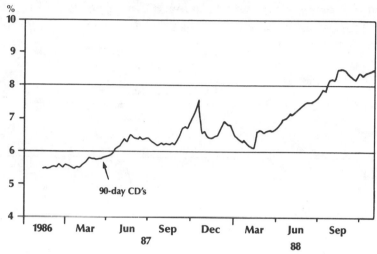

Rates paid by major banks on new certificates in blocks of $1 million or more.
Source: *Investor's Daily.*

Fig. 18. 90-day CD rates

Of course, the 1987 credit squeeze wasn't identical in every detail to those of the past (say, 1974 or 1980). History never repeats itself exactly. One of the foolers in the 1987 episode was that the "yield curve" remained positive. In other words, short-term interest rates stayed well below long-term rates. Before the crash, some analysts argued from the positive slope of the yield curve that the Federal Reserve was really conducting a loose, easy monetary policy. That idea was, I think, blown out of the water on Black Monday.

My own view, and I voiced it several times in *Personal Finance* during the last few months before the crash, was that the Fed had tightened the credit screws considerably, indeed perilously. Not only did interest rates surge, but—as a direct consequence—money growth (however you care to define money) slowed to a crawl. In the 12 months ended January 1987, as Figure 19 shows, the basic M1 money supply grew a sizzling 17.5 percent. By December 1987, the growth rate in M1 had plummeted to 3.5 percent—the slowest growth rate for M1 in 17 years.* "Jamming on the brakes" is hardly an exaggerated metaphor for what hap-

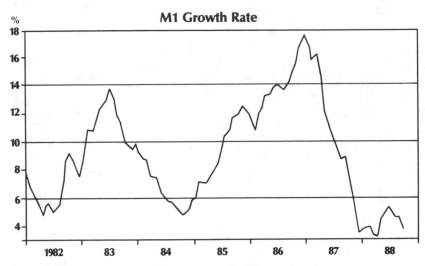

M1 Growth Rate

12-month growth in M1 money supply. **Source:** Federal Reserve Board.

Fig. 19. M1 growth rate

pened. Never before had the central bank so quickly engineered such a drastic turnaround in policy.

Debt: The Looming Backdrop

If tight money was the proximate cause of the crash, the ultimate cause—the looming background to the economic drama of our times—was the gigantic buildup of debt, public and private, over the past 40 years but especially during the Reagan era. Debt always poses a risk to any enterprise because when cash flow sags

*M1 consists of cash, checking accounts (including NOW accounts) and traveler's checks.

the debt remains and must be serviced. When an entire economy is awash in debt, the slightest hint of a contraction in cash flow can spark a financial panic.

Wall Street, going into the crash, was enormously leveraged—a gentle way of saying "deep in hock." Margin debt had quadrupled since the 1982 stock market low to $44 billion in September 1987. Moreover, speculators could buy and sell futures contracts on 5 percent down, a privilege that Jesse Livermore and the pool operators of the 1920s never dreamed of. As stock prices plunged on Meltdown Monday, forced selling by futures traders to meet margin calls intensified the panic and begot more selling. Leverage, and not computerized trading per se, was the market's Achilles heel.

But Wall Street's excesses before the crash pale in comparison with the borrowing binge that consumers, businesses and—the biggest debtor of all—the U.S. government have carried on for the past decade. You've doubtless heard the grim statistics:

• Household debt service (interest and principal payments) as a percentage of personal income is at an all-time high.

• Corporate debt-to-equity ratios (even adjusting the "equity" portion up to current market values) stand at all-time highs.

• The federal debt has more than doubled, to $2.5 trillion, in just eight years. As a percentage of gross national product, the government's debt has reached its highest level since the end of World War II.

• The nation's total public and private debt is more than twice the GNP, a much higher ratio than in 1929 (see Figure 20).

These grim statistics remind us that the entire economy is highly leveraged and accident prone. When the stock market crashed, investors were really just expressing—for a moment—the doubts in the deep recesses of their minds about the ability of the U.S. economy to make good on this mountain of debt.

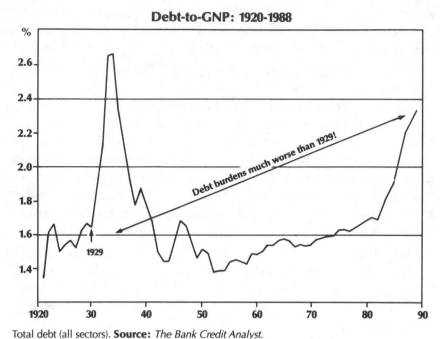

Total debt (all sectors). **Source:** *The Bank Credit Analyst.*

Fig. 20. Debt-to-GNP: 1920-1988

Sound and Fury, Nothing More?

Analyzing the causes of the crash is a fairly straightforward exercise. It's more difficult, however, to interpret the "meaning"— if any—of the crash for the future of the economy and investment markets. Today's extraordinary debt burdens do suggest that the *risk* of a 1930s-style depression is greater now than at any time in the past 50 years. But the crash itself doesn't guarantee that an economic debacle will follow, either sooner or later.

For one thing, the existence of the federal deposit-insurance agencies militates against a wholesale collapse of the banking system such as occurred in the 1930s. As long as bank customers know that the U.S. government ultimately stands behind their deposits, a confidence-killing run on the nation's banks is unlikely. And as long as people retain their confidence in the integrity of the bank-based payments system, economic life will go on more or less as before. Despite all the ink spilled in recent years about the banks' problems, popular faith in the banking system remains well-nigh unshakeable: the stock market crash actually caused an inflow of funds into the banks, not an outflow, as investors pulled money out of equities and stashed it in what they perceived to be a safe haven.

Another factor that the doomsayers and superbears may not have reckoned with is that cooperation among international policymakers has improved greatly in the past two decades. When the dollar sank perilously in 1978-80 and again in 1987, foreign central banks eased credit while the Federal Reserve tightened. The net effect was that everyone helped bolster the dollar. Contrariwise, when a superstrong dollar was decimating America's export industries in the mid-1980s, central banks overseas agreed to tighten credit while the Fed loosened. Together, the world's central bankers brought the dollar down.

Never mind that these initiatives sometimes overshot their goals. The point is that the leading industrial nations are now working more closely together than ever before in the post-World War II era to harmonize their respective economic—and particularly, monetary—policies. Local examples of this increased cooperation include the new U.S.-Canadian free trade pact and the forthcoming dismantlement of trade barriers among the European Common Market countries in 1992. Economic holocausts typically occur when countries are turning inward, not when they're strengthening ties with their trading partners.

From a contrarian standpoint, one of the best reasons for believing that a big-D depression will *not* result from the 1987 crash is that so many people—inside as well as outside of government—are aware of the danger. When an economic or financial problem is well-known, market forces will generally launch a preemptive first strike to keep the situation from getting out of hand. Recall America's struggle with inflation in the late 1970s. As the end of the decade approached, more and more seers began to argue that hyperinflation was around the corner. (Several books playing this theme hit the bestseller list, as I noted in Chapter 3.)

The markets reacted with alarm to these pronouncements. Bond prices plunged, driving long-term interest rates to heights never before seen in U.S. history. The dollar sank to horrifying depths—to the point where European shopkeepers, long 'accustomed to taking dollars from U.S. tourists, started to refuse payment in greenbacks. Eventually, the clamor became so great that the government had to respond. Against his wishes, Jimmy Carter appointed a well-known inflation hawk, Paul A. Volcker, to head the Federal Reserve Board in 1979. The moment he nominated Volcker, Carter must have known that his chances of re-election in 1980 were doomed. But the psychological pressure from the markets was overwhelming. For all practical purposes, Carter had no other choice but to install an inflation-fighting strongman at the central bank.

1987: Popular Premonitions of Doom

In the months leading up to the 1987 stock market crash, forecasts of a coming depression began to appear with increasing frequency in the popular press. A spate of gloom-and-doom books rocketed up the bestseller charts, including *Blood in the Streets* by James Dale Davidson and Sir William Rees-Mogg; *The Panic of '89* by Paul Erdman; *Beyond Our Means* by Alfred L. Malabre Jr.; *The National Debt* by Lawrence Malkin; and the runaway favorite, *The Great Depression of 1990* by Ravi Batra. Investment banker Peter G. Peterson, who served as Secretary of Commerce under Richard Nixon, weighed in with a deeply pessimistic article for the October 1987 *Atlantic* called "The Morning After." Never before had so many forecasts of imminent economic destruction been given such a wide and respectful hearing in the midst of prosperity.

The central message of all these books and articles was that America—from the federal government down to the man in the street—was digging itself hopelessly into debt. We had gone on an orgy of overspending and overconsumption. Our savings habits were in shambles. If we didn't change our ways, but fast, an economic cataclysm was inevitable. In fact, some of the gloom-and-doom prophets maintained that the cataclysm was inevitable regardless of what efforts we might make as a nation at reforming ourselves.

Much of what the latter-day gloomsters have been saying about the dangers of debt rings true, as I pointed out earlier in this chapter. The markets, however, are well aware of these megarisks—and the markets are already forcing the United States in the direction of fiscal prudence. Even before the crash, the growth rate in federal spending had dropped from a peak of 18 percent in 1980 to less than 4 percent in 1987 (see Figure 21). With the rate of increase in the government's expenditures slowing, the

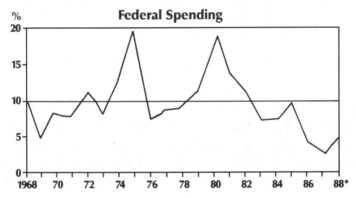

*1988 = six months. Percentage growth in federal expenditures, calendar years. **Source:** Federal Reserve Bank of St. Louis, Treasury Dept.

Fig. 21. Federal spending

budget deficit narrowed $70 billion in 1987 and 1988 from its 1986 peak—and will continue to narrow, barring a steep recession, for the next several years. The Gramm-Rudman law, which mandates a balanced budget by 1993, should help President Bush hold Congress' feet to the fire.

Thus, the stock market crash could turn out to be the "preemptive first strike" (or, more likely, one of several such shocks) that will prevent the U.S. government from going off the deep end in debt. In Washington, the crash solidified the feeling that the

United States simply can't afford major new spending programs. One of the remarkable aspects of the recent presidential campaign was that neither candidate, for the first time in the memory of most people now living, proposed a significant increase in *any* category of federal expenditure.

The Crash and the Private Sector

As important as the government's finances are for the overall economy, however, the private sector looms much larger. (The federal budget amounts to only about one-quarter of the GNP, and the GNP actually *understates* private economic activity.) It's worth recalling that the private sector is where the crash occurred: in the market for common stocks, which are certificates of title to private capital goods. Hence, any enduring impact from the crash is likely to be greatest in the private sector.

Superficially, it seemed that the private economy, a year or two after the crash, had come through pretty much unscathed. The GNP continued to expand at a healthy clip, and the unemployment rate dropped to a 15-year low in the spring of 1989. Widespread complacency about the economy's strength spurred a binge of corporate leveraged buyouts, culminating in the record-breaking $21 billion RJR Nabisco deal in October 1988. (In a leveraged buyout, takeover artists arrange for a company to borrow money to buy back essentially all of its own stock.) A headline story in *Investor's Daily* during the fall of 1988 proclaimed: *"No End in Sight for Current U.S. Expansion."*[1]

Beneath the surface, though, cracks were beginning to appear in the economy's seemingly solid foundations. Housing starts continued to drop in 1988 and 1989, as they had in 1987. The Commerce Department's index of leading indicators, which is designed to "lead" or foreshadow economic trends, fell during most of 1989—much as in 1979, a transition year from growth to recession. Money growth (M1, M2, etc.), after a blip in the first half of 1988, settled back to its plodding pace of the year before as the Federal Reserve once again boosted interest rates. To underscore its independence and inflation-fighting resolve, the Fed actually hiked its discount rate (the rate at which commercial banks can borrow directly from the Fed) *during the Republican National Convention* in August 1988, an unprecedented demonstration of political willpower. And the Fed remained stingy with credit in 1989.

Given the huge debt burden hanging over American business and the bad loans infesting the nation's banks and thrifts, a thoughtful observer might wonder how much "slowing" this economy can take before it rolls over into recession. If an economic slump does begin within the next year or two, it could snowball rather quickly, leaving a bloody trail of bankruptcies and bank failures.

Such a turn of events, even if it didn't culminate in a 1930s-style depression, would strike fear into the hearts of consumers and investors as well as corporate managements. Debt growth in the overall economy would slow dramatically, reinforcing a pattern that has already been in place since 1986 (see Figure 22). Indeed, a recession may be just what the economy needs right

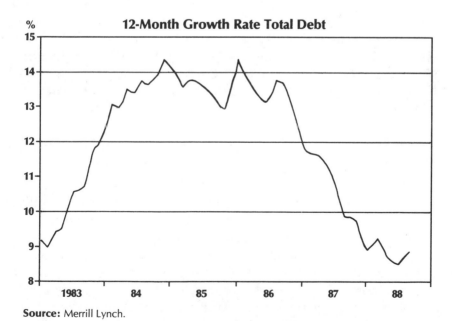

Source: Merrill Lynch.

Fig. 22. 12-month growth rate total debt

141

now to complete the shift, which began in the early 1980s, from high inflation to low or no inflation. Apparently, a psychological shock is still necessary to teach borrowers and lenders alike that low inflation is here to stay and that excessive debt carries unacceptable risks. If a recession were to descend in the next few years, with sharply rising unemployment and debt defaults, people who haven't learned the lesson yet might finally do so. Farmers and oilmen learned in the early 1980s. Now, perhaps, the yuppies and corporate paper traders will take their turn in the school of hard knocks.

No iron law dictates that a recession must follow within a certain number of months after a collapse in stock prices. Over the years, the lag time has varied widely. Nonetheless, in the past century, every decline of 30 percent or more in the stock market during peacetime has led, sooner or later, to an economic contraction. I see no particular reason why this instance should wind up as the exception.

Only a year after the crash, most economists and Wall Streeters were already shrugging it off as a "value correction" or a "market break." *The Wall Street Journal,* in an October 1988 story, captured the euphoria beautifully with the headline *"Bullish Brokers Say Buy-Buy to Crash."*[2] To a contrarian's ears, such whistling past the graveyard suggests that the ultimate effects of Meltdown Monday have yet to be felt. Eventually, they will be—but probably *not* in the form of a simple replay of the 1930s. Too many gloom-and-doomers are already prepared for that scenario.

More likely, the economy will hit a series of painful, frightening bumps in the next few years, which will at last persuade Americans to clean up their individual and collective balance sheets. Purged of its unsustainable debt load, the U.S. economy will then be in a position to grow dynamically in the latter part of the 1990s and into the first decade of the 21st century. If we assume "normal" (6 percent a year) growth of corporate earnings and dividends, the Dow Jones Industrial Average should trade above 4000 and perhaps above 5000 before revelers in Times Square celebrate the New Year's eve of the new century.

But first, the nation must settle a few outstanding accounts. The rest of the world will no longer allow us to borrow and spend our way to prosperity without any restrictions. We must change our habits, from the federal budget in Washington to the family budget in Peoria. The process is already well under way, but it must—and will—continue. Occasionally, it will hurt. That, at bottom, is the sobering message of Black Monday.

Where Were the Warning Bells?

From an investment standpoint, one of the major surprises of the Crash of 1987 was that so many of the traditional contrary indicators failed to warn that a market decline of historic proportions was in the offing. Advisory sentiment, as measured by the *Bullish Consensus* and *Investors Intelligence* polls, reflected a fair degree of optimism, but not the runaway euphoria that has traditionally characterized primary turning points in the stock market. For example, the highest reading on the *Bullish Consensus* poll in August 1987 was only 69 percent. During the entire year, it never reached the low end of the overbought range (70 percent). By contrast, the advisors were 88 percent bullish at the June 1983 peak.

Anecdotal evidence also showed that investor sentiment was somewhat more subdued at the August 1987 top than at previous major market tops. A few magazines ran euphoric cover stories— such as *Barron's*, which headlined its issue two weeks before the peak, "Memo to the Pros: In Case You Haven't Noticed, the Bull Market Is Beating the Pants off You."[3] And the day the Dow touched 2722, some gurus were excitedly announcing that prices could only go higher. The head equity trader at one brokerage firm told *The Wall Street Journal*: "In a market like this, every story is a positive one. Any news is good news. It's pretty much being taken for granted now that the market is going to go up."[4]

On the other hand, a veteran technician quoted in the same edition of the *Journal* said he was troubled by "fuzzy-cheeked market analysts" who were talking about "this new era of investing where stock is going to keep going up forever because of foreign investors. Sooner or later," this analyst predicted, "the supply and demand situation will be reversed." Thus, even at the absolute top of the market, there was an uncommon amount of nervousness about the bull's prospects.

Most remarkable of all, perhaps, the cover of the August 31 *U.S. News and World Report* depicted a bull riding a roller-coaster, with the car at the top of the highest hump. The headline asked, "The Bull Market: Time to Get Out?" Granted, most of the advisors interviewed in the article argued that it was *not* time to get out. But the amazing thing is that the question was even asked.

In short, the euphoria that might have been expected at a once-in-a-lifetime market peak never materialized in 1987. One reason may be that the stock market's internal health was shaky for several months leading up to the crash, a fact that many intelligent analysts took note of. Valuations had reached some of the greatest extremes ever in terms of dividend yields, book values and corporate earnings.

Moreover, indicators of market breadth revealed that fewer and fewer stocks were participating in the upswing as the Dow lunged toward its final peak. The advance-decline line—the cumulative total of stocks rising in price each day minus those declining—peaked in March 1987, five months before the Dow. Likewise, the roster of stocks touching new yearly highs hit its high in February 1987, six months before the Dow.

Worst of all, as I pointed out earlier in this chapter, the Federal Reserve was squeezing credit. Money-supply growth plunged in the seven months preceding the market's 1987 peak (turn back to Figure 19). Historically, growth in the money supply has had a close correlation with movements in stock prices. An accelerating rate of money growth generally boosts the market, while decelerating money growth hinders stocks.

Because so many market watchers knew about—and talked about—these problems, the traditional top-making euphoria never really took hold. What, then, is the most important lesson contrarians can learn from the crash? I've already stated it in Chapter 1. You can't afford to ignore the fundamental and technical background when you appraise the mood of the market.

Each market cycle is to some extent unique, and the intensity of bullishness or bearishness among investors will depend to some degree on such factors as whether the Fed is promoting easier or tighter money, whether P/E ratios are high or low and whether the great mass of stocks are following the pattern set by the market averages. When the market's fundamental or technical health is slipping, investor sentiment—even at the top for prices—won't rise to the heights of euphoria that prevail when the backdrop is more encouraging. By the same token, when the fundamental or technical picture is improving, the market can make a solid bottom without sinking to the depths of pessimism that would be necessary in the absence of such "good news."

In other words, you should continually ask yourself: "Is the market overdoing it?" Are investors too cheerful, given the news background and the market's own internal dynamics (including value benchmarks)? If so, you should sell. Are investors too gloomy, given recent developments? If so, you should buy. Look for excesses. There were plenty of them in the summer of 1987.

Chapter 9

The Income Investor
Fights Back

One thousand dollars left to earn interest at 8 percent a year will grow to $43 quadrillion in 400 years, but the first hundred years are the hardest.—Sidney Homer, *A History of Interest Rates*

For most of recorded history, investing for income has been a losing battle. If it were possible to amass a fortune by collecting interest and dividends, surely many of the ancient noble families of Europe, and even some of the old patrician families of America (the Adamses of Massachusetts, for example, and the Lees of Virginia) would long since have become "quadrillionaires."

Sad to say, just the opposite is what usually happens: great fortunes disintegrate, devoured by taxes, inflation, depression, war, revolution, expropriation, bad management or simple waste. Over long periods, it seems, the "miracle of compound interest"— once lightheartedly dubbed the Eighth Wonder of the World— never really gets a chance to show its stuff.

In America, with our relatively stable economy and legal system, inflation has for the past half century or so been the income investor's most implacable foe. Almost every year since Franklin D. Roosevelt took the United States off the gold standard in 1934, the purchasing power of the dollar has dwindled—but never at a uniform rate. If lenders knew what rate of inflation to expect in coming years, they could hedge themselves by demanding an interest rate high enough to protect the "real" (inflation-adjusted) value of their principal.

147

But under a system of fiat currency, unbacked by any tangible asset (such as precious metals), no one can be certain of the future value of money. For decades, as I pointed out in Chapter 1, bond buyers repeatedly underestimated the degree to which the U.S. government would debauch the dollar through inflation. In late 1988, a notice in *The Wall Street Journal* caught my eye: it announced the final redemption of a tranche of bonds issued by one of the Bell telephone companies in 1948—40 years previously. The bonds bore a coupon interest rate of 3 percent.

From date of issue to maturity, the principal (face value) of these bonds lost approximately 80 percent of its purchasing power. Even if all the interest coupons had been plowed back to buy more bonds at the higher and higher interest rates that became available in later years, an investor who bought these Bell bonds in 1948 would have earned a compound return of only about one-half of 1 percent a year in constant, real dollars. A passbook savings account would have performed better—and spared our hapless bondholder the agony of seeing the market value of his investment decline almost continuously from 1948 to 1981.

Fool Me Twice, Shame on You

Today's income investor, however, has wised up to the inflation game. As inflation raged out of control in the late 1970s and early 1980s, investors finally began to demand a huge interest premium over the current inflation rate to compensate for the risk of higher inflation to come. For almost the entire decade of the 1980s, real interest rates—the nominal rate of interest minus the prevailing inflation rate—hovered at the highest levels in 50 years (see Figure 23).

Even in late 1988, long after the double-digit inflation of the Jimmy Carter era had wilted away, garden-variety Treasury bonds with 20 or more years to maturity were still paying a premium of 500 basis points (5 percent) over inflation. Wary investors refused to believe that the threat of accelerating inflation was gone for good. In August 1988, when bond yields peaked for the year, a spate of newspaper and magazine articles growled about the dangers of inflation. An Associated Press story was headlined

Real T-bond Yield

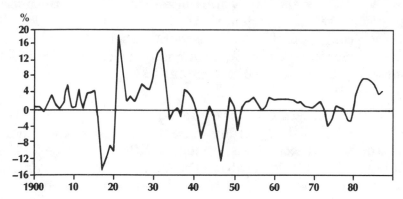

Yield on long-term Treasury bonds minus 12-month inflation rate. **Source:** Weiss Research Inc., P.O. Box 2923, W. Palm Beach, FL 33402.

Fig. 23. Real T-bond yield

"Some Experts Fear Return of High Inflation." *Business Week* ran a column (August 8) titled "The Winds of Inflation Are Blowing a Little Harder" and *USA Today* warned: "Inflation Fear Growing with the Economy." At the time, consumer prices were rising at only a 4 percent annual pace.

From 1980 onward, the attitude of bond investors shifted 180 degrees, from "Hit me again, it feels good" to "Fool me once, shame on me; fool me twice, shame on you." Instead of complacently accepting higher and higher inflation rates, bond buyers learned to sell at the slightest blip in the cost of living. Twice during the decade, in 1984 and again in 1987, bond prices plummeted (interest rates soared) on inflation fears, forcing the Federal Reserve to show its inflation-fighting resolve by tightening money and credit. Each time, investors refused to buy bonds again until it became apparent that the inflation danger had subsided. The income investor finally decided to fight back. And he won in a knockout.

What he won was, in effect, a commitment from the nation's central bank to defend the integrity of the dollar from the ravages

149

of inflation. To be sure, the United States, at this writing anyway, hasn't yet reached the happy state of zero inflation (or the not-so-happy state of outright deflation). But tomorrow, who knows? Several recent appointees to the Federal Reserve Board have endorsed schemes—such as a commodity price rule to govern monetary policy—that could eventually suppress inflation altogether.

Equally interesting in this context, the Federal Reserve Bank of Cleveland published a study in September 1988, co-authored by one of its staff economists, under the title, "The Case for Zero Inflation." Regional Federal Reserve banks often send up trial balloons in the form of scholarly articles and monographs to prepare the public for a change in policy. A consensus may well be forming within the Fed to aim for zero inflation within the next several years.

Even if the Fed were inclined to disregard the wishes of domestic bond buyers (which it isn't), foreign investors wouldn't allow the United States to pursue a highly inflationary monetary policy. One consequence of the massive build-up of debt by Americans in the past decade is that, for the first time in this century, we owe foreigners more money than they owe us. If foreign investors start to lose confidence in the purchasing power of the dollar as a result of our central bank's monetary policy, they'll dump dollar-denominated paper (from bank accounts to Treasury bonds), driving the exchange value of the dollar down and U.S. interest rates up. Ironically, when Richard Nixon established freely floating exchange rates for the dollar on the world's currency markets in 1973, he thought he was escaping, once and for all, the discipline of the gold standard. Today, floating currency rates act much like the gold standard of old—as a brake on the Fed's ability to inflate.

The Real Trouble with Real Rates

Will today's high real interest rates last indefinitely? In the first edition of this book, published in 1985, I said no—and my hunch has grown stronger with the passage of time. In words that now seem almost uncomfortably prophetic, I argued: "Today's sky-high interest rates may, I think, be foreshadowing a financial crisis that could bring down the curtain on the postwar credit boom and, eventually, cause interest rates to collapse." The financial crisis, or at least the first installment of it, occurred on Black Monday, 1987. If the stock market crash does lead, sooner or later, to an economic contraction, as I suspect it will, the aftershocks of that slump may well break America's long romance with debt and allow money rates—both real and nominal—to plummet.

To begin with, a wave of defaults by households, corporations and possibly even some city and state governments would tend to curb demand for credit, both during the recession and long after. Deadbeats generally don't bother to apply for new loans, at least not for a few years after filing bankruptcy. Furthermore, and perhaps more important, horror stories of foreclosures and repossessions would discourage financially sound borrowers from taking on more debt. Many, in fact, reading the signs of the times, would probably decide to pay down their obligations rather than assume new ones.

Of course, the financial habits that Americans have developed over a generation or more won't change overnight. For as long as most people can remember, buying on time has been the smart way to beat the rising cost of living—and the taxman. (Until recently, the government allowed liberal deductions for interest payments on consumer loans.) But the next downturn in the economy, even if it doesn't degenerate into a 1930s-type deflationary depression, will probably leave a gaping gash in the "fly now, pay later" psychology.

The key point to keep in mind is that our fellow citizens have *encumbered their cash flow* to an unprecedented degree. Not only are borrowers carrying some of the largest debt balances in history, relative to their incomes, but the cost of servicing that debt (principal and interest payments) is consuming a larger fraction of their cash flow than ever before. Take a look at Figure 24 to see what I mean. This graph portrays corporations' interest expense as a percentage of their profits before interest and taxes. Since 1965, the interest bite out of corporate cash flow has soared fivefold. To put it another way, the margin of safety between a typical corporation's cash flow (a variable quantity) and its inter-

Corporate Interest Expense

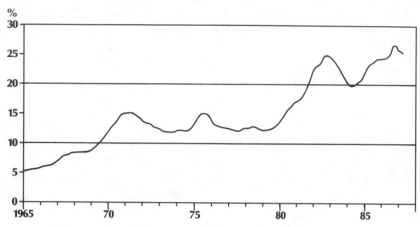

Earnings calculated before interest and taxes. **Source:** First Boston Corp.

Fig. 24. Corporate interest expense

est expense (a more or less fixed quantity) has shrunk by a factor of 80 percent. A relatively small drop in corporate cash flow could cause a relatively severe problem with debt service. This is the dark side of leverage, visible only in hard times.

Corporations aren't the only players on the economic scene who have burdened their cash flow with a skyrocketing interest tab. Individuals at one end of the spectrum, and the federal government at the other, have done the same thing. In 1952, interest payments on mortgage debt and consumer installment debt combined amounted to just a little over 2 percent of Americans' disposable personal income or take-home pay (see Figure 25). Today, interest payments eat up 8 percent of the average American's paycheck—and remember, that number doesn't include repayments of principal, which are mandatory with most consumer loans. For individuals, the interest burden alone has quadrupled in a little more than one generation.

Uncle Sam, the biggest single debtor of all, is also facing a worsening cash squeeze—the inevitable consequence of chronic overspending. (The federal budget hasn't shown a surplus since

1969.) Interest on the national debt amounted to only 12 percent of the government's revenues in 1950. By the end of fiscal year 1988, that figure had nearly doubled, to 23.6 percent. The government's interest bill now ranks a close third behind national defense and Social Security among the largest expenditure categories of the federal budget.

With the enormous leverage on the balance sheets of individuals, corporations and the federal government, it isn't difficult to see how the next economic downturn—whenever it happens and

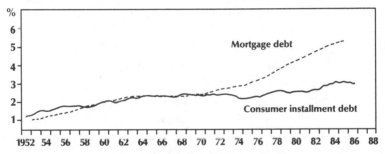

Interest Paid On Debt
(As a Percent of Disposable Personal Income)

Source: *Bank Credit Analyst,* BCA Publications Ltd., 1988.

Fig. 25. Interest paid on debt
(as a percent of disposable personal income)

even if it isn't quite so gruesome as the gloom-and-doomers expect—could create a widespread, long-lasting aversion to debt. If demand for credit shriveled, interest rates would almost certainly plunge. However, the bull case for bonds doesn't rest on speculation about the shape of the next recession. Several long-term megatrends are already working quietly to curb the U.S. economy's appetite for credit.

The Graying of America

There are few certainties in economic life. One near-certainty, though, is that the U.S. population will be growing older over the next 20 years or so. The Baby Boom generation (those born between roughly 1946 and 1961) is aging. Because the succeeding generation—the children of the Boomers—has been much smaller in number, the average age of the population will climb inexorably as the dawn of the 21st century approaches.

What does an aging population suggest about interest rates? Young people, especially those in the 25-to-34-year-old bracket, tend to be heavy borrowers. Many are buying their first home, typically on a small down payment because they've accumulated relatively little capital. (Shelter, as a rule, is the largest single expense of a person's lifetime.) Some, as their careers blossom, are trading up to a more expensive home, buying a new BMW or vacationing at exotic watering spots around the world. This latter subgroup, popularly known as the "yuppies," is so conspicuous that it has become (somewhat unjustly) a symbol for anyone in the 25-34 age bracket. Nonetheless, it's fair to say that consumption is king for most Americans in their yuppie years, whether they qualify as authentic yuppies or not.

People in later middle age (45 to 54 years old) are working toward a different set of financial goals. Most have reached a plateau in their careers. They aren't inclined to move into a bigger house, partly because they can't afford to and partly because they don't need one: their children are grown up (or nearly so) and leaving home. Instead, the middle-aged "nerd" is thinking more about putting children through college and, ultimately, settling into retirement. To achieve these goals, the middle-aged person knows he must watch his consumption and step up his savings rate. Late-middle-aged people are America's champion savers and investors.

Figure 26 shows how the balance between "yuppies" (consumers) and "nerds" (savers) has shifted over the years, and where the Census Bureau predicts that the ratio is headed in coming decades. During the 1950s and early 1960s, a period of extremely low real interest rates, the proportion of 45-to-54-year-old savers in the general populace surged. Then, from 1966 to 1986, the balance reversed: as Baby Boomers streamed into the workforce, the proportion of 25-34-year-old consumers rocketed. Inflation soared, ultimately producing today's sky-high real interest rates.

Since the 1986 peak, however, the yuppie/nerd ratio has begun to fall—and it will continue to fall steeply until the year

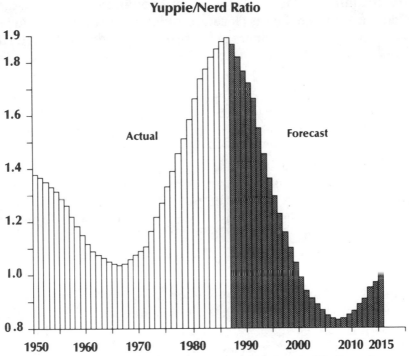

Yuppie/Nerd Ratio

Yuppies = 25 to 34 year olds, Nerds = 45 to 54 year olds. **Source:** U.S. Census Bureau, Comstock Partners.

Fig. 26. Yuppie/nerd ratio

2007. In fact, by 2007, if the Census Bureau's projections (usually pretty accurate) are anywhere near the mark, *savers will outnumber consumers by an even wider margin than in the low-inflation halcyon days of the early 1960s.*

The Budget Wars: Truce in Sight?

Another long-term plus for bonds is that the federal government finally seems to be getting a grip on its budgetary problems. When the Gramm-Rudman budget-balancing law was passed in 1986, many observers dismissed it as another gimmick. Yet Gramm-Rudman has added subtly to the pressure being exerted on Congress by two Republican presidents, the financial community and the Federal Reserve to curb spending. Each year from now until 1993, Gramm-Rudman calls for a reduction in the federal budget deficit—until the deficit is closed completely at the end of the period. In any year that Congress fails to meet its deficit target, the president is empowered to order spending cuts across a wide front.

The mere threat of Gramm-Rudman cuts has all but snuffed out major new spending initiatives in Congress since 1986. If you don't believe it, turn back to Chapter 8 and study Figure 21 again. In calendar year 1987, federal spending actually grew more slowly than the rate of inflation, implying that the size of the U.S. government shrank in real terms for the first time in a quarter-century. Preliminary estimates for 1988 indicate that federal spending was once again almost unchanged in dollars of constant purchasing power.

On the revenue side of the ledger, the growing surplus in the government's Social Security accounts will also tend to lower the unified budget deficit—and could even produce an overall budget surplus as early as the mid-1990s. This emerging Social Security surplus has stirred up a wasp's nest of controversy and misunderstanding among economists and politicians alike. It simply means that the government is now taking in more money in the form of Social Security "contributions" than it's paying out in benefits. In fiscal year 1988, for example, the surplus was $38 billion, double the previous year's figure.

Far from going bankrupt, the Social Security system—thanks to the massive tax increases enacted several years ago—is turning into a cash cow. According to some private projections, barring a depression, the Social Security surplus will cancel out the

156

entire deficit in the government's other accounts between 1994 and 1996. And official estimates suggest that the Social Security surplus will continue to mushroom from there, soaring to a peak of more than $500 billion a year by the year 2015 (see Figure 27).

There's a risk, of course, that Congress will try to raid the Social Security surplus in order to finance increases in current spending. If the solons do reach their hands into the cookie jar, however, I suspect that the nation's politically potent legion of retirees—to say nothing of the millions of aging yuppies whose retirement security is riding on that surplus—will slam the cover

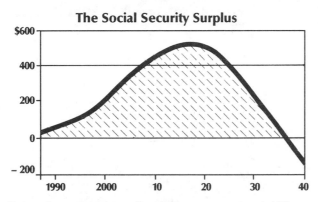

The Social Security Surplus

Projected annual surpluses of tax receipts over payments in billions of current dollars for calendar years. **Source:** *The New York Times.*

Fig. 27. The Social Security surplus

down. Eventually, to support themselves in retirement, the Baby Boomers will need every penny of the huge Social Security surplus that is slated to be built up over the next 25 years. It seems unlikely to me that any politician who attempts to spirit that money away for other purposes will stay in office long.

As the government's unified (i.e., including Social Security) budget deficit narrows, the Treasury will be issuing fewer and fewer bonds to the public. But the plot thickens. Once the unified budget swings into surplus in the mid-1990s, the Social Security system (which is allowed to invest only in Treasury securities) will be buying *all* the new Treasury paper that comes to market.

In fact, the trustees of the Social Security system will be forced to start buying older Treasury securities back from the public. By 2015, some economists calculate, the Social Security trust fund will own all the bonds, notes and bills that the Treasury has ever issued. The supply in private hands will completely dry up.

Frankly, I don't think this mind-boggling state of affairs will ever come to pass. But I do accept the idea that the growing Social Security surplus will sharply curtail the supply of T-bonds available in the marketplace as the turn of the century draws

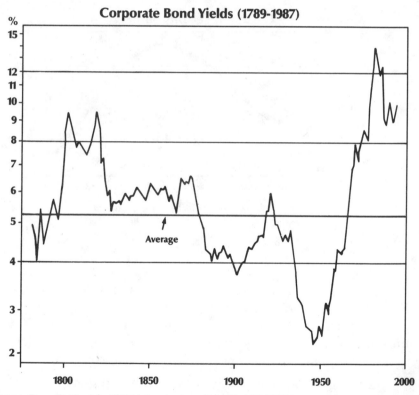

Source: Tracy G. Herrick, 1150 University Ave., Palo Alto, CA 94301.

Fig. 28. Corporate bond yields

near. Result: most likely, interest rates will plunge to levels that prevailed 20 or 30 years ago.

Many investors forget that the stratospheric interest rates of the 1980s are, in history's eye, an aberration. Figure 28 plots the annual average rate on high-grade corporate bonds from the founding of the republic up to now. Over that 200-year span, prime-quality corporate bonds have yielded an average of 5.4 percent. As I write, such bonds are paying well over 9 percent after trading almost as high as 11 percent at the peak in yields on Black Monday, 1987.

As the graph illustrates, bond yields have wandered well above the mean—and well below—in the past 200 years. But when they deviate far to one side or the other, they always manage somehow to swing back to the middle. I'm not expecting miracles, but a drop back to the 5-6 percent area for corporate bonds (4-5 percent for Treasurys) would seem to be well within the realm of possibility sometime in the first half of the 1990s. For bondholders, the next decade could prove to be a golden age as falling interest rates drive up the market value of existing long-term paper.

Lengthen Your Horizons

In the first edition of this book, I recommended bonds strictly as a short-term speculation. However, I also suggested that "some-day, perhaps in the not-too-distant future, bonds will offer such high yields that prudent income investors will buy them and put them away for 10 or 20 years, or more." That day has now arrived. The Federal Reserve has proved it can keep inflation in the low single digits over an entire business cycle. Demographic factors are pointing to lower credit demand and higher savings rates in future years. And prospects are brightening for a resolution of the federal government's seemingly endless budget crisis. Therefore, given today's exceptionally high real interest rates, a buy-and-hold strategy for bonds once again makes sense—for the first time in more than 40 years.

Anyone who buys long-term Treasury bonds in the 8-10 percent range and sits on them to maturity is likely to chalk up an outstanding real return over almost any time frame of five to 25 years or more. By choosing your entry points carefully, however, you can substantially improve your results. The best time to buy bonds is at the height of a credit squeeze, when interest rates are soaring and the newspapers are filled with excited reports about the mortal sickness of the bond market.

A classic example was March 1980. At the climax of the worst sell-off in U.S. bond market history, *The New York Times* published an article titled, "Living Without a Bond Market,"[1] which related how British industry has managed to do without long-term fixed-rate financing. The implication was that the U.S. bond market was dying, too. To a contrarian, it should come as no surprise that the *Times* article coincided almost perfectly with a major bottom in bond prices (a major peak in interest rates).

More recently, in October 1987, another rush of panicky commentary about the bond market filled the air. "You need a helmet to avoid the shells," a managing director of Bear Stearns told *The Wall Street Journal* about two weeks before bond prices made their final lows. "Everybody is trying to get out the same window."[2] Two days before the bottom, a comment by a Chicago mutual fund manager revealed that even value-oriented investors who knew better were giving up: "This is not a good time to sell—and probably is a good level at which to buy...But there's no one out there who wants to be a hero, no one who is willing to stick his neck out."[3] Turn back to p. 47 for an almost identical opinion voiced at the bottom of the great 1973-74 bear market for stocks.

Fortunately, it wasn't literally true that *no one* was "willing to stick his neck out" and buy Treasury bonds at 10 percent or more in October 1987. In the October 14 issue of *Personal Finance,* three trading days before the bottom, I wrote:

> *This may be it—the last great buying opportunity for bonds in the 20th century. If you miss it, you'll never forgive yourself....Bonds today are the closest thing you'll ever find to a free lunch.*

In addition to frantic bond bashing by the "experts," Earl Hadady's *Bullish Consensus* commodity poll, discussed in Chapter 4, can also give you a clue to important turning points in the bond market. (The figures for bonds and bills are printed every week in *Barron's*.) Hadady's poll tracks advisory sentiment on Treasury bond futures, which serve as a reliable proxy for the bond market as a whole. When the bullish consensus on bonds drops to 20 percent, or averages in the low 20s for three or four weeks in a row, the bond market is usually close to a significant bottom. (The four-week average at the 1987 low was less than 24 percent.) On the other hand, when the bullish consensus swells to 80 percent or averages in the upper 70s for several weeks in a row, as it did at the cyclical peaks for bonds in May 1983 and April 1986, it's time to batten down the storm hatches.

Admittedly, credit crunches and spectacular buying opportunities for bonds don't come along often—once every two or three years, at best. Nonetheless, you can still make above-average returns in the long-term bull market I expect for bonds if you "buy the dips." After the Black Monday bottom, bond prices soared into early 1988, then pulled back sharply. During this normal correction, many advisors turned sour on bonds again. Newspaper commentary grew somber and hostile: "Almost every analyst believes interest rates are going up," said *The Wall Street Journal* in early May 1988[4] (my emphasis). The bullish consensus fell to 34 percent a few weeks later. It was another good entry point for long-term investors.

Quality vs. Junk: The Great Debate

Some bond mavens who share my concerns about the U.S. economy's debt overload have spent most of the past decade inveighing against lower-quality or "junk" bonds. One day, no doubt, junk paper and the underwriters who peddle it will get their comeuppance—probably during the next recession. Defaults will spread like prairie fire, gutting the performance records of mutual funds, insurance companies, S&Ls, pension funds and other institutions that have so eagerly and uncritically snapped up this high-yield, high-risk merchandise. As in the 1930s, a debacle in the junk sector of the market could turn investors away from lower-grade bonds for many years to come.

So far, though, obituaries for the junk market have been decidedly premature. Studies by Prof. Edward Altman of New York University[5] and others have shown that, even after you take into account the greater default rate for junk bonds, a diversified portfolio of lower-rated issues has provided a higher total return (interest plus capital gains) than gilt-edged Treasury bonds for the past decade or more. Over almost any recent five-to-10-year period, high-yield mutual funds as a group have outperformed high-quality funds as a whole.

In view of this record, it strikes me as unreasonable for investors to reject lower-grade bonds out of hand. At certain stages of the business cycle, junk bonds may offer returns far out of proportion to their real risk. As I've noted elsewhere, the investing public's *perception* of risk tends to become irrationally exaggerated when the fundamental economic news flowing into the market is bad. Likewise, when the news is good, the public's perception of risk tends to become abnormally relaxed.

The best opportunities for buying junk bonds typically occur late in a recession, when investors start to wonder whether marginal bond issuers can continue to service their debt. The spread between the yield on high-grade obligations and lower-grade paper yawns as prices for the junk issues drop more sharply. On the other hand, it's usually best to buy high-grade bonds near a peak in the economy, when investors begin to fret more about accelerating inflation than about the danger of debt defaults. At this stage of the cycle, yield spreads between high-grade and lower-grade paper generally tighten.

A handy yardstick for measuring whether the market is in a manic (buy Treasurys) or a depressive (buy junk) state is the *quality ratio,* pictured in Figure 29. This ratio is simply the yield on 30-year Treasury bonds divided by the yield on medium-grade corporate bonds (rated BBB by Standard & Poor's or Baa by Moody's). You can track this ratio yourself on a daily basis by referring to the "Yield Comparisons" table published in *The Wall Street Journal.* When the yield on long Treasurys is low relative

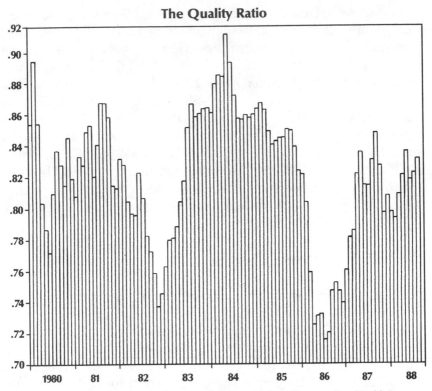

The Quality Ratio

Monthly frequency through August 1988. 30-year Treasury/BAA Corporate Bond Yield. **Source:** Board of Governors of the Federal Reserve, Comstock Partners.

Fig. 29. The quality ratio

to what you can earn on medium-grade corporates (the ratio is 76 or below), the market may be putting too high a premium on quality. Consider buying "junk" bonds for their ultra-high yields. By the same token, when the ratio climbs to 86 or higher, the market is becoming overconfident about the strength of the economy. Few investors are worrying about credit risk. Take the cue and sell your junk bonds in favor of the highest-quality IOUs you can find—Treasurys or AAA-rated corporates.

If you decide to dabble in junk bonds, make sure you put together a diversified portfolio. Don't try to pick just three or four of "tomorrow's Chryslers." One lemon could throw you for an enormous loss. Instead, I recommend that you buy shares in a mutual fund that invests in lower-rated paper. Two well-managed junk bond funds are *Fidelity High Income Fund* (82 Devonshire St., Boston, MA 02109, 800-544-6666, 617-523-1919, minimum $2,500) and *T. Rowe Price High Yield Fund* (100 E. Pratt St., Baltimore, MD 21202, 800-638-5660, 301-547-2308, minimum $1,000). Both were recently yielding over 11 percent. For investors in the top federal tax bracket, the *Vanguard Municipal Bond Fund—High Yield Portfolio* (P.O. Box 2600, Valley Forge, PA 19482, 800-662-2739, 215-648-6000, minimum $3,000) pays about 7.5 percent tax free. It has been one of the best-performing tax-exempt junk funds of the past five years. All of these are no-load funds (no sales charge).

Closed-End Bond Funds

Closed-end funds are another type of bond fund to consider, either for trading purposes or for a long-term holding. These funds issue a fixed number of shares, which trade on a stock exchange or over the counter. You must buy or sell your shares through a stockbroker. (By contrast, open-end mutual funds like Fidelity and Vanguard deal directly with the public, continuously issuing and redeeming their shares at a price based on the value of the fund's portfolio.) Sometimes, you'll find that shares of a closed-end bond fund are selling at a discount to the fund's underlying assets. In effect, you can buy a dollar's worth of bonds for less than a buck— occasionally as little as 90 cents.

Closed-end bond funds usually perform about as well as the open-end funds, but yield slightly more because of the discount. As with the open-end funds, I prefer the lower-quality (higher-yielding) funds when the quality ratio is low, and the higher-grade funds when the quality ratio is high. My recommended list includes the funds below. Take care, however, to buy them *only* when they're trading at a discount of 5 percent or more to NAV. *Barron's* publishes the discount (or premium) for the leading closed-end bonds funds every week.

At panic bottoms in the bond market, the discount usually widens, making closed-end funds an especially attractive buy. In the spring of 1980, for instance, the discount on most closed-end bond funds was running about 20 percent, with some funds trading at as much as a 30 percent discount to their underlying assets. Later in the year, when the bond market rallied sharply, the discounts narrowed or vanished. Several closed-end funds racked upgains of 40 percent or more—on top of a 14 or 15 percent current yield!

High-Grade Funds

- Current Income Shares (NYSE: CUR)
- Fort Dearborn Income Securities (NYSE: FTD)
- INA Investment Securities (NYSE: IIS)
- Vestaur Securities (NYSE: VES)

High-Yield Funds

- Independence Square Income Securities (OTC: ISIS)
- State Mutual Securities (NYSE: SMS)
- USLIFE Income Fund (NYSE:UIF)
- First Australia Prime Income Fund (NYSE: FAI)*
- Global Yield Fund (NYSE: PGY)*

*Invests in foreign securities

For the buy-and-hold investor who wants a minimum of fuss and bother, I suggest U.S. Treasury bonds with the longest possible maturity (25-30 years). Despite our government's fiscal profligacy in recent decades, Treasury paper is still among the most creditworthy in the world. In addition, most—though not all—Treasury issues are *noncallable*. This means that the government can't call them in early for redemption if interest rates drop. By contrast, most corporate and municipal bonds allow the issuer to call them long before the maturity date—in some cases, as little as five years after issue.

If I'm right that a downward megatrend for interest rates began in 1981 and could continue for the next 10 to 20 years, you'll be glad that you locked in today's high T-bond yields. Investors who buy callable bonds, or (worse yet) bonds that mature in just a few years, will find themselves reinvesting their principal payments at lower and lower rates. For many retired people who rely on interest income for living expenses, the "coming interest rate shock" could bring an unwelcome pinch in the pocketbook. My advice: Extend your maturities now!

Several mutual funds invest exclusively in Treasury bonds. One I favor because of its low overhead is the no-load *Vanguard Treasury Bond Portfolio* (P.O. Box 2600, Valley Forge, PA 19482, 800-662-2739, 215-648-6000; $3,000 minimum). However, all open-end bond funds, Vanguard included, present a significant disadvantage for the long-term investor: as interest rates decline, you can expect Johnny-come-lately investors to flood in. The fund's managers will be forced to put this torrent of new money to work at lower and lower rates, diluting the fund's yield to existing shareholders.

Therefore, to avoid the problem of dilution, my preferred approach is to buy T-bonds outright—and have them registered in your own name. Virtually all stockbrokers deal in bonds, as do many commercial banks. Shop around, though, to make sure you're getting the best combination of price and commission. You can eliminate all commissions by purchasing Treasury bonds directly from the government through your regional Federal Reserve Bank. (The Richmond Fed publishes a helpful booklet on the subject titled, "Buying Treasury Securities from Federal Reserve Banks." Send a $3 check to the Federal Reserve Bank of Richmond, P.O. Box 17622, Richmond, VA 23261.) The Treasury normally sells 30-year bonds once every calendar quarter, around the 10th of November, February, May and August. Minimum purchase is $1,000.

A final note on the blessings of Treasury paper: the interest is exempt from state income taxes. In high-tax states like California, New York or Massachusetts, this feature can make a big difference in your bottom-line return. Be sure to deduct your state income tax from any competing investment—like corporate bonds or out-of-state municipals—when comparing T-bond yields with other long-term rates.

Multiply Your Wealth with Zeros

Zero coupon bonds are the ultimate play on falling interest rates. As the name implies, zeros pay no current interest, only a lump sum at maturity. Accordingly, they sell at a discount to their final maturity value. (U.S. savings bonds are a familiar species of zero-coupon bond.) The longer the term to maturity, the deeper the discount. Also, the higher the prevailing level of interest rates, the deeper the discount. Thus, a zero priced to yield 9 percent to maturity in 20 years will sell for about $172 per $1,000 of face value. A zero yielding 10 percent to maturity in 25 years will fetch only $87 per $1,000 face value. Table 9 shows these two factors—term to maturity plus the level of interest rates—interact to determine the price of a zero.

For the speculator with a time horizon of, say, three to five years, zeros offer enormous potential for profit if interest rates drop sharply. Let's say you buy a 20-year zero at 9 percent for $172. In three years, if market rates drop to 6 percent, what will this bond be worth? As you can see from the table, a 17-year zero

Table 9 Market Value of Zero Coupon Bonds

Yrs mat	5.0%	5.5%	6.0%	6.5%	7.0%	7.5%	8.0%	8.5%	9.0%	9.5%	10.0%
30	$227	$196	$170	$147	$127	$110	$95	$82	$71	$62	$54
25	290	258	228	202	179	159	141	125	111	98	87
20	372	338	307	278	253	229	208	189	172	156	142
18	411	377	345	316	290	266	244	223	205	188	173
16	454	420	388	359	333	308	285	264	244	227	210
14	501	468	437	408	382	357	333	312	292	273	255
12	553	521	492	464	438	413	390	369	348	328	310
10	610	581	554	527	503	479	456	435	415	395	377
9	641	614	587	562	538	515	494	473	453	434	416
8	674	648	623	599	577	555	534	514	494	476	458
7	708	684	661	639	618	597	577	558	540	522	505
6	744	722	701	681	662	643	625	607	590	573	557
5	781	762	744	726	709	692	676	659	644	629	614
4	821	805	789	774	759	745	731	717	703	690	677
3	862	850	837	825	813	802	790	779	768	757	746
2	906	897	888	880	871	864	855	847	839	831	823
1	952	947	943	938	933	929	925	920	916	911	907

167

priced to yield 6 percent will sell for $366 per $1,000 face value—a total return of 113 percent.

Of course, if interest rates head substantially higher next week or next month, the market value of your 20-year zero will erode. But only for a while: eventually, the bond *must* mature at 100 cents on the dollar, as long as the issuer doesn't default. Hence, while highly speculative over the short term, long-dated zeros are actually a quite conservative investment over the long pull. From the moment you buy, your return is locked in for the life of the bond. And recently, those returns have looked mighty enticing: a 20-year zero compounding at 9 percent will automatically multiply your stake nearly six times. That's just about as good a performance as the stock market has turned in over most 20-year periods in this century. Moreover, it's far better than stocks have done over some disappointing 20-year stretches. From 1961 to 1981, for instance, the total return on the Standard & Poor's 500 index, including reinvested dividends, was less than 4-to-1 or a meager 6.8 percent a year, compounded.

Private corporations, as well as state and local governments, are among the entities that issue zeros. But again, I generally prefer Treasury zeros because they're safer (remember, you won't see any of your money until maturity) and they're noncallable. A drawback to Treasury zeros—most corporates, too—is that you're required to pay income tax annually on the implied interest that accrues on the bonds, even though you don't receive any cash until maturity. You can sidestep this tax, however, by stashing your zeros inside an IRA, Keogh or other retirement plan.

Because the Treasury doesn't issue zeros directly to the public, you must buy them through a broker. (Wall Street trade names for zeros include CATS, TIGRS, RATS, COUGRS and STRIPS. All carry essentially the same features, although only the STRIPS are universally recognized as exempt from state income tax.) A nationally known discount broker that offers IRAs and Keoghs with no start-up or annual maintenance fees is Vanguard Discount Brokerage Services (800-662-7447).

Joker in the Deck

What could go wrong with the scenario I've painted of falling interest rates over the long term? If the gloom-and-doom school is correct and a depression cripples the U.S. economy in the next few years, the Federal Reserve (under pressure from panicky politicians) might attempt to bail out debtors large and small through massive infusions of cheap money. Hyperinflation would ultimately result. Short of a depression, though, the Fed will probably decline to rescue more than a few dozen of the "essential" banking institutions (like Continental Illinois and First RepublicBank). The authorities will inject enough money into these sick giants to prevent a wholesale deflationary bust, but not enough to fire up inflation in the grand old style of Richard Nixon and Jimmy Carter.

In any event, worries about a hyperinflationary resolution to the international debt problem fall into the category of "too much, too soon." For now, the free market—through the mechanism of today's high real interest rates—is forcing central banks everywhere to squeeze inflation out of the world economy. When (and if) inflation gives way to deflation, investors can make a fresh appraisal of what governments are likely to do in response to that new reality. Until then, I believe, the great 1980s bull market for bonds will continue to romp. As a famous B-grade actor said upon looking up from his 200-year bond chart, "You ain't seen nothing yet."

Chapter 10

High Yields with a Hedge

I beseech you, in the bowels of Christ, think it possible you may be mistaken. —Oliver Cromwell

Fair enough. You're *almost* convinced that inflation is down for the count and that bonds will roll up handsome returns over the next decade or two. But down deep, a little voice tells you to keep an anchor to windward, just in case an inflationary storm does unexpectedly blow up. Contrarians make mistakes, too, after all. The high real yields that bonds can deliver seem enticing, but you also want protection against the possibility of an accelerating decline in the purchasing power of the dollar.

The main drawback to most bonds in a period of rapid inflation is that their yields are fixed. Once you buy an ordinary bond, you receive the same semiannual interest payment until the bond matures, regardless of increases in the cost of living.

"Mild" inflation poses little threat to the investor who buys bonds at today's interest rates. If consumer prices rock along at a steady 3-4 percent a year (low inflation by the standards of the 1970s), bonds yielding 8, 9 or 10 percent provide an ample inflation hedge in themselves. To maintain the purchasing power of his income, a bondholder need only plow back a portion of each interest check into more bonds.

If, say, you're earning 9 percent a year on a $1,000 Treasury bond and the inflation rate is 4 percent, you should reinvest at least $40 of the $90 of interest that you collect annually from Uncle Sam. If you spend more than $50 of your interest, you're eating into your seed corn and diminishing the purchasing power of your principal. Failing to replenish your real principal can hurt

171

over the long term: the real value of your interest income will also dwindle as the years go by.

But the big problem with bonds comes when inflation quickens to a gallop *after* you've bought your bonds. In an environment of rapid inflation, you must plow back a larger fraction of your interest income just to maintain your purchasing power. In other words, you must take a cut in your present lifestyle to prevent further erosion in the future. Who wants to own bonds under those circumstances?

Common stocks and real estate are two assets that offer the prospect of a rising stream of income to combat inflation. But not all types of stocks and not all forms of real estate are equally suited to the task. In general, I believe that the kinds of stocks and the classes of real estate that will provide the highest, most dependable returns over the next decade (and thus, the best inflation hedge) will be *those that most closely resemble bonds*. Let me explain.

Virtues and Vices of Common Stocks

For the past two generations, Wall Street's claque of PR men have sung the virtues of common stocks as a hedge against inflation. And it's true that common stocks (or equity-type mutual funds), when held for reasonably long periods of, say, 10 years or more, have usually chalked up inflation-beating returns. But here's the rub: investors who bought common stocks when dividend yields marketwide were low, as is the case now, often fell way behind inflation for maddeningly long stretches of time, sometimes a decade or more.

Take the example of the luckless chap who bought the stocks in the Standard & Poor's 500 index in November 1968, at the close of the go-go era. Even after reinvesting all his subsequent dividends, our investor would have found that, net of inflation, his portfolio was still under water in July 1984—almost 16 years later![1] Remember, too, that I haven't deducted income taxes in this example.

What went wrong? When Mr. B.A. Chump bought his stocks, the dividend yield on the S&P was a meager 2.9 percent. Over the long pull, reinvested dividends account for approximately half of the total return generated by common stocks. (The rest comes from rising share prices.) Therefore, if you start with an abnormally low dividend yield, you virtually foredoom yourself to mediocre results. You can forget about beating inflation.

Today's stock market isn't "cheap" by any stretch of the imagination. While the current dividend yield of 3.2-3.4 percent on the S&P 500 isn't as skimpy as the 2.6 percent that prevailed at the manic top in August 1987, it still ranks in the lowest quarter of stock market experience since 1926. Presumably, the market's total return (capital gains plus reinvested dividend income) over the next decade or so will also fall into the lowest quarter of historical experience, or somewhere between 6 and 8 percent a year, compounded. As I write, you can do as well as that with riskless zero coupon Treasury bonds. Thus, *stocks in general* offer you no more of a shield against inflation right now than bonds do.

Fortunately, not all stocks are as pricey as the market averages. One group in particular, the electric utilities, has been trading for several years at well over twice the dividend yield of industrial stocks (see Figure 30) and a little over half the market price/earnings ratio (Figure 31). These are among the most extreme readings for utility shares in modern market history. From the end of World War II until the mid-1960s, utility stocks often sold for a *higher* P/E and a *lower* dividend yield than the market as a whole.

Investors in the 1950s and 1960s thought of utilities as a growth industry. So boundless was Wall Street's enthusiasm for utility shares that in 1965, at the peak of their popularity, the average utility stock sold for 20 times earnings. Some utilities in fast-growing service areas were even more richly priced: Texas Utilities had a P/E of 30 and Tampa Electric, 35—sky-high multiples that the market nowadays accords to only the most glamorous growth companies.

In their 1965 heyday, electric utilities sported an average dividend yield of only 3 percent—less than the yield on the Dow Jones

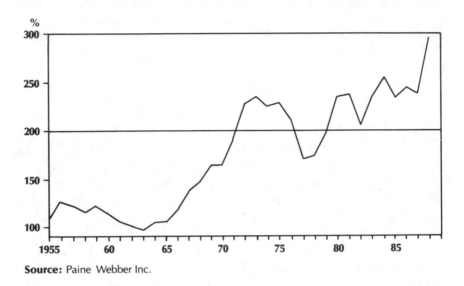

Relative Yield, S&P Electrics vs. Industrials

Source: Paine Webber Inc.

Fig. 30. Relative yield, S&P electrics vs. industrials

Industrial Average! (In late 1989, the typical utility yield was over 7 percent, not far below the yield on long-term government bonds.) Most utilities were selling back then for two or three times their book value per common share.* Nowadays, most utilities are trading around 1 to 1.5 times book value and some troubled nuclear companies are quoted substantially below book.

Utilities Light the Way

What makes today's low valuations for electric utility stocks so amazing is that these shares have actually performed in line

---

*A company's *book value* (also known as net asset value or stockholders' equity) is what is left of the company's assets after all its liabilities have been paid off. To put it another way: what the company *owns* minus what it *owes*. This is the portion of the company that belongs to the stockholders.

Relative P/E, S&P Electrics vs. Industrials

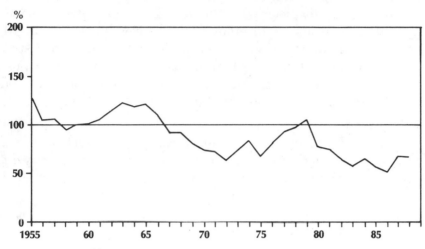

Source: Paine Webber Inc.

Fig. 31. Relative P/E, S&P electrics vs. industrials

with—or better than—industrial stocks on a total return basis for the past decade or more. Counting both price gains and reinvested dividends, the Standard & Poor's index of industrial stocks produced a compounded annual return of 16.3 percent from January 1, 1975 to December 31, 1987. Over the same 13-year stretch, the S&P electric utility index produced an even richer return—16.6 percent! Thanks to their ultra-high dividend yields, the tortoise-like utilities have beaten the jackrabbit industrials for eight out of the past 14 years (1988 included).

With that kind of track record, you would expect investors to be banging down the doors of the New York Stock Exchange to buy utility shares. Not so, however. Most big-time security analysts and portfolio managers are obsessed with the idea that the utility industry is now stodgy, "mature," lacking growth opportunities. Wall Street can't get excited about an industry that routinely delivers 3-5 percent annual increases in earnings and dividends.

175

On the other hand, if the rosy growth prospects that investors envision for other industries in the next few years don't pan out, the slow but steady progress of the utilities might not seem so unappealing. Utilities could enjoy a major revaluation, bringing their P/Es and dividend yields closer to those of the broad stock market averages. And all the while, you'll be holding stocks that— in addition to their high, bond-like dividend yield—offer a modest inflation hedge through regular hikes in the payout.

Many advisors automatically steer away from utilities that are constructing, or have recently completed, nuclear power plants. Others, taking a more extreme position, refuse to buy *any* utility with *any* nuclear exposure—even companies that are operating low-cost, trouble-free plants built a decade or more ago. This aversion to nuclear power by some investors has created opportunities for the contrarian. In today's market, utilities with a large commitment to nuclear energy (completed plants or plants under construction) generally trade at a higher dividend yield and a lower price-earnings multiple than similar stocks without the nuclear element.

While I don't recommend that you focus exclusively on nuclear companies, many of the best values in the utility industry come from this sector. Here are a few stocks I currently rate a buy, both nuclear and non-nuclear, with their prices and dividend yields as of September 29, 1989. The further you go down the list, the riskier the company—and the greater your potential for capital gains as the company's prospects brighten:

Non-nuclear; moderate yield; very safe dividend
Kentucky Utilities (NYSE: KU, 19 5/8), 7.1%
Orange & Rockland Utilities (NYSE: ORU, 29 1/4), 7.7%
PacifiCorp (NYSE: PPW, 40 7/8), 6.8%

Nuclear construction completed long ago; very safe dividend
Dominion Resources (NYSE: D, 43 1/2), 7.4%
Wisconsin Public Service (NYSE: WPS, 23 1/8), 7.0%

Nuclear construction recently completed; safe dividend
Carolina Power & Light (NYSE: CPL, 44), 6.5%
Kansas City Power & Light (NYSE: KLT, 33 3/4), 7.6%
SCEcorp (NYSE: SCE, 35 3/4), 7.2%

Nuclear construction recently completed; dividend safe for the foreseeable future, but needs to be monitored closely
Commonwealth Edison (NYSE: CWE, 37 3/8), 8.0%
New England Electric (NYSE: NES, 26), 7.8%
New York State Electric & Gas (NYSE: NGE, 26 1/2), 7.7%
Pacific Gas & Electric (NYSE: PCG, 20), 7.0%
Southern Company (NYSE: SO, 27 1/8), 7.9%

Most of these companies, incidentally, sponsor automatic dividend reinvestment plans (DRIPs), which let you plow back your dividends to purchase additional shares of stock. If you wish, you can build your stake even faster by making optional payments into the plan. Most utility DRIPs charge ultra-low brokerage commissions (SCEcorp's fee, for instance, is only 4 cents per share) or none at all.

The best time to buy utility stocks is after interest rates have risen sharply for several months to a year. (Because power companies frequently issue new stock to finance their construction budgets, prices of utility shares go down and dividend yields go up when interest rates rise.) A fine buying opportunity presented itself in mid-1984 and again in the spring and summer of 1987. If your contrarian instincts tell you it's time to buy bonds, then it's probably time to buy utilities, too.

The Return of the REIT

Besides utilities, another way to earn a high and rising stream of income that can insulate you against inflation is through real estate investment trusts (REITs). Unlike most forms of real estate ownership, REIT shares are completely liquid: you can buy or sell them anytime because they trade just like shares of stock, either on an exchange or over the counter. In principle, REITs are really nothing more than closed-end funds specializing in real estate.

Although some REITs invest in mortgages, I suggest that you stick with REITs that own land and buildings outright—the so-called equity REITs. Mortgages held in the portfolios of most REITs are *not* federally insured. If you want to dabble in mortgage securities, you're better off taking a somewhat lower yield with government-backed GNMA certificates. In a severe recession, I suspect that a shockingly large percentage of the mortgage loans written by REITs in recent years would default. Foreclosure proceedings could drag on and on, and your REIT might recover only a fraction of its money in the end. This is precisely what happened when REITs last went on a lending binge in the early 1970s.

Financially sound equity REITs nowadays yield about 7-8 percent. That's double the average dividend yield of industrial stocks, making REITs a reasonably good bond substitute. Even though the conventional wisdom views them as plodding performers, REITs—like utilities—have outdistanced industrials over the long pull on a total return basis. From January 1, 1976 to December 31, 1987, the "all REITs" index compiled by the National Association of Real Estate Investment Trusts rolled up a compounded annual return (including dividends and price gains) of 17.3 percent. Over the same 12-year time span, the Standard & Poor's 500 stock index returned only 14.5 percent a year. Yet the REITs achieved these superior returns with far less volatility than industrial stocks: on Black Monday, the S&P fell 23 percent, while the all-REITs index dropped only 11 percent.

The main disadvantage of REITs, compared with owning real estate yourself, is that they can't pass any tax deductions through to their shareholders. In my judgment, however, the advantages of REITs far outweigh the drawbacks. In addition to instant liquidity, you get professional management plus diversification (most equity REITs own at least a dozen properties, and some of the larger trusts own many more). All this in an investment that may retail for as little as $10 to $20 a share!

My favorite equity REITs feature low debt and a record of frequent dividend increases over the years. Several to consider, with their current dividend yields:

• *Burnham Pacific Properties* (ASE: BPP, 19 7/8), 6.8%

- *New Plan Realty Trust* (NYSE: NPR, 16 3/4), 6.1%
- *United Dominion Realty Trust* (OTC: UDRT, 18 3/4), 6.4%
- *Weingarten Realty* (NYSE: WRI, 30 3/8), 5.8%.

I might point out in passing that the last REIT on the list, Weingarten, owns a bunch of shopping centers in Texas, with a concentration in the Houston area. This well-managed trust offers a contrarian play on the recovery of the battered Texas economy. If you believe, as I do, that Texas will rise again, you should own a piece of Weingarten. For a copy of the trust's financial reports, write Weingarten Realty at 2600 Citadel Plaza Dr., Houston, TX 77008 or call 713-868-6361.

Your Rainy-Day Reserve

Utilities and REITs can provide you with a growing, inflation-beating stream of cash. But the income investor trying to survive this era of overindebtedness and uncertainty should also channel a portion of his wealth into top-quality short-term instruments like Treasury bills, money market funds, bank CDs and savings bonds.

I see nothing wrong with keeping six months' living expenses at all times in these liquid interest-bearing vehicles. Yields on short-term paper have easily outrun inflation in recent years, even after deducting the maximum federal income tax (28 percent). *Liquidity*—the ability to turn an asset into cash quickly, without loss of principal—is so scarce and so highly prized nowadays that the investor who has it can command handsome real (inflation-adjusted) rates of interest. In late 1989, for example, three-month Treasury bills yielded almost 8 percent compared with an inflation rate of just over 4 percent.

As long as short-term interest rates remain well ahead of inflation, it will pay you to "stay liquid." A sizable chunk of cash and cash equivalents in your portfolio gives you the flexibility to deal with financial surprises that may overtake your family or the economy as a whole. In the bad old days of the 1970s, you had to accept a negative real interest rate—you were losing money after inflation and taxes—as the price for this insurance. Today, you

179

can enjoy the security of money market assets while collecting a generous return that keeps you ahead of inflation and taxes. The income investor is calling the shots!

Banks often pay lower yields on their money market accounts than you can earn on quality money market funds— sometimes as much as two full percentage points less. True, banks can boast $100,000 of FDIC insurance. But, given the shaky condition of the FDIC, I don't think you're taking any more risk with a conservatively run money market fund than with a bank deposit. If you're deeply concerned about safety, you should probably buy Treasury bills directly from the Federal Reserve or buy shares of a money market fund that invests exclusively in U.S. Treasury securities. One such fund is *Capital Preservation Fund* (755 Page Mill Rd., Palo Alto, CA 94304, 800-4-SAFETY, 415-858-2400, $1,000 minimum).

For most purposes, though, a plain-vanilla money fund that invests in private bank and corporate obligations will fit the bill. As in the bond arena, I recommend the Vanguard Group's money market funds because of their extremely low expense ratios. More of the "gross" flows through to your pocket. Vanguard sponsors three no-load money market portfolios—Prime, Federal and Insured, each with a $1,000 minimum. (The insured portfolio carries private insurance, which I think would be of doubtful value in a *real* financial crisis.) The fund group also offers several tax-free municipal money funds. For a prospectus, call Vanguard at 800-662-2739 or 215-648-6000.

Don't rule out U.S. savings bonds either, as an income vehicle with a built-in inflation hedge. Series EE bonds now pay an adjustable interest rate equal to 85 percent of the open-market yield on five-year Treasury notes. So, if accelerating inflation drives interest rates up, your yield will also rise. And if rates drop, you're guaranteed a minimum yield of at least 6 percent as long as you hold your bonds five years or more.

Interest income on savings bonds is exempt from state and local taxes, and there's no federal tax until you redeem the bonds or they mature (whichever occurs first). Currently, the government is issuing EE bonds with a 10-year maturity, but you can automatically defer tax on the first 10 years' interest for a second 10-year term. Denominations start at $50 face value ($25 purchase price) and range up to $10,000 face. You can buy savings bonds at almost any bank.

The likelihood of falling inflation and falling interest rates in the years ahead seems strong. If I'm correct, utility and REIT shares should go up in price because each dollar of income they produce will tend to be more valuable as interest rates decline. (*Exception*: in a deflationary depression, many utilities and REITs would probably cut their dividends, negating the advantage of lower interest rates.) Cash equivalents like money market funds and savings bonds will preserve your principal and modestly enhance your wealth through periodic payments of interest income.

At the same time, utilities, REITs and cash equivalents provide some cushion against an unexpected resurgence of inflation—though not against runaway inflation (20, 50, 100 percent a year). Their payouts can ratchet upward in an inflationary environment. Conventional fixed-coupon bonds, by contrast, don't furnish much of a hedge against accelerating inflation, beyond the fat inflation premium already built into today's bond yields. As much as I love bonds, I would never advise you to put your entire portfolio into them. "Think it possible you may be mistaken." Keep your hedges trimmed and watered for growth.

Chapter 11

If Inflation Roars Again

Without gold we fold.—slogan of *American Gold News*
(now defunct)

Show me an honest politician, and I'll show you a society with no inflation. *Inflation*, defined as an increase in the money supply that results in a general rise in prices, is an all but universal phenomenon nowadays, common to virtually every country—whatever the form of government. South Africa suffers from inflation, as does the Soviet Union. Kings and presidents may come and go, but the cost of living climbs relentlessly higher. Until the world can agree on a fixed monetary standard, like the gold standard of old, some degree of inflation is almost bound to continue.

Of course, there have been interludes of falling prices, even in recent times. The United States experienced seven months of net *deflation* in the wake of the 1986 oil crash—the nation's longest deflationary period in more than 30 years. Moreover, prices for certain selected goods may decline even in the face of a general inflation. (Personal computers are cheaper today than they were five or six years ago, for example.) But the long-term trend for most prices is always up, because most politicians—from Solon the Athenian to Jim Wright—prefer to pursue inflationary policies.

A little inflation is an appealing choice for politicians because it allows them to finance their spending sprees with a hidden tax. It's a tax they need never vote on or defend to their constituents. To impose it, they merely spend money. If they spend more money than they can raise in visible taxes, they run a budget deficit and borrow money (sell bonds) to pay the government's bills.

So far, no inflation. But when the government runs a massive budget deficit (as the United States did under Ronald Reagan through most of the 1980s), the nation's central bank—our Federal Reserve—can do either of two things. Under the first alternative, the Fed can shrug its shoulders and let the Treasury sell its bonds and bills to the public at whatever interest rate the market may require to move the merchandise. However, since rising interest rates tend to depress economic activity (by increasing the cost of buying on credit), such a course would evoke shrieks of outrage from politicians.

Instead, the Federal Reserve does what it knows the politicians want it to do: it buys some of the debt itself on the open market, paying for its purchases with money created out of thin air. This added demand tends to push up prices for Treasury bonds and bills, which is the same thing as lowering interest rates. The new money begins to percolate through the economy, driving up prices as more money chases the same quantity of goods. This, in simplified terms, is how the inflationary engine works.

Even if the long-term "supercycle" of worsening inflation has reversed, as I believe it has, mini-cycles of rising inflation will continue to occur as countertrends within the primary trend. During those phases (1985-87, for example), you should arrange your portfolio to include a larger share of assets that will benefit from accelerating inflation. (I'll discuss portfolio building more fully in Chapter 13.) When the primary trend reasserts itself and inflation rates start to fall again, you should pare back your inflation hedges to a minimum and stress "disinflation" assets like bonds and utilities in your portfolio.

Ever since the inflation supercycle peaked in 1980, a buy-and-hold strategy has produced poor results for investors in oil, agricultural commodities, precious metals and other tangibles. By the standards of the 1970s, bull markets for inflation hedges have been weak and short, while bear markets have been powerful and long. Just the opposite is true of assets (such as bonds) that benefit from low inflation: a buy-and-hold strategy in the 1980s has generated handsome profits, covering a multitude of timing errors. Long, sweeping bull markets have carried prices to unimagined heights, while the intervening corrections have been relatively brief and shallow. Investors who plan to dabble in the market for inflation hedges in the next few years would do well to keep this pattern in mind. Timing could make or break you.

The Midas Metal

Gold has been the classic inflation hedge throughout history. Over the centuries, the Midas metal has retained its purchasing power while one paper currency after another has been thrown into the ash heap.[1] In the short term, however—and here by "short term" I mean any period shorter than your lifetime—the price of gold can fluctuate wildly, rising far above or plunging far below the metal's "normal" purchasing power. (During most of the 1980s, for instance, gold has traded at its highest prices in 200 years *relative* to the basket of goods and services in the Consumer Price Index.) To keep your head above water in a volatile market, contrary thinking is essential.

The first rule of successful gold investing is not to get enthralled with specific predictions about the price. To profit from a bull market in gold, you don't particularly need to know whether the price two years from now will be $500, $1,000 or $10,000 an ounce. What you do need to know is whether the cyclical outlook for inflation is up or down. As long as inflation is accelerating, gold will tend to advance. Similarly, once the inflation rate begins to slow, the price of gold will usually drop. Figure 32 illustrates the close connection between gold and the inflation cycle.

Monitoring the media as I suggested in Chapter 3 can help you identify major turning points in the inflation cycle and the price of gold. Watch for enthusiastic predictions of zero inflation or even deflation by respectable advisors. During 1985 and 1986, when gold and gold-mining shares were in the dumps, *Business Week* published two cover stories that hinted at a change in the wind: "Living with Disinflation" (July 15, 1985), which announced that "The U.S. will probably enjoy low inflation for the foreseeable future"; and, more conspicuously, "America's Deflation Belt" (June 6, 1986), which identified mining as one of the three "depressed industries" whose troubles were "hurting a wide swath of the country." The other two industries, by the way, were oil and agriculture, both of which rebounded nicely in 1987-88.

On a more advanced level, I pointed out in Chapter 4 how the *Bullish Consensus* poll can help you gauge investor sentiment in the gold market (or any other commodity market). A third contrary indicator that applies specifically to gold is depicted in Figure 32. Armchair analysts can track it every day in *The Wall Street Journal* or *The New York Times*.

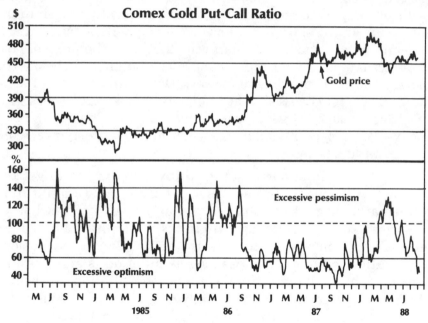

Source: Davis/Zweig Futures, Inc., P.O. Box 5345, New York, N.Y. 10150.

Fig. 32. Gold put-call ratio

Puts and Calls

The *gold put-call ratio* measures the mood of the speculators who buy gold futures options on the Commodity Exchange (Comex) in New York. (A Comex call option lets you *buy* a 100-ounce gold futures contract at a specified price within a stipulated time frame; a put lets you *sell* a contract under the same conditions.) Like options traders in other markets, people who buy gold options on the Comex are for the most part trend followers with atrociously poor judgment. As the graph shows, they buy calls most heavily when the market is close to a peak, and they buy puts most heavily when the market is near a bottom.

You calculate the gold put-call ratio by adding up the put volume (i.e., the number of puts purchased) over the 10 most recent trading days and dividing it by the call volume over the same period. A speculator buys a call if he thinks the market is headed up, and a put if he thinks the market is headed down. Therefore, a high ratio of puts to calls (say, 1.4 or higher) implies that gold speculators are snarlingly bearish. A low put-call (say, below 0.5) suggests that the speculators are ravingly bullish. At these extremes, the majority is nearly always wrong. During a strong bull market, the call-put ratio will usually range from 0.3 to 0.9, with the lowest readings near the ultimate peak for prices; in a powerful bear market, the ratio will normally surge into a range of 0.7 to 1.5, with the highest readings near the ultimate bottom for prices.

The gold put-call ratio is a useful tool for contrarians who want to trade gold options and futures "against the crowd." (Several techniques for making money in options and futures are described in Chapter 12.) However, it's equally valuable for timing the movements of physical bullion and mining shares. In March 1985, for example, the 10-day put-call ratio soared to an incredible 1.6 as the price of gold bullion slipped to a five-year low of $282 an ounce.

Frenzied gold bears were buying five puts for every three calls—a truly amazing statistic when you consider that most options traders are by nature optimistic (why else would they play such a high-risk game?). In virtually every options market, speculators purchase many more calls than puts. This burst of pessimism provided convincing evidence that gold and gold stocks were close to rock bottom.

The put-call ratio also warns of trouble at the top. In early 1983 and again in the spring and summer of 1987, it fairly shouted that the gold market was dangerously overbought. Euphoric gold bulls were buying three calls for every put. The gold market collapsed soon afterward.

As with most sentiment indicators, it's often difficult to tell immediately whether the gold put-call ratio is signaling a change in the market's primary trend or simply an intermediate correction against the primary trend. But in general, *the more extreme the reading, the more severe the reaction is likely to be.*

After the turn has occurred, you can judge whether it was of long-term or only intermediate-term significance. If, for instance, the market has been weak for months but a sickly rally pushes the put-call ratio way down (signaling too much optimism), look out for a sharp, nerve-jarring relapse. Beware of any market move that attracts too many followers too quickly. On the other hand, if the market climbs sharply *without* attracting a flood of call buying, prices may be able to keep climbing. A bull market must climb a wall of worry.

By the same token, a bear market must slide down a chute of overconfidence. If the put-call ratio (or any other sentiment indicator) shows that investors are quickly turning pessimistic whenever prices dip, the primary uptrend will likely resume. But if overconfident investors keep buying calls at lower and lower price levels, the market will probably drop further. A primary downtrend is under way.

Bullion or Shares?

Physical gold serves a different investment function from the shares of companies that mine precious metals. In a strong up market for bullion, mining shares will generally appreciate even faster. The reason is that a mining company's costs are more or less fixed. When the price of its product (bullion) is climbing rapidly, the company generates additional revenues for the same amount of physical output. These extra dollars flow directly to the bottom line. Thus, in a bull market, a mining company's profits tend to rise by an even greater percentage than the price of bullion. Of course, the same leverage works on the downside, too. In sum, mining shares are much more volatile, both up and down, than bullion.

As a matter of fact, mining shares are among the most volatile issues in the entire stock market. Conservative investors who can't stomach the roller-coaster action in mining shares should emphasize bullion in the inflation-hedge sector of their portfolios. In addition, I recommend a small holding of bullion, not to exceed 5 percent of your net worth, as insurance against The Unthinkable—a worldwide financial crisis in which all the banks came tumbling down a la the 1930s. The probability of such a crisis is still remote, but it's nothing to laugh at. When all other financial assets fail, gold shines. It never defaults, because (unlike a bank deposit) it isn't somebody else's liability.

If you plan to take physical possession of your gold, a course I strongly recommend for your "insurance" stash, I suggest that you purchase bullion coins (coins that sell for close to their bullion value). Three popular issues are the American Eagle, the Canadian Maple Leaf and the Austrian 100 Coronas. The Eagle and the Maple Leaf contain exactly 1 troy ounce of pure gold and generally retail for about 5 percent above the spot price of gold. On the other hand, the 100 Coronas (thanks in part to its odd weight of .9802 ounces of fine gold), usually trades at a premium of only 1 or 2 percent over melt value. Contrarian bargain hunters favor Coronas!

Choosing a reputable coin dealer is crucial. In recent years, investors have lost hundreds of millions of dollars by ordering gold and silver from boiler-room outfits that had no intention of delivering the merchandise. Several well-established firms that I recommend for their quality service and low markups are: *James U. Blanchard & Co.* (2400 Jefferson Hwy., Jefferson, LA 70121, 800-322-6267, 504-837-3010), *Liberty Coin Service* (300 Frandor Ave., Lansing, MI 48912, 800-321-1542, 517-351-4720) and *Sam Sloat Coins* (136 Main St., Westport, CT 06881, 800-243-5670, 203-226-4279).

Investors who buy gold purely for an inflation hedge—rather than as insurance against a breakdown in the financial system—don't need to take physical possession of their metal. It's easier and cheaper to open a bulk storage account with one of the major stockbrokers (Dean Witter, Merrill Lynch, Paine Webber, Prudential-Bache, Shearson Lehman Hutton, etc.). Commissions are typically smaller than the bid-ask spread on coins, and many firms will allow you to lock in a selling price immediately with a phone call to your broker. The brokerage firm stores the metal for you, charging a small annual fee. But you can request delivery at any time.

If you're afraid of the sales pressure you might encounter with a Wall Street brokerage firm, look into the certificate storage programs of *Citibank* (399 Park Ave., New York, NY 10043, 800-223-1080) and *Benham Certified Metals* (755 Page Mill Rd., Palo Alto, CA 94304, 800-447-GOLD). Minimum to open an account with either organization is only $1,000. An interesting feature of the Citibank program is that you can pay for your metal on your Visa card. No carrying charge is imposed if you pay when you receive your next Visa statement.

Is silver a worthy investment substitute for gold? In the past decade, "poor man's gold" has experienced much wider price swings than gold itself—wider, even, than the mining shares. In the spring of 1987, to take the most striking recent example, silver doubled in six weeks. During the same period, the price of gold climbed only 16 percent. Because of its volatility, silver is suitable primarily for investors who have already amassed some gold and want to diversify into a faster-paced market. Silver will give you all the excitement you're looking for—and more.

Normally, silver will follow the same direction as gold, although in recent years the white metal has had a tendency to peak sooner than its senior partner and bottom later. The most economical way to hold silver bullion is through a storage account, such as those mentioned above. Physical silver, whether in the form of ingots or coins, is bulky and expensive to store on your own.

A compromise vehicle that gives you exposure to both gold and silver bullion is *Central Fund of Canada,* a closed-end fund traded on the American Stock Exchange (ticker symbol CEF). This fund doesn't attempt to trade the swings of the metals market. Instead, it sits passively on a hoard of bullion, together with a smattering of cash and mining shares (designed to generate enough income to cover the fund's expenses). As of September 30, 1988, the dollar value of Central Fund's portfolio broke down as follows:

Gold bullion	52.9%
Silver bullion	40.5
Cash & other	6.6
Total	100.0%

Because Central is a closed-end fund, its shares (which are also listed on the Toronto Stock Exchange) can sell for a premium or a discount to the fund's underlying net asset value, depending on supply and demand in the marketplace. As a contrarian would guess, Central shares usually trade at a small discount when investors are eager to buy gold and silver bullion (near the top of the market). In fact, in the spring and summer of 1987, during the most recent gold mania, Central fetched a *premium* over NAV for the first time in its history (see Figure 33). At the February

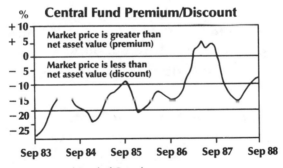

Source: Central Fund of Canada.

Fig. 33. Central Fund premium/discount

1985 bottom for gold, when nobody wanted to hear about precious metals, Central sold at a huge discount of more than 25 percent. You could buy a dollar's worth of bullion for less than 75 cents! If you're interested in precious metals, you'll find it worthwhile to monitor Central Fund's discount as a sentiment indicator—even if you never intend to buy a single share. Along with the other

191

gauges I've discussed previously, this barometer can give you valuable insight into the prevailing psychology in the metals market.

Central's net asset value and discount or premium are published every week in *Barron's* under "Mutual Funds/Closed-End Funds." *The Wall Street Journal* also publishes this information once a week, usually on Monday. As a rule of thumb, I would buy Central whenever it trades at a discount of 25 percent or more, and sell it at a discount of 5 percent or less. Central Fund, I might add, is an excellent tool for bringing gold and silver bullion into your self-directed IRA, Keogh or corporate pension fund "through the back door." In the eyes of the law, you're buying shares of an investment company; you're not buying bullion. So legal restrictions on bullion investments inside a retirement account don't apply.

Mining Stocks: Your Own Grubstake

Mining shares are a pretty homogeneous group. Silver stocks generally move in the same direction as gold stocks, though not necessarily at the same pace. (The number of "pure" silver-mining companies in North America has shrunk in recent years as more and more silver producers have diversified into gold to provide a more stable earnings base.) Moreover, among the gold shares, individual issues usually show similar percentage gains or losses during any significant market swing. The main exceptions are:

• *The South African kaffirs*, which have behaved erratically in the past few years as a result of political pressures on their mother country; and

• *The junior companies,* most notably the exploratory penny mining shares (those selling for less than $1), which typically rise further in a bull market than the major mines do—and fall further in a bear market.

Since mining shares normally go up or down together, I would advise most investors not to hunt for "the big hit." Instead, the easiest and most profitable strategy is to buy a diversified portfolio of shares when the mood of the market is gloomy, and gold and silver stocks are cheap. Sell off chunks of your portfolio when the crowd is enthusiastic and prices are high.

Numerous mutual fund families sponsor gold funds, which furnish you with instant diversification. I recommend the following no-load and low-load funds. All except the Blanchard fund permit you to switch into a companion money market fund with a toll-free telephone call. The Blanchard fund, under the supervision of noted Toronto metals analyst Peter Cavelti, performs its own market timing, building up a cash position and writing call options when Cavelti feels that market conditions aren't favorable to precious metals.

Benham Gold Index Trust*
755 Page Mill Rd.
Palo Alto, CA 94304
800-472-3389, in Calif. 800-982-6150
$1,000 minimum

Lexington Goldfund
P.O. Box 1515
Saddle Brook, NJ 07662
800-526-4676, 201-845-7300
$1,000 minimum

Blanchard Precious Metals Fund
41 Madison Ave.
New York, NY 10010
800-922-7771, 212-750-0555
$3,000 minimum
$120 account-opening fee

Scudder Gold Fund
160 Federal St.
Boston, MA 02110
800-225-2470, 617-439-4640
$1,000 minimum

Fidelity Select American Gold*
82 Devonshire St.
Boston, MA 02109
800-544-6666, 617-523-1919
$1,000 minimum
2% sales charge; 1% redemption fee

Vanguard Specialized
Portfolios—Gold &
Precious Metals
P.O. Box 2600
Valley Forge, PA 19482
800-662-2739, 215-648-6000
$1,500 minimum
1% redemption fee

*Fund has a policy against investing in South African securities.

Unfortunately, there aren't any no-load funds devoted exclusively to silver-mining shares. If silver stocks strike your fancy, though, you can form a basic portfolio by purchasing equal dollar amounts of *Callahan Mining* (NYSE: CMN), *Coeur d'Alene Mines* (ASE: CDE) and *Hecla Mining* (NYSE: HL), three leading producers. Speculators who would like to play the penny gold and silver shares should work with a broker who keeps close tabs on this Wild West-style market. I recommend Jerry Pogue of *National Securities Corp.* (500 Union St., Suite 210, Seattle, WA 98101, 800-426-1608, 206-622-7200). Minimum account: $3,000.

The Currency Casino

Besides precious metals and mining shares, certain foreign currencies can offer a cozy refuge when the winds of inflation are blowing hard. Traditionally, U.S. investors have looked to the Swiss franc as the world's strongest and safest paper currency. From 1972 to 1978, for example, the Swissy soared more than 160 percent against the dollar, providing an excellent hedge against the reckless monetary policies of the Nixon-Carter era. And again, from 1985 to 1987, when the Federal Reserve under Paul Volcker created an excess of dollars, the Swiss franc doubled against the greenback.

The Swiss National Bank's firm commitment to keep inflation under wraps is the most important factor behind the enduring investment appeal of the franc. Another, no doubt, is Switzerland's bank-secrecy laws. In recent years, however, investors seeking to diversify out of dollars have increasingly turned to the powerhouse of the East—the Japanese yen. Japan has been even more successful than Switzerland in curbing inflation over the past decade, and yields on bank deposits denominated in yen tend to be somewhat higher than in francs. As a result, even after the Swiss franc and other "hard" European currencies (such as the German mark and Dutch guilder) began to crumble against the dollar in 1988, the yen gave ground grudgingly.

Making money in foreign currencies was a cinch in the 1970s. As with gold, the value of most foreign currencies versus the dollar had been fixed for decades by government fiat (the Bretton Woods agreement of 1944). By the time the Bretton Woods system collapsed in 1971, it was apparent to anyone who could see beyond the self-serving propaganda of the Nixon administration that the dollar had to fall. Inflation was accelerating in the United States and our balance of payments had slipped into deficit. The world was holding too many dollars. Accordingly, as soon as exchange rates were allowed to float freely, there was only one way for the hard currencies to go vis-a-vis the dollar—up.

Since the 1980s dawned, things are no longer so simple. America, despite occasional lapses, has begun to get a grip on its inflation problem through a combination of tighter monetary policy and slower growth in government spending. The dollar, in consequence, has enjoyed at least one extraordinarily strong bull market, from 1980 to 1985, and may well be embarking on another as I write. Nowadays, if you buy foreign currencies too high, you can pay a terrible price: a dollar-based inflation hedger who jumped into the Swiss franc at its peak in November 1978, for example, would have lost more than 50 percent of his principal by February 1985.

The classic contrarian indicators from the news media will often help you spot major turning points in the dollar's fortunes. In Chapter 3, I cited the famous "Superdollar" cover story that *Business Week* published in the fall of 1984, just before the dollar nosedived. *Fortune* called the next primary bottom for the dollar in December 1987 with its cover on "The Dollar and the Deficits." Two days after the dollar hit its low on December 31, 1987, a cartoon appeared in *The Washington Post* and other newspapers (Figure 34), depicting a dollar bill with a grocery bag over the head of a spooked George Washington. When even the cartoonists (not known for their sophisticated understanding of international economics) start to poke fun at the dollar, it's fair to assume that market sentiment has reached a lopsided extreme.

Another news item to watch for: at important turning points in the foreign-exchange markets, tourists change their habits. In the spring of 1985, the noontide of the dollar's glory, *The New York Times* reported that shrewd denizens of the Big Apple were chartering flights to London for weekend shopping sprees.[2] The depressed pound made British merchandise look cheap to Americans—cheap enough to justify flying across the pond for a bargain or two. Two years later, the situation was reversed. This time, the dollar was low and the foreign currencies were high. Tourist traffic from Europe and the Far East soared 50 percent between 1986 and 1987. Charter flights coming into America were

Dollar Cartoon

Reprinted with special permission of King Features Syndicate, Inc.   JIMBORGMAN CINCINNATEN ENQUIRER 1987

Fig. 34. Dollar cartoon

jammed. A lower-level Austrian bureaucrat who planned to take his family on a vacation tour of the United States in the summer of 1987 told *The Wall Street Journal*: "Who knows when the dollar will be like this again? It's now or never."[3] As I've said before, the average guy isn't stupid. When he pays cash on the barrelhead, he's a canny judge of value.

Another tool for determining whether the dollar is overvalued or undervalued is called *purchasing-power parity (PPP)*. Briefly, this theory asserts that, in a system of freely floating exchange rates, a dollar should buy essentially the same amount of goods and services in the United States as it does elsewhere. When it doesn't, the exchange rate is (temporarily) out of whack and will eventually head back toward PPP.

Measuring PPP is a rather complicated task. But you can save yourself a few steps by watching for low-cost, freely traded consumer items—such as books, magazines and dress patterns—marked with a foreign-currency price as well as a dollar price. In late 1987, for instance, I sat next to a British man on an airplane who was reading a book issued by the London branch of an American publishing house. A quick comparison of the sterling and dollar prices showed that if I had bought the book in London (exchanging my dollars for pounds), it would have cost me about 25 percent more than in New York. Since the book was identical in both countries, I concluded that the pound was about 25 percent overvalued.

Minor differences between a currency's market value and its purchasing-power parity aren't worth your attention. However, when the gap yawns to 20 or 30 percent (or more), you'll generally find it profitable to speculate that the rubber band will snap back. When foreign currencies are undervalued, consider opening a bank account overseas in Swiss francs, Japanese yen or other sound monetary units. Switch back into dollars when these other currencies become overvalued. Canada's giant Royal Trust Co. has a subsidiary in Vienna that has dealt with English-speaking clients for many years. Royal Trust Bank (Austria) offers savings accounts in a wide variety of currencies. Minimum deposit for CDs, which pay the best interest, is $3,000 or the equivalent. You may write Royal Trust at Rathausstrasse 20, 1010 Vienna, Austria.

If the thought of opening an account with a foreign bank puts you off (it shouldn't), you can accomplish much the same result with a money market fund called *International Cash Portfolios* (251 S. Lake Ave., Suite 600, Pasadena, CA 91101, 800-826-0188, 213-681-3700). This fund consists of seven portfolios, each of which is invested in money market instruments of a different currency: Australian dollar, British pound, Canadian dollar, German mark, Japanese yen, Swiss franc and U.S. dollar. There's also a global cash portfolio for investors who want broad diversification. Minimum to open an account: $2,500. A sales charge of 1.25 percent applies to all but the U.S. dollar portfolio. Telephone switching between portfolios is free.

For speculative maneuvers in the currency markets, see Chapter 12.

Real Estate: Success from Distress

While precious metals, mining shares and foreign currencies aren't the only assets you can buy to hedge yourself against inflation, they're certainly the most liquid. You can sell them quickly, anytime, without having to make drastic price concessions. Nonetheless, the theory of contrary opinion applies to any market, including the less-liquid tangibles like real estate, rare coins, gemstones, art and antiques.

197

I discussed an indirect form of real estate ownership, REITs, in Chapter 10. However, most people who invest in real estate for an inflation hedge prefer to own their property directly—because of the tax advantages. For readers who plan to roll up their sleeves and make a direct investment in property, here are some thoughts on how to carry out a successful contrarian real estate strategy.

The key point to keep in mind is that you should *buy into distress and sell into prosperity*.[4] In real estate, the finest buying opportunities typically emerge during or just after a recession, when most potential buyers are wary of the market. The best time to sell is when the economy looks strong and investors are eager to buy. But you don't necessarily have to wait for an officially defined national recession to occur before you buy investment property. Real estate isn't a monolithic market; it's intensely local, and even within a geographical area one sector of the real estate market may be experiencing a downturn while another is surging.

During the first half of the 1980s, for instance, farmland values crashed 50 percent or more in states like Illinois, Indiana, Iowa, Missouri and Nebraska, reflecting the collapse of commodity prices. Meanwhile, farmland in New England soared, thanks to the increasing urbanization of the region. Office buildings in Dallas declined in value, while prices of single-family homes in the same metropolitan area kept rising. The long "Reagan recovery" that began in late 1982 (the longest peacetime business expansion in U.S. history) left many pockets of distress in local real estate markets. To profit from these anomalies, however, you needed a keen microeconomic eye to spot them and, in some cases, a willingness to invest outside your own locality.

In general, the following criteria will help you know that an important bottom is forming for a particular real estate market:

• *News reports focusing on the problems of the real estate industry.* You'll read and hear about unemployed construction workers, builder bankruptcies, real estate agents looking for second careers, soaring mortgage delinquencies and the unaffordability of housing at current interest rates.

• *Price cuts by builders through rebates, below-market financing or other gimmicks.* Landlords will offer a free month's (maybe as much as a free year's) rent to lease up their buildings.

• *Housing starts at or near a multiyear low.* Often, housing prices remain flat or continue to drop even after housing starts begin to turn up. If you find a pattern of low housing starts, stable-to-lower prices and rapidly falling interest rates, jump in! The bear market is probably ending.

• *High vacancy rates* for apartments or office buildings in the area, as compared with previous years.

• *A peak in the local unemployment rate,* followed by a month or two of declines. If people are out of work or afraid of losing their jobs, they aren't going to bid aggressively for real estate. Hence, prices are likely to be low.

• *Uncommonly courteous real estate brokers.* This is a subjective indicator, but nevertheless one of the best. When brokers have plenty of time on their hands, they tend to be less pushy and more eager to please. They'll pamper you. They won't rush you to sign on the dotted line. Real estate investing is much more enjoyable under such circumstances.

The opposite characteristics signal a top:

• *Glowing news reports about the booming real estate market*, perhaps tempered by worries about rising mortgage rates.

• *A peak in housing starts* (or permits issued by your local building inspector), followed by several declines. This is a powerful warning.

• *Low vacancy rates in apartments and office buildings,* sparking a construction spree. When you see construction crews working on every vacant lot in town, you should think about selling.

• *A multiyear low for the local unemployment rate,* followed by two or three seemingly innocuous upticks.

• *Rude, hard-nosed brokers.* A favorite broker's line at the top of the market (it was used on me in 1979 when I was looking for my first house) is: "If you don't buy now, you'll never be able to afford a home again." Brokers don't want to bother with browsers at the peak of the boom. They want to pile up commissions fast. The universal hard sell will tip you off that the market is about to go bust.

For many people, a major drawback to direct investing in real estate is the amount of capital required. Limited partnerships, which pool the resources of many individuals, can erase or at least mitigate this disadvantage. Although there are no doubt many contrarian real estate syndicators throughout the country, one I know and recommend is *J.W. English Real Estate Inc.* (191 N. Hartz Ave., Danville, CA 94526, 800-423-8423, 415-838-8100).

The principal of this firm is Dr. John Wesley English, who started buying distressed apartment properties in Houston in 1983. He was early (the Houston market didn't bottom until 1987), but he held on through the oil crash and all his partnerships remained solvent. Wes is an outstanding negotiator. In one case, he persuaded a desperate seller to *pay* him $79,000 to take an apartment building off the owner's hands—better than a "nothing down" deal! Minimum investment for Wes English's partnerships is typically $30,000.

Collectibles and Other Tangibles

During the late 1970s (the glory days of inflation hedging), many Americans invested in collectibles—including art, antiques, rare coins, rare stamps and gemstones. While many of these items have risen fabulously in value over the long term, they pose some serious disadvantages for the investor who isn't prepared to hold them for at least five to 10 years. To begin with, you buy at retail and sell at wholesale prices. The spread between the price you pay and what a dealer pays you when you sell is enormous. Dealer markup typically comprises 20 to 50 percent of the retail price.

Fine differences of quality, which may be noticeable only to a trained eye, can make a dramatic difference in price. This is especially true with rare coins and gemstones. Unless you're willing to become an expert yourself, you must rely on experts to grade your merchandise for you. Unfortunately, most dealer-experts tend to grade loosely when selling *to* you but oh-so-strictly when buying *from* you!

Despite these disadvantages, collectibles can rack up stunning gains for the patient long-term investor. Rare coins, in particular, have performed superbly over the decades. The numismatic market is also the most highly developed of all the collectible markets, with the largest number of auctions and even a dealer teletype network that provides current price quotations.

The most important rule a contrarian should observe when investing in rare coins (or any collectible) is: *Avoid fads.* Buy quality items that have attracted a steady following of collectors over the years, but don't buy *anything* when it's "hot." In the spring of 1984, for example, many coin dealers were touting U.S. $20 gold pieces of the Saint-Gaudens design (minted 1907-33) as a device for sidestepping IRS regulations that require dealers to file a report when you sell gold bullion. My mailbox was crammed with advertising flyers making this pitch.

The $20 Saint-Gaudens is, of course, a staple of the numismatic market, with a long history of upward price movement. But the promotional hype pushed the price of this double eagle far out of line with prices of other U.S. gold coins—all of which were equally exempt from the IRS reporting requirements. At one point, uncirculated "Saints" were fetching more than $1,000 apiece, two-and-a-half times their melt value. The same week that I warned *Personal Finance* readers about this absurdity, quotations began to fall. Within seven months, the Saints had plunged 30 percent. In early 1989, you could buy them for $525 each, even though the price of gold was higher than during the mania five years earlier.

If you plan to invest in rare coins, I suggest that you work with a low-pressure dealer like R.W. Bradford, proprietor of *Liberty Coin Service* (300 Frandor Ave., Lansing, MI 48912, 800-321-1542, 517-351-4720). Bill Bradford has a remarkable eye for bargains, and he *hates* fads. Buy the classic U.S. coins when the market is quiet and dull and sell them when stockbrokers and other self-styled "financial planners" start peddling them to a greedy and gullible public.

It's unlikely that inflation in America will again approach the double-digit rates of the late 1970s for many years. Nonetheless, as long as the nation adheres to a fiat money system, issuing currency with no backing in real goods, inflation will remain a risk for the investor. Hard assets—from gold and silver to foreign currencies, real estate and Chagall lithographs—will continue to find a place in the prudent investor's portfolio, though in much more modest quantities than would have been appropriate a decade ago. During cyclical lulls in inflation, when the crowd assumes that the monster is dead, the shrewd contrarian will start building up his defenses, just in case. When the dragon roars again and the public tries to protect itself by rushing into hard assets, it will be time to sell.

Chapter 12

More Bang for the Buck

Give me a place to stand, and I will move the world.
—Archimedes on leverage

Not everyone is cut out to be a speculator. Some people just don't like to take big risks and would prefer to earn a modest payback on their investments rather than throw themselves open to the possibility of a major loss. Others, especially people in their later years, can't afford to speculate. If they squander their savings on ill-advised ventures, time may never give them an opportunity to make up their losses. Retired people, as a rule, should concentrate on preserving their wealth rather than multiplying it through high-risk enterprises.

In this chapter, I'll discuss several techniques that only the diehard speculator—the compulsive high roller—will want to try. If you don't fit that category, pass on to Chapter 13, or read what follows for entertainment only!

All the speculative vehicles I describe in this chapter exploit the principle of leverage. In simple terms, *leverage* means making money with other people's money. The speculator puts up a small amount of money, which he can afford to lose entirely, in hopes of making a much larger profit. Buying stocks and bonds on margin (or selling them short) is probably the oldest and most familiar form of leveraged speculation. More recent inventions include warrants, options and futures contracts.

It's entirely possible, as some respected contrarians have suggested, that the boom in leveraged speculations during the 1980s marks the last days of a financial era—and foreshadows the approaching Big Bust that deflation seers have prophesied for so long. The stock market crash of 1987, and the role that program trading played in aggravating it, certainly lend credence to this view. But I think it's a mistake to advise *everyone*, under all circumstances, to avoid these instruments. As a matter of fact, if a deflationary depression is coming, investors may not be able to preserve the value of their capital except through short selling and other aggressive tactics. By observing a few basic rules, contrarian speculators can greatly reduce their risks and increase their odds of making sizable profits.

The Ten Commandments of Speculation

Here are 10 principles to follow if you plan to venture into the exciting world of leveraged speculation. Most of them aren't original with me. I'm especially indebted to the late Charles R. Stahl, gold trader and for many years editor of *Green's Commodity Market Comments,* who laid down many of these rules for speculators at the annual Contrary Opinion Forum in Vermont back in 1967:

1. *Speculate with money you can afford to lose.* If you're trading with money that you know you'll need next month for a down payment on a new house, or next year for your child's college tuition, emotions will cloud your judgment. Make sure you've set aside an adequate liquid reserve to pay for life's necessities before you attempt to speculate.

2. *Always keep more than the broker's required margin on deposit in your account.* When you buy securities on margin, trade commodity futures or "write" (sell) options, you must deposit a minimum amount of money (margin) with your broker to assure that you'll meet your obligations. Never deposit only the minimum margin, because a relatively small market movement against you could wipe out your stake. With commodity futures, put up at least twice the required margin and preferably more.

3. *Limit your losses.* Determine in advance how much risk you're willing to bear. When you enter a transaction, give your broker a standing order to offset (close out) your position if your losses reach a predetermined point. It's essential to set loss limits

in advance because, if the market goes against you, you'll conjure up a multitude of excuses to persuade yourself that you should hold on in the face of mounting losses. Accept losses gracefully. As long as you don't lose more than a predetermined amount of money, an opportunity will come for another try.

4. *Never speculate if your personal life is in disarray.* If your wife is sick or your teenage son is in trouble with the police, the paranoia and self-doubt that constantly bedevil risk takers will torment you even more. Controlling your emotions is crucial to success as a speculator.

5. *Don't play every horse.* Most of the time, most markets aren't going anywhere. There simply aren't any big profits to be made. Resist the temptation to "keep your money working" on some speculation, somewhere, all the time. In most markets, good buying or selling opportunities come no more than once or twice a year. The rest of the time, you should put your idle funds into Treasury bills or other money market instruments, sit back and count your interest.

6. *Undertrade.* This rule is a corollary of the Second and Fifth Commandments. Once you've decided how much of your capital you want to set aside for speculation, don't commit more than a portion of it to any single trade. If, for instance, you've allocated $5,000 to buying options, don't buy more than $1,000 worth of options at any time. If you see an interesting opportunity that would bring your total exposure to more than a 20 percent of your capital available for speculation, get rid of one or more existing positions before you enter the new trade.

7. *Never trust the market.* When a speculation begins to show a profit, many people relax and complacently assume that the profit will last. Too often it doesn't. The market reverses itself and pretty soon the speculator is taking another loss. As soon as your speculation moves into the profit column, enter a standing order with your broker to sell (or cover your short sale) if the price slips back to your entry point. If your profits keep expanding, move the stop order up (a *trailing stop*) to protect your hard-won gains.

8. *Handle charts with care.* Most technical analysts put a great deal of stock in price charts. Prices are said to form a variety of

205

patterns from pennants, islands and W's to head-and-shoulders tops and saucer bottoms. Technicians also claim to see critical *support* and *resistance* levels on price charts. (If the market previously made an important reversal at a certain price level, that price theoretically becomes support if the reversal was from down to up, and resistance if the reversal was from up to down.) Furthermore, trendlines drawn along the market's lows or highs are thought to provide support or resistance, respectively. The odds are better than 50-50, technicians believe, that prices won't drop below a support level or rise above a resistance level. If prices do break through these barriers, technical gurus say, the market is likely to keep going in the direction of the breakthrough.

In my own experience (and a host of academic studies tend to corroborate my findings), chart patterns *by themselves*—including trendlines and support/resistance levels—possess little or no forecasting value. As I'll detail more fully later in this chapter, however, one type of technical analysis can prove helpful when used in conjunction with other contrarian indicators. *Rate-of-change analysis,* which looks at the velocity or "speed" of a market's price changes, can often help you spot important turning points before they occur or as they're occurring. Read on!

9. *When you make a profit, withdraw half of it.* The speculator who executes a successful trade is sorely tempted to pyramid his profits—to reinvest all the gain in a new speculation. The danger, though, is that a severe loss on the second trade may wipe out the profits on the first. Whenever you roll up a nice gain on a trade, withdraw half and put it out of harm's way, in Treasury bills or a similar safe, interest-bearing vehicle.

10. *Resist the impulses of the crowd.* In other words, think like a contrarian. Don't chase markets that have run up sharply, or sell markets short that have been collapsing for some time. Any profits you might make from following the existing trend are likely to be insignificant, and the risk of a painful reversal is high.

The Magic of Margin Accounts

A margin account with your stock broker can greatly enhance your profits from trading stocks and bonds—if you're prepared to follow the Ten Commandments of Speculation. When you buy on margin, you deposit a down payment with your broker, who lends you money to purchase securities.

The interest rate you're charged on the margin loan floats up and down with the rate the brokerage firm pays to borrow from the bank (the *broker loan rate* or *call money rate*). At most full-service brokerage firms, the margin rate is close to the bank prime rate, but some discount brokers make margin loans for a point or more below prime. You can keep the loan as long as you want—brokers don't fix any repayment schedule. The interest is added to your debit balance daily. However, you must always maintain a large enough margin deposit in the account to satisfy your broker that the loan is safe.

The Federal Reserve Board, which regulates broker loans, currently requires you to put up an initial margin deposit equal to at least 50 percent of the purchase price of any stocks you buy on credit. If the value of the stocks in the account drops, your broker may send you a *margin call*, demanding that you deposit more collateral to secure the loan. On the other hand, if the value of the stocks goes up, you can draw funds out of the account as long as you meet the broker's minimum *maintenance margin*.

Let's look at the arithmetic of a margin purchase to see how you can leverage your profits. We'll assume that you bought 100 shares of XYZ stock at $20 a share, and that the margin rate stayed at a steady 10 percent for one year. You deposited the minimum 50 percent margin and borrowed the rest of the purchase price from your broker. At the end of a year, XYZ stock was trading at $40 per share. Table 12.1 shows how your profit from a margin purchase would compare with your profit from a straight cash purchase.

Table 12.1 Profit Comparison

	Cash purchase	Margin purchase
(a) Proceeds of sale	$4,000	$4,000
(b) Cost of stock	2,000	2,000
(c) Net profit	2,000	2,000
(d) Initial cash outlay	2,000	1,000
(e) Interest expense	0	100
(f) Total cash outlay	2,000	$1,100*
(g) Percent profit on total cash outlay (c/f)	100%	182%*

*A taxpayer who had interest or dividend income could write off the $100 interest expense (up to the amount of the interest or dividend income) as an itemized deduction on his federal income tax return. Thus, the true cash outlay could be less than $1,100 and the profit more than 182 percent.

When a stock rises swiftly, the speculator who puts up 50 percent margin can earn almost twice as much profit as the more conservative investor who buys for cash. But interest expense always puts a drag on a margin account. In our example, unless XYZ stock gains at least 10 percent within a year (disregarding the tax benefit of deductible interest), you would have been better off to buy the stock for cash. Furthermore, leverage can work in reverse: on 50 percent margin, your losses pile up twice as fast (compared with a cash purchase) if the stock drops.

Because of today's historically high interest rates, I generally don't recommend buying stocks on margin. There are better ways to leverage your stock market profits, and some of these alternative methods—writing put and call options, for example—allow you to *collect* money rather than paying it out.

Margin buying makes far more sense with bonds. First of all, the leverage is greater: you need only deposit 30 percent of the purchase price when you buy corporate bonds on margin, and as little as 10 percent when you buy Treasury bonds. However, I don't recommend that you buy anything on 10 percent margin, not even bonds, unless you're supremely confident of your timing. A minor drop in the market could wipe out your margin deposit.

The beauty of buying bonds on margin is that bonds nowadays pay a generous rate of interest, offsetting the interest you owe on your margin loan. When long-term bonds are really worth buying for speculation, they pay a higher interest rate than the broker-loan rate, which is tied to short-term money market rates. Hence, you make money on the spread between long-term and short-term rates, much as a bank does by borrowing short and lending long. A broker who specializes in obtaining low interest rates on large ($500,000 and up) margin loans for bond purchases is Jay Goldinger of *Capital Insights Inc.* (190 N. Canon Dr., Beverly Hills, CA 90210, 800-421-4323, in Calif., 800-321-2644).

It's generally not a good idea to buy bonds on margin when the yield curve is inverted—when short-term money costs more than long-term money. But if, after a panic selloff in the bond market, you find that short rates have dropped below long rates, buying bonds on margin can reap spectacular profits. From May 1984 to April 1986, for example, you could have rolled up a total return (interest plus capital gains) of more than 600 percent on your money if you had purchased long-term Treasury bonds on 10 percent margin!

Selling Short—and Avoiding the Pitfalls

Probably the most valuable use of a margin account is for selling short. A short seller is a speculator who tries to make a profit from a drop, rather than a rise, in the market. Most investors, and many brokers, are reluctant to sell short because theoretically, the losses from an ill-considered short sale can mount to infinity. When you sell a stock short, you sell shares that you don't actually own. Instead, you borrow the stock from your broker and sell it.

Naturally, you hope to replace the borrowed stock (cover the short) later at a lower price than you received when you sold. For a short seller, the lower a stock goes, the better. If the stock drops all the way to zero, you earn your maximum profit—100 percent. But if the stock rises instead, you'll lose money when you cover your short. In theory, the stock could keep going up forever, and you would have to buy back the shares at an infinitely high price.

Novice speculators often balk at short selling because the risk-reward ratio seems unfair—an infinite risk versus a maximum reward of 100 percent. Moreover, Uncle Sam taxes any profits you earn from a short sale as a short-term capital gain (ordinary income), regardless of when you cover your short.

However, short selling isn't as risky or unprofitable as it appears at first blush—if you respect the Ten Commandments of Speculation, especially #3 (limit your losses). To begin with, no stock soars to infinity, and if you sell short when the market is bubbling with euphoria after a sharp runup, the odds of a major decline vastly outweigh the likelihood that the market will stage another dramatic advance.

Moreover, you don't need to pay any margin interest on a short sale (because you're borrowing stock, not money). But you do obligate yourself to pay any dividends that may accrue on stocks you sell short. If you wish, you can put up income-producing securities such as Treasury bills as collateral for a short sale, thereby avoiding any cash outlay. For short sales of stock, the cash margin requirement is 50 percent of the value of the stock sold short. However, if you put up securities as collateral, the market value of the securities must equal the value of the stock you're selling short.

Once you've decided that the market looks vulnerable, selecting stocks to sell short isn't especially difficult. As veteran short seller T.J. Holt is fond of saying, "Short the overpriced favorites." As a rule, the stocks that rise the most during a bull market—the stocks the crowd loves best—fall the most during a bear market. Here are some characteristics that flag a stock as a good short-sale candidate:

- *Price-earnings ratio twice or three times the market average*

- *Minuscule dividend yield* (or none at all)

- *Price gain far in excess of the market indices over the past 12 months.**

*Paradoxically, stocks that have lagged the market averages may also make good short sales if their poor relative performance is due to rapidly deteriorating earnings or an excessive debt burden.

- *Heavy insider selling* (preferably one or more transactions worth $500,000 apiece)

- *Company or its industry featured in a puff piece on the front cover of a national newsmagazine*

- *Company's product (often a fad item or vanity product) attracting intense competition, with profit margins beginning to sag*

Most of the stocks that came down hardest in the collapse of the 1983 and 1987 speculative manias shared these characteristics. In both cases, hundreds of glamorous stocks with P/Es of 20, 30 or more crashed. (Remember Osborne Computer in 1983, or Home Shopping Network four years later?) For the legions who thought that these overrated growth stocks could only go up, up, up, it was a hair-raising toboggan ride. Short sellers, on the other hand, loved every minute of it.

The New World of Options

Options trading has exploded in recent years, almost to the point of becoming a mania. You can now buy or sell ("write") options on more than 300 stocks (and a variety of stock indices), as well as bonds, foreign currencies, precious metals, agricultural commodities and oil, to name just a few dishes on the menu.[1] A *call* option gives you the right (but not the obligation) to buy a certain quantity of an asset—say, 100 shares of stock—at a fixed price (the *strike price*) during a specified period. Speculators buy calls when they expect the price of the underlying asset to go up.

A *put* option allows you to sell a given quantity of the underlying asset (again, for example, 100 shares of stock) at a fixed price during a specified period. Speculators buy puts to profit from a decline in the market.

The appeal of options lies in their enormous leverage. When you buy an option, the price you pay (the *premium*) is usually a small fraction of the value of the underlying asset. For instance, if Sears Roebuck stock is trading at $40 per share, you may be able to buy a call option, entitling you to purchase 100 shares at 40 within the next three months, for only $2 per share. If Sears stock gained only $6 within the next three months—a 20 percent rise—the value of the call would triple.

Incredible? Let's briefly review the arithmetic. You agreed to pay $2 per share for the option. To triple your money, the option must appreciate to at least $6 by the expiration date. If Sears stock is at 40 or *below* on the expiration date, your call option will expire worthless. It wouldn't make any sense for you to exercise your option, paying $40 apiece for 100 Sears shares, because you could buy Sears on the open market for 40 or less. But if Sears rises above 40, your option will possess *intrinsic* value on the expiration date, because it will enable you to buy Sears stock for 40—less than the going market price.

Should Sears trade at 42 at the end of the option's life ($2 above the $40 strike price of the option), you would break even. Your option would expire with an intrinsic value of $2—exactly what you paid for it. You would double your money if Sears rises another $2 (to 44) and you would triple your money if Sears tacked on yet another $2 (to 46). In short, a $6 gain in Sears shares would net you a 200 percent profit (a 3-for-1 return).

The same analysis applies with put options, except that the option builds up intrinsic value as the price of the underlying asset (Sears stock, in our illustration) drops below the strike price of the option. Let's assume that you could buy a put on Sears, exercisable at $40 per share within the next three months, for $2 per share. If Sears dips to 38 at the end of the option's life, you'll break even; at 36, you'll double your money; at 34, you'll triple your money, and so on.

Of course, you pay a price for such spectacular leverage. If you buy "out of the money" options—those with no intrinsic value, but only time value—the probability that you'll end up with a loss is extremely high. Don't fall for the specious argument, advanced by many brokers, that your risk is limited when you buy options. True, your risk is contractually limited to the purchase price of the option (the premium). However, a large percentage of options either decline in value or, worse, expire with no value at all because the market doesn't go in the direction the buyer expected or doesn't go as far as expected. Speculators who buy an out-of-the-money option and hang on to it until expiration face over-whelming odds that they'll lose their entire investment.

It should therefore come as no surprise that the vast majority of option buyers lose money over time. Nonetheless, by following the Ten Commandments of Speculation—particularly the stop-loss rule and the trailing-stop rule—you can substantially improve your likelihood of success. Here are some specific guidelines for trading options:

• *Never allow a loss on an option to exceed 30 to 40 percent of the purchase price.*

• *Buy in-the-money or near-the-money options only.* For calls, "in the money" means that the price of the underlying asset is above the strike price (exercise price) of the option. For in-the-money puts, the underlying asset is trading *below* the strike price of the option. In-the-money options are much less likely to expire worthless than out-of-the-money options.

• *Close out all options—winners as well as losers—no later than two or three weeks before the expiration date.* The time value of an option decays rapidly in the last few weeks of the option's life. Even if your option appears to be safely in the money, sell. The clock is ticking, and your risk of losing everything if the market moves sharply against you is mounting rapidly.

• *Buy calls when everyone else is buying puts, and buy puts when everyone else is buying calls.* In the stock market, the best time to buy calls is when the 10-day ratio of puts to calls on the Chicago Board Options Exchange has soared to 0.8 or higher (see p. 89) at the end of a steep market decline. Buy puts when the put-call ratio has slipped sharply, to 0.4 or lower. If you're interested in trading Comex gold options, you might track the gold put-call ratio described in Chapter 11. For bond options and foreign-currency options, your best trading guide is probably Earl Hadady's *Bullish Consensus* poll, described in Chapter 4. (The consensus is also invaluable for the gold trader.) As a contrarian, you'll want to buy calls when the vast majority of advisors are bearish and puts when the advisors are bullish—just the opposite of what the crowd is doing.

Don't Buy Options, Sell!

Every dollar that option buyers lose flows (after brokerage commissions) into the pockets of option sellers. Since a large majority of out-of-the-money options expire worthless, it follows that the seller of an out-of-the-money option who waits patiently for it to expire stands a good chance of making money. Speculators with the financial resources to play the seller's side of the options game can build a fortune on those odds.

Selling (or *writing*) options turns off most unsophisticated speculators, for a couple of reasons. To begin with, there doesn't seem to be much money in it. Most stock options sell for $500 or less, and—even under the best of circumstances, assuming the option expires totally worthless—the option writer can't earn more than the premium received for the option. Option writing doesn't promise the instant returns of 100, 200 or 300 percent on your investment that are possible when you buy options.

Furthermore, some option-writing strategies pose what appear (superficially, at least) to be grave risks. Think back to our Sears Roebuck example. If you sell a Sears call with a $40 strike price, you've promised to deliver, upon request, 100 shares of Sears for $40 apiece at any time between now and the option's expiration date. You would sell the call if you thought Sears was likely to go down, or at least remain flat, over the life of the option.

But what if Sears goes up sharply instead—to 44, 46, or 48? The call buyer would exercise his option and, if you didn't already own 100 shares of Sears, you would have to go into the marketplace and buy them. (Selling an option without owning the underlying asset is called *naked* option writing.) Because Sears could theoretically soar to infinity, the call buyer's unlimited profit might become your unlimited loss.

Selling naked puts can also saddle you with massive losses, as some unlucky option writers discovered during the 1987 stock market crash. In our example, when you sell a Sears 40 put, you've promised to buy, if asked, 100 shares of Sears at $40 each between now and the option's expiration date. Should Sears go up or remain flat, you'll turn a profit. But if Sears drops precipitously (to 36, 34 or 32, say) and the put buyer exercises his option, you could end up buying Sears stock from the put owner at a price far above the prevailing market—for a huge loss to you.[2]

To avoid these potentially horrendous risks, many advisors suggest that option writers stick to selling *covered* calls against stocks, bonds, currencies, gold and other optionable assets that the investor already owns. And it's true that the premiums you collect from covered option writing can boost your income and smooth out the fluctuations in your portfolio.

But naked option writing—the activity that *everybody* seems afraid to engage in—can bring the well-financed speculator steady profits of 20 percent a year or more, with far less risk than is commonly believed. Consider an analogy. A life insurance company would go bankrupt if all its policyholders died at once. But insurance companies survive—and make a handsome living— precisely because they know that the probability of such an occurrence is all but nil. The premiums an insurance company collects more than compensate for the occasional claim the company must pay out.

Likewise, the intelligent option writer recognizes that most out-of-the-money options expire worthless. As long as you take the proper steps to limit losses on the relatively few transactions that go against you, the probabilities argue that over the long run, you'll rake in far bigger profits as an out-of-the-money option writer than will the speculator who buys options in hopes of making a quick killing. Because options are a wasting asset with a finite life, time is on the side of the patient seller—and is working against the impetuous buyer.

You can significantly pare the risks of option writing by observing the Ten Commandments of Speculation, especially the stop-loss rule. In general, I suggest that you give your broker a standing order to buy back any option if its market value rises to twice the premium you received for writing it. This procedure will help ensure that you never risk more than you stand to gain on an option sale. Unless your stop-loss point is reached, or you have reason to believe that the market is about to reverse gears, allow your options to run until they expire. You'll save a second commission.

In a flat market, you can expand your profits and lower your risk further by selling a put and a call simultaneously at the same strike price. This maneuver is called a *straddle*. In the Sears case, you would have sold a put *and* a call, both with an exercise price of $40, collecting $4 of premiums in the process. As long as Sears stayed above 36 and below 44—a pretty wide band—you would clear a profit. If Sears drifted around dead center for three months (not especially likely, but possible), you would pocket $4 for each straddle, rather than the $2 you would have made if you had simply bet that the stock was going up (write a put) or down (write a call).[3]

How do you know when to sell options? Sell calls when the crowd is buying—when the put-call ratios are low and most advisors are brimming with optimism. When the crowd is clamoring for puts (the put-call ratios are high) and most advisors are wearing long faces, sell puts. As an option writer, you can do the great mass of option buyers a humanitarian favor by fulfilling their secret craving for a chance to lose money.

Perhaps the best feature of option writing is that it doesn't consume any cash, except when you must buy back your options at a loss. To begin selling options, you can deposit cash or (preferably) income-producing securities such as Treasury bills with your broker as margin. Thus, any profits you make on your option writing merely sweeten the yield from your Treasury bills. The option buyer, by contrast, is obliged to pay for his options up front. For the speculator who meets the financial qualifications (many brokerage firms require $50,000 net worth or more), writing options can be less risky than buying them, and far more profitable in the long run.

Commodities: Stacking the Odds in Your Favor

Like options, commodity futures capture a speculator's imagination with the promise of awesome leverage. For example, by plunking down a margin deposit of a little more than $2,000, you can buy a contract on the Comex for future delivery of 100 ounces of gold. If the price of gold climbs $20 (roughly a 5 percent gain at current prices), you'll double your money; if it drops $20, your stake will be wiped out.

In Chapter 4, I described the contrarian commodity-trading system devised by Earl Hadady, publisher of *The Bullish Consensus*. It's possible to make decent commodity profits by this method alone, trading contrary to the consensus of advisors. However, the mere fact that a market has gone to an extreme of optimism or pessimism doesn't always keep prices from shooting off even further in the direction of the prevailing trend. Thus, I suggest that commodity traders double-check their reading of the sentiment indicators by comparing it with the message from a set of "momentum" indicators—more properly known as velocity or rate-of-change indicators.

Before a market can go up, it must stop going down. (The reverse is also true.) Momentum indicators are designed to tell you when a trend is *slowing* and therefore may soon be stopping. Unlike trend-following indicators, such as moving averages—which can only confirm a trend change after the fact—momentum indicators can alert you to an impending trend change before it happens.

The simplest way to construct a momentum indicator is to compare the current market price with its value at some point in the past. If you're a short-term trader, you might want to focus on the market's 10-day rate of change, for example. Say the price of gold today is $420 and two weeks (10 trading days) ago it was $400. The 10-day rate of change is plus 5 percent. If, several weeks from now, the price of gold bounces up to a new high of $430, but the 10-day rate of change is only 2 percent, the indicator is telling you that the momentum of the market's advance is ebbing. This divergence between prices and momentum, if coupled with excessive optimism among the professional advisors (as revealed by the *Bullish Consensus* poll), would signal an opportunity to sell gold short at $430.

Traders with a longer-term perspective might use a 13-week momentum indicator, or a 26-week, or even a 52-week. The longer

217

the period, the more significant are the signals generated by the indicator. Figure 35 illustrates a 13-week momentum oscillator for gold. As you can see, gold's upward momentum made three

Change in the Price of Gold

In dollars per ounce. **Source:** *Bank Credit Analyst.*

Fig. 35. Change in the price of gold

descending peaks in October 1986, April 1987 and December 1987. Meanwhile, the spot price of gold made three rising peaks. The first divergence between price and momentum, in April 1987, was accompanied by a wave of hysterically bullish sentiment in the gold market, prompting me to write an article in the April 15, 1987 *Personal Finance* titled, "The Tide May Be Ebbing for Gold."A trader with a time horizon of several months could have snared excellent profits by selling gold short near its "unconfirmed" April 1987 high of $475.

When the final high occurred in December of that year at $502, momentum diverged from price for a second time. This double failure sounded the death knell for the 1985-87 bull market for gold. (A double momentum failure is usually fatal; a triple failure is nearly always fatal.) Whether you were planning

218

to hold your position for two weeks, two months or two years, the December 1987 high was an ideal place to short gold in the futures market.

Several commodity charting services publish, alongside their price charts, graphs of one or more momentum indicators. I particularly recommend Commodity Trend Service's weekly *Futures Charts* (P.O. Box 32309, Palm Beach Gardens, FL 33410, $415 per year or $230 for financial commodities only). CTS computes a 14-day, 14-week and 14-month momentum indicator known as a *stochastic oscillator*. Basically, the stochastic oscillator looks back and asks: Where does the market now stand compared with its price range over the period in question? Is the market near its low, near its high or somewhere in between? The market's current price is expressed as a percentage of the historical range (0 to 100). Then this figure, averaged together with the preceding numbers in the series to smooth out statistically meaningless fluctuations, is plotted on the graph.

From the commodity trader's standpoint, the best time to trade against the prevailing trend is when the long-term (monthly) and intermediate-term (weekly) stochastics are extremely overbought (75 percent or higher) or extremely oversold (25 percent or lower) and the daily stochastic shows that momentum is diverging from prices. A striking example from recent experience is, once again, gold in December 1987.

At the yellow metal's peak that month (which turned out to be a major cyclical peak), the monthly and weekly stochastic readings were both severely overbought: 84 percent on the monthly and 74 percent on the weekly. The weekly stochastic, like the 13-week rate-of-change indicator I mentioned earlier, had been diverging from the gold price for more than a year. As the coup de grace, the ultrasensitive daily stochastic, depicted in Figure 36, revealed that momentum made a lower peak on December 11, the day the gold price topped out, than it had achieved two weeks previously. Gold was ready to roll over and die.

Even after gold touched a primary peak in December 1987, the market afforded several good entry points for short sellers. The monthly stochastic soon turned down into neutral territory,

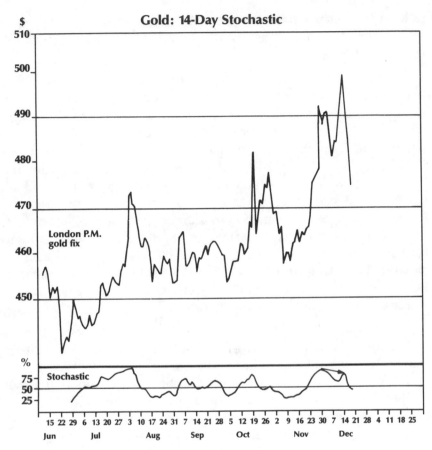

Fig. 36. Gold: 14-day stochastic

Source: *Commodity Trend Service.*

but twice in 1988—in June and again in December—the price of gold mounted strong knee-jerk rallies, driving up the weekly stochastic back into the overbought region. On both occasions, the daily stochastic produced a divergence between momentum and price. This warning flag signaled that gold's rebound was losing steam (despite the enthusiastic cheers of goldbugs). A short seller who seized the hour could have made out exceedingly well, even after missing the primary top.

Keep an Eye on the Clock

Momentum or rate-of-change analysis can give you a leg up in the high-stakes arena of commodity speculation. You can also make your task somewhat easier by developing an appreciation for the value of time. The problem I pointed out in the context of option buying also applies to most commodity futures. If you buy a futures contract, you're generally fighting against the clock. As I write, for example, the price of a gold contract expiring a year hence is more than $30 per ounce higher than the current or *spot* price of gold. Gold for delivery eight months from now is $20 an ounce higher than spot.

In other words, the price of gold must rise $20 an ounce within the next eight months, and $30 an ounce within the next 12 months, if the speculator who buys those contracts today is simply to break even. Let's assume that you deposit $2,000 with your broker today as margin to buy a 100-ounce gold contract expiring in eight months. If price of gold remains steady for the next eight months, your entire margin will go up in smoke. Any interest earned on your margin deposit can't begin to compensate for the erosion in the value of the contract.

Built into the price of most futures contracts is a carrying charge, which represents the cost of buying and storing the commodity until the contract matures. The more distant the delivery month, the greater the carrying charge. For short sellers, the premium of the distant contracts over the nearby contracts is a major advantage; for buyers, it's a major disadvantage. (The reverse order typically prevails in the interest-rate futures. The more distant Treasury bill and Treasury bond futures, for instance, typically sell at lower prices than the nearby contracts. This phenomenon hinders the short seller, but aids the buyer.)

If you're planning to trade for the long term, it's wisest—other things being equal—to buy commodities (like bonds) that feature a negative carry and sell those (like gold) with a positive carry. Otherwise, the carrying charge will eat inexorably into your equity, much as the wasting time value of an option gobbles up the buyer's premium. Try, wherever possible, to position yourself on

221

the receiving end of the carrying charge. That way, the passage of time will benefit you even if the spot market doesn't budge an inch.

Many people feel uncomfortable with leveraged speculations—and rightly so. The speculator who taps other people's money to multiply his own always takes a greater risk than the investor who pays cash on the barrelhead. (Don't forget: leverage can multiply your losses, too!) For the speculator willing to follow a disciplined approach, however, contrary thinking provides a method for reducing the risks and increasing the rewards of leveraged vehicles such as futures, options and margin accounts.

But should you fool around with these volatile instruments at all? Only you can resolve that issue, as we'll see in Chapter 13.

Chapter 13

Be Your Own Person, Virginia

Make your decisions based upon what you are, not what you or someone else thinks you should be.—Harry Browne

Several years ago, an attorney friend from out of state and his family were visiting for a couple of days at our home. Their eldest child and our eldest (both daughters, two years old at the time) soon discovered that each wanted to wear the same clothes as the other. If one had a frilly dress on, the other nagged for a frilly dress. If one was wearing red sneakers, the other wanted to wear red sneakers. Finally, my friend, exasperated, bellowed to his daughter, "Be your own person, Virginia!"

As adult investors, of course, we don't need an irate parent to tell us to think and act for ourselves. Nevertheless, I suspect from the queries I receive as editor of the nation's largest investment newsletter that many people are searching for a guru to follow, someone who will take the responsibility for making decisions out of their hands. Too often, brokerage-house clients, customers of bank trust departments, newsletter subscribers, and—alas— even readers of investment books blindly accept an advisor's recommendations without stopping to weigh for themselves the arguments behind the advice.

Why are so many people so eager to abdicate responsibility for making their own financial judgments? One factor, no doubt, is the widespread superstition that advisors with prestigious credentials know more about the future than anybody else does. We live in the Age of the Expert. If we don't understand something, we assume that somebody with a Ph.D. or MBA after his name does. Yet the markets, with their unpredictable ways (people are never completely predictable), succeed in making fools of the experts time and again. Remember how the panel of experts at *Fortune* magazine told us in 1981 that Continental Illinois Bank was one of the best-managed companies in America?

Another, and even more powerful, reason why many investors want to be led by the hand is that they believe in the "gospel of the track record." If an advisor has made dazzling profits for his clients recently with a series of accurate predictions or timely market maneuvers, the world assumes that he must know something nobody else knows. As a result, advisors with a "hot hand" often develop a cult-like following of investors who have all but given up thinking critically. Like worshipers, they wait upon their master's words until, inevitably, the cult leader's magic touch fails and his clients run up horrendous losses.

Then the disenchanted investors jump ship and sign on with another advisor who appears to have found The Formula. It never occurs to them that they're sacrificing their minds and wills—their own self-respect—to the whims, passions, foibles and errors of another imperfect human being. *Everybody* is doing it and *everybody* (for a while) seems to be making money, so they go along—until they discover that, in the end, *everybody* was mistaken.

Please understand: I'm not suggesting for a moment that you shouldn't take advice. Others may have studied the markets more closely and more deeply than you have. By drawing on their research and experience, you can save yourself the time and money it would take to investigate the universe of investment opportunities yourself. But make sure you apply your own critical judgment to your advisor's *conclusions* and *recommendations*. Ask yourself these questions:

• Has this advisor made a logical case for this recommendation, or is he engaging in wishful thinking? Does authoritative rhetoric conceal flaws in the argument?

• What possible unforeseen factors have been left out?

- Is this advisor merely repeating the conventional wisdom, or is he looking behind the obvious to anticipate some surprise that will push prices up or down?

- Am I taking this advice because I think it's correct or because I believe in the advisor's track record (i.e., he has been right in the past)?

- What happens to my investment if this advice doesn't pan out?

Thinking for yourself doesn't mean that you must personally handle every detail of managing your investments. For instance, I believe it's entirely appropriate for investors of moderate means to participate in the stock market through a mutual fund—not because the fund's managers are so much smarter than you are, but because a mutual fund gives you the safety of diversification among 30 or 50 or more stocks. If it's a no-load fund, it also slashes your transaction costs (primarily brokerage commissions). But there are hundreds of no-load stock funds to choose from, with radically different investment policies and objectives.[1]

You must decide for yourself which type of fund suits your financial goals—and your temperament. Nobody can determine for you how much risk you're willing to accept and how large a return you wish to seek. Don't let some broker or newsletter writer, who has little to lose by giving risky advice, push you into trading options or futures if those tactics will keep you tossing and turning at night. On the other hand, don't allow your friendly bank trust officer to convince you that the only assets a prudent investor should own are blue chip stocks. If you lack the time or the expertise, by all means hire someone to help you manage your investment portfolio. But see to it that your portfolio reflects your personality and your priorities—not somebody else's.

Risk and Return

The most basic decision you need to make when designing an investment portfolio is how much risk you can afford to take. How large a loss could you accept on your investments without jeopardizing your long-term financial goals—buying a home, starting your own business, putting the children through college, ensuring yourself a comfortable retirement? Generally, the riskier the investment, the greater the potential return, although not always, as we'll see shortly.

Table 13.1 illustrates the spectrum of risks posed by 10 popular investments. For this purpose, I'm defining "risk" crudely but simply as the largest price drop that the asset experienced for any single year in the 10 years from 1978 to 1987.

Several interesting conclusions emerge from the table. To begin with, the five riskier investments—the bottom half of the list—produced a smaller average gain over the 10-year period (132.5 percent) than the five safer investments (171.5 percent). Thus, the traditional correlation between risk and reward was turned upside down. If we had taken intrayear fluctuations into account, the Black Monday crash on Wall Street would have pushed common stocks into a much higher risk category and the traditional risk-reward trade-off would have applied once again. (The Dow dropped 36 percent from August to October 1987.) But it's remarkable how often the familiar rules of risk and reward are violated in real life. Money market funds, the least risky investment of all, provided an above-average return over the 10-year period in the table. Meanwhile, silver, the most volatile item on the list, produced the lowest return.

In theory, the safest asset should have yielded the lowest return and the riskiest should have generated the highest return. But these are unusual times! In the early years of the 1978-87 period, when "everybody" was frantically hedging against inflation, silver became grossly overpriced and interest-sensitive instruments such as T-bills became severely underpriced (yields soared far above the inflation rate). It took the better part of a decade for the markets to redress this imbalance.

Moral of the story? Historical measures of risk and return are useful, but watch out for psychological factors that can throw the traditional correlation out of kilter. I would argue, for example, that the lingering inflation phobia in the marketplace has, in recent years, kept bond yields at exceptionally high levels compared with dividend yields on common stocks. In the summer of 1987, the ratio of bond yields to stock yields surged to an all-time high—and at this writing, it remains on a historically high plateau. As a result, the conventional view that "stocks outperform bonds, but bonds are safer" may prove inaccurate over the next few years. Because of the unusual disparity in yields, bonds may furnish a higher return than stocks, with lower volatility (lower, at least, on a total-return basis).

Regardless of your taste for risk, I would suggest that you keep at least six months' worth of living expenses in the form of liquid assets (Treasury bills, money market funds, bank accounts, savings bonds, etc.). If your cash cushion is thinner than that, you're not ready to build an investment portfolio at all. Hold enough cash equivalents to let your mind rest easy.

Table 13.1 The Risk-Reward Tradeoff

Current value of Investment	Largest one-year % price drop (1978-87)	$10,000 invested in 1978
Money market funds	None	$25,860
Single-family home	None	21,600
S&P 500 stocks	9	41,390
Swiss bank account	11	22,200
Treasury bonds	15	24,700
Commodity basket	18	11,430
Rare coins	24	35,170
Gold	29	28,590
U.S. stamps	33	27,140
Silver	57	13,900

Any income is assumed to be reinvested, except for single-family home.

Your Risk Profile

Statistics may seem coldly authoritative, but you should remember that the risk-reward table reflects only the *historical* performance of stocks, bonds, gold and the like—and then only over a 10-year period. Past performance, as mutual fund advertisements say, is no guarantee of future performance. Because the future never exactly resembles the past, it's impossible to measure risk with scientific precision.

Nonetheless, experience suggests that, as a rule, prices fluctuate more widely for some types of assets than for others. Zero coupon bonds bounce around more than Treasury bills. High tech stocks and rare coins take deeper nosedives than single-family homes. Depending on your tolerance for risk, you should emphasize either more stable or more speculative assets.

To give you some idea of what your risk profile might be, I've prepared the questionnaire below. I invite you to fill it out and score yourself. The average score indicates your risk profile. By matching your risk profile in the left-hand column with the investment strategies in the right-hand column, you can form a rough estimate of how much investment risk you can afford to take. The average risk of all the assets in your portfolio (right-hand column) should equal your risk profile (left-hand column).

I should add that I've based the risk rankings largely on the past performance of each type of investment but also partly on my own "guesstimate" of the future volatility of each asset. Needless to say, I give no guarantee that all my hunches will prove correct. If you disagree with my rankings, I welcome you to amend the table to suit your perceptions of risk. But I suspect that you'll end up ranking most of the investments in the same categories I did, or perhaps one or two steps above or below.

Profile Analysis

Directions: Circle the answer that most nearly applies to you. Write that number in the space at right. Then add up the numbers and divide by 9 to get your average score.

Age
My age bracket is:

(7) under 35 (5) 35-49 (3) 50-57 (2) 58-65 (1) over 65 _____

Income
My annual income from all sources is (in thousands):

(1) under $25 (3) $25-34 (5) $35-49

(6) $50-100 (7) over $100 _____

Annual Expenses
In relation to income, my annual expenses approximate:

(1) over 95% (3) 90-95% (4) 80-89%
(6) 60-79% (8) under 60% _____

Number of Dependents
I currently have these dependents (including nonworking spouse):

(7) 0 (6) 1 (5) 2-3 (3) 4-5 (1) 6 or more _____

Estimated Value of Assets
Market value of my house, cash value of life insurance, savings and investments (in thousands):

(1) under $50 (3) $50-149 (5) $150-249
(7) $250-499 (8) $500 or more _____

Liabilities
My mortgages, installment loans and long-term debts in relation to assets approximate:

(8) under 30% (6) 30-49% (4) 50-69% (2) 70-90%
(1) over 90% _____

Savings
I have cash on hand or other liquid assets in savings to equal expenses for:

(1) 2 months (3) 4 months (5) 6 months
(6) 1 year (8) over 1 year _____

Life Insurance
My life insurance coverage equals (in thousands):

(6) $300 or more (4) $200-300 (3) $150-299
(2) $50-149 (1) under $50 _____

Health Insurance
My health insurance coverage, counting Medicare but not Social Security disability benefits, includes:

(1) Basic (3) Major medical plus basic
(5) Catastrophic, major medical, and basic
(7) Catastrophic, major medical, basic, and disability _____

Score_____

229

Risk Profile (average score from profile analysis) and Investment strategies

1: Bank savings accounts, money market funds, Treasury bills, fixed annuities, universal life policies

2: Bank CDs, government securities and high-grade corporate and municipal bonds, all with maximum maturity of five years

3: Single-family home (for rental), high-grade utility stocks, adjustable-rate bonds

4: Low P/E stocks and mutual funds invested in low P/E stocks, middle-grade utility stocks; government, corporate and municipal bonds with maturities up to 10 years

5: Gold; quality growth stocks and mutual funds; convertible bonds; variable annuities; tax-sheltered income partnerships; high-grade long-term bonds; foreign currencies; covered option writing

6: Aggressive-growth mutual funds; troubled utilities; silver; office and apartment buildings; junk bonds and long-dated zero coupon bonds

7: Mining shares; oil-drilling partnerships; junior mortgages; penny stocks; option buying, naked option writing

8: Distressed real estate; margin accounts and short selling; rare and exotic investments such as stamps, coins, art, antiques, gems, rare books, and other collectibles

9: Commodity futures

Don't assume, just because your risk profile is 4, 5 or 6, that you shouldn't own *any* penny stocks, rare coins or other assets in the higher-risk categories. If you fit into the middle of the scale but your portfolio is heavily weighted with assets in the low-risk categories (1 to 3), you might allocate a modest percentage of your portfolio to high-risk assets. What counts is the *average* risk of your total portfolio, not the risk of each individual component.

An 85-year-old millionaire dowager who keeps 98 percent of her fortune in Treasury bills and 2 percent in penny gold shares is hardly speculating! Even if her penny stocks went to zero, her Treasury bill interest would make up the loss within two or three months. The average risk of her portfolio, according to the ranking system outlined above, would amount to a lowly 1.1.

To take another example, a 40-year-old insurance salesman with an annual income of $40,000 and a risk profile of 4 should ideally strive for an average risk of 4 in his total portfolio. Here's how it might be done:

Table 13.2 Risk Profile vs. Total Portfolio

Investment	Percent of portfolio	Risk category
Bank accounts and money funds	20	1
Universal life policy	5	1
3-year Treasury notes	10	2
Low P/E stocks	15	4
Gold coins	5	5
Convertible bonds	5	5
Aggressive mutual fund	10	6
Real estate partnership (office buildings)	10	6
Zero coupon bonds	10	6
Naked options	5	7
Average risk*	100	4

*Weighted according to the percentage of the portfolio represented by each asset.

Normally, a person with a risk profile of 4 wouldn't dabble in naked options (ranked 7). But because our insurance salesman had a large reserve of liquid assets (20 percent), he could safely afford to put a small percentage of capital to work in naked option writing.

Note, too, that our salesman has spread his risks among 10 different categories of investments. If inflation flares up, the gold coins and real estate would tend to gain in value. On the other hand, zero coupons and convertible bonds should profit if inflation and interest rates gradually decline. The low P/E stocks and mutual funds stand to benefit if the economy grows normally. In a deflationary depression, the Treasury notes, bank accounts (or money funds) and universal life policy would maintain our salesman's purchasing power—assuming, as I do, that the U.S. government, the banks and the insurance companies could survive such a cataclysm.

Diversification is the better part of valor in an uncertain world. By all means, play the probabilities as you see them. Skew your portfolio toward inflation hedges when the crowd is moaning about deflation, and toward deflation hedges when popular opinion is buzzing about inflation. Invest for an economic recovery when the pundits are universally chattering about a depression, and anticipate a slump when *Time* magazine proclaims that all is well. But never bet all your chips on a single favorite scenario. The markets may not oblige, and what will you do then? Diversification protects you from your own ignorance, stupidity and greed.

Save More, Risk More, Make More

Why can't some people "afford" to live with greater investment risks than others? Personality, broadly defined, has something to do with it. But the profile analysis zeroes in on some more easily measured criteria that reveal your "financial personality"—age, for example. In general, people can accept more risk when they're young, and less when they're old. Working people in their 20s and 30s can usually look forward to a long parade of paychecks before retirement. Hence, younger investors can typically recoup through savings any losses they might incur on high-risk ventures.

By contrast, it's more difficult for older investors—especially retirees with Social Security as their main source of income—to make up a major loss through savings. They're more likely to need all or nearly all their current income for living expenses.

More important than age, however, are your saving and spending habits. As the questionnaire implies, a person who saves diligently and keeps debts to a minimum can afford to take greater risks (in search of a higher return) than the person who is always financially strapped. The saver has this advantage over the spender *almost regardless* of age or income bracket. Therefore, it's crucial to make a systematic savings program the cornerstone of your long-term wealth-building effort.

Rudyard Kipling, England's poet of empire, once wrote that "any fool can waste, any fool can muddle, but it takes something of a man to save, and the more he saves the more of a man does it make of him." Whether saving is in fact a "manly" virtue or not, many of us find it hard to practice. We know we should be putting more aside, but we don't.

Mark and JoAnn Skousen, in their delightful book, *Never Say Budget!*[2], suggest that you can make saving easy by *paying yourself first*. Determine how much you want to save out of your income weekly, monthly or at whatever interval suits you. (The Skousens recommend salting away 10 percent of your gross take, but some people in the upper income brackets should, I think, be able to save considerably more.) Then, when you receive your paycheck, immediately deposit the stipulated amount in your chosen savings vehicle. *Pay yourself* before you pay any of your other bills—mortgage, utilities, credit cards, you name it. This approach automatically regulates your spending without requiring you to draw up a formal budget. If the money is gone, you can't spend it!

Many people who begin a savings program allow it to lapse after a few months. You can keep your resolution from flagging, the Skousens suggest, by enrolling in a payroll-deduction plan sponsored by your employer. (Often, company profit-sharing plans will match some or all of your contribution, boosting your return substantially.) Or, if your employer doesn't offer such a plan, many mutual funds allow you to purchase shares through automatic monthly withdrawals from your checking account.

Occasionally, you may feel tempted to raid your savings to pay for some frivolous expense. To help you resist the siren call, the Skousens suggest that you *make it difficult to withdraw your savings.* An Individual Retirement Account (IRA) serves this purpose, since the government imposes a penalty tax if you make a premature withdrawal. Company profit-sharing plans, too, usually discourage withdrawals.

Another savings vehicle that gives you an incentive not to withdraw early is a deferred annuity. With a deferred annuity, any interest, dividends or capital gains aren't taxed as long as you leave them in the account. If you withdraw more than a small sum within the first few years, the insurance company that issued the annuity will generally charge you a 5 to 7 percent penalty. In addition, Uncle Sam socks you with a 10 percent penalty tax if you withdraw annuity funds before age 59 1/2.

One of the lowest-cost annuities I've seen lately is Guardian Life's *Value Guard II,* available through any local Guardian agent (for literature, call 800-221-3253, in N.Y., 800-522-7800). This annuity offers several investment options, including a money market fund, a bond fund and two stock funds. Minimum to open an account is only $500, and you can make additional contributions of $100 or more at any time. Since Value Guard imposes no sales charge, 100 percent of your money goes to work immediately.

Slash Your Mortgage in Half

Making extra payments on your home mortgage is a widely overlooked savings technique. Assume for a moment that you're Mr. and Mrs. Average American, buying an average newly built house for $120,000 (roughly the average price). You come forth with the average down payment of about $30,000 and you take out a fixed-rate mortgage for $90,000 at 10 percent for 30 years. Over the life of the loan, you'll pay a shocking $194,472 in interest. Your $120,000 house will have cost you $30,000 down, $90,000 loan principal, and $194,472 interest for a total of $314,472—more than two-and-a-half times the price you supposedly paid for the house! This is the miracle of compound interest, in reverse.

On the other hand, most lenders allow you to make optional prepayments of principal in addition to your required monthly payment. Every dollar of principal that you pay off early saves you interest and shortens the term of your mortgage. In our example, you can effectively earn 10 percent a year, compounded monthly, by making extra principal payments on your mortgage. Few investments as safe as your home boast such a high return.

Table 13.3 shows how much interest you can save—and how far ahead of schedule you can extinguish your mortgage—if you slip in a few extra dollars with your monthly mortgage payment. Once again, I'm assuming a $90,000 loan for 30 years at 10 percent. You'll see that if you make an extra optional payment each month of $150 or more, you'll cut your total interest cost over the life of the mortgage by half.

For some reason, this idea drives real estate agents wild. When I first intimated to readers of *Personal Finance* that they could slash their mortgage costs by prepaying some of the principal, I received almost a dozen letters from distraught realtors who had one objection or another to the plan. Of course, real estate agents aren't going to be pleased with a scheme that encourages people to stay put and pay off their debts rather than "trading up" every couple of years. After all, how does a realtor bring home the bacon?

Making extra payments on your mortgage won't benefit you if your mortgage was written years ago at a low interest rate (less than 8 percent, say). Furthermore, if you follow this program, your tax deduction for mortgage interest will slowly ebb away. That's a minor drawback, however, since the Tax Reform Act of 1986 has sharply curtailed the value of deductions by slashing the top tax bracket to 28 percent. Even if you expect to move within a few years, the extra principal payments you make now will increase the equity in your present home so that you'll probably qualify to buy a more expensive home next time.

Table 13.3 Prepayments of Home Mortgage Principal

The following table shows how you can pay off a 30-year mortgage of $90,000 with a fixed interest rate of 10 percent by making optional monthly payments.

Optional monthly payment	Time to pay off	Interest saved
$25	25 years 5 months	$36,387
50	22 years 5 months	58,538
100	18 years 7 months	86,201
150	16 years 1 month	103,428
200	14 years 3 months	115,466
300	11 years 9 months	131,483
500	8 years 9 months	149,120

Before you start paying down your mortgage, however, remember that you can't withdraw your money, except by selling the house or taking out a home-equity loan. Moreover, making optional payments doesn't free you to skip your regular payments—if you lose your job, for instance. Be sure to build up your holdings of liquid assets (Treasury bills, money funds and so on) before trying to bulldoze your mountain of mortgage debt.

In the 1970s, the heyday of borrow-and-spend, paying off your mortgage early wasn't chic. Thrift in general wasn't chic. (Did you ever see a *Time* magazine cover on "The Savings Boom"?) But, unnoticed by most people, high interest rates have been changing the economics of saving and spending. Savers are no longer the suckers—not when they can earn 8-10 percent on their money, with little risk, in a low-inflation environment.

Someday, the crowd will rediscover the virtues of saving, but probably not until *after* a nerve-wracking deflation has driven the prime rate back down to 2 or 3 percent. For now, however, only a minority of Americans—contrarians by instinct—recognize that saving, not borrowing, is the key to getting ahead in today's brave new financial world. If you grasp this insight, you'll undertake a systematic savings program and invest your savings in a liquid, well-diversified portfolio that reflects your taste for risk. With patience and persistence, you can bring your most cherished long-term financial goals within reach, whether your ambition is to buy a new home or a vacation hideaway, launch your own business, educate your children or enjoy retirement to the fullest.

Epilogue

It Pays to Be Contrary

I find more and more that it is well to be on the side of the minority, since it is always the more intelligent.—Johann Wolfgang von Goethe

Contrary thinking, as I've tried to show throughout this book, isn't some kind of negative philosophy for crackpots and cranks. Rather, being a contrarian encourages you to stretch your mind and envision possibilities that others don't yet see. Contrary thinking is really nothing more than *thinking for yourself*—one of the highest privileges granted to the human species.

Lower animals live almost entirely according to instinct. They eat, sleep, mate and migrate without reflecting on what they're doing. And, indeed, since human beings share some psychological characteristics with the rest of the animal kingdom, we often act on instinct, too—for better or for worse. Put us in a crowd, and we'll frequently yield to the emotions and impulses of the herd. As Humphrey Neill pointed out (and as every demagogue down through history has known), "A crowd never reasons, but follows its emotions; it accepts without proof what is 'suggested' or 'asserted.'"[1]

But a unique feature of our humanity is that we can also rise above the crowd. Individuals can reason. In Neill's words, "A 'crowd' thinks with its heart...while an individual thinks with his brain."[2] Unlike the other animals, we can ask *why* (or why not). It would never occur to a Canada goose and her gander, for example, to debate whether they should fly south for the winter. The herd instinct, a collective feeling, would decide for them. Human beings, on the other hand, can give you *reasons* why Miami or Toronto is a better place to spend the winter.

Contrary thinking is a philosophy that celebrates the value of the individual over against the undifferentiated masses. In a crowd, we feel driven to imitate others. We're afraid to be the oddball. Ironically, however, it's always the "intelligent minority"—the few individualists in the crowd—who set the pattern that the rest of the crowd follows. In 1964, the Beatles were the nonconformists who wore long hair when the masses of men preferred butches and flattops. By 1970, virtually *everybody* had changed styles. Long hair was no longer a mark of individuality but of conformity.

Thus, the essence of contrary thinking—and contrary investing—is to be a trend *setter*, rather than a trend *follower*. All the great trailblazers of history were contrarians who broke out of the narrow mind-set of their contemporaries (and often had to face ridicule or persecution for their trouble). Einstein was written off as a slow learner by his second-grade teacher. Dr. Jenner was attacked by mobs for vaccinating people against smallpox. Luther was excommunicated. Socrates was poisoned.

Of course, you may not go down in the history books as a hero or a genius like one of those luminaries. As an investor, your goal is more modest—to make money and keep it. But the route to investment success is the same course they charted:

- Think for yourself.

- Don't settle for pat answers.

- Challenge the conventional wisdom. Be skeptical of "experts."

- Look beyond the obvious.

- Steer away from fads.

- Control your emotions, especially fear and hope.

- When the truth is unpleasant, don't try to ignore it. Admit your mistakes while there's time to correct them. Beware of self-deception.

I can't guarantee that you'll make a fortune by adhering to these precepts, nor can I assure that you'll never suffer a loss. But these principles will give you a far better chance of investment success than all the academic degrees you can earn and all the computer programs you can buy. *Attitude* is everything!

What Is Stopping You?

Candidly, we must all admit that too often we unthinkingly embrace the opinions and prejudices of others, usually out of laziness, or a lack of courage or imagination. In the investment markets, we wait until we notice that others are making handsome profits before we buy (after prices have already gone up) and we wait until we observe that others are losing big money before we sell (after prices have already dropped).

In retrospect, our crowd following can make us look foolish, like the emperor who finally acknowledged to himself that he wasn't wearing any clothes. Why did so many of us buy stocks at the blowoff peak in August 1987 when we had refused to buy them at the panic bottom in August 1982? Why did others among us jump into gold at $850, only to sell in disgust at $300? Because we were allowing the crowd to do our thinking for us. We had set our minds on autopilot. Emotionally, it was easy to go along with what nearly everyone else seemed to be advising and doing. It was also a mistake.

To be a trend setter at a major market turning point is sometimes lonely and uncomfortable, even scary. (The more frightened you feel when going against the crowd, the better your investment decisions will probably turn out to be.) People will wonder why you're behaving so strangely, and you may need to deflect a few smirks and guffaws. But the contrary investor takes the joshing in stride because he knows that the odds are running strongly in his favor. In due time, his daring is likely to be vindicated—spectacularly. His goal is to remain cool, logical and detached when everyone else is fired up, irrational and obsessed with the day-to-day, hour-to-hour meanderings of the market. Although he may look crazy for the short term, he's confident that he'll enjoy the last laugh.

To prevent your confidence from melting at market extremes, you must *train yourself* in the habit of contrary thinking. For most of us, it doesn't come naturally, even though we can see the logic of a contrarian approach. Learn to treat bad news as good news, and vice versa: be cheerful after prices have fallen sharply (because the ultimate bottom is approaching) and grow cautious after prices have risen steeply (because the final peak is drawing near).

Remember that the degree of risk in the market is probably the opposite of what the crowd—and your emotions—are telling you. As the market approaches a low, the chances that a new buyer will lose money vanish to zero, even though most people are too frightened to buy. Likewise, as the market nears a top, the odds that a new buyer will lose money mount to 100 percent, even though most people are too greedy to sell.

Reading widely (and critically) can help you develop your own independent viewpoint. For the budding contrarian, I recommend that you pay special attention to books and periodicals that take an untrammeled, maverick approach to economics, the investment markets and human nature. The publications listed in the resources section at the end of this book will sweep the cobwebs out of your mind and give you a refreshing alternative to the dogmas you hear repeated daily in the mass media.

After you've practiced thinking "contrarily" for a while, you'll be amazed at how many fine investment opportunities (both buying and selling) present themselves throughout the year, every year. Crowds gather regularly in the stock market, the bond market, the commodity market, the metals market, the real estate market and every other market. If you know how to recognize the symptoms of crowd hysteria, a contrarian strategy can help you roll up profits in any market you choose.

A Strategy for All Seasons

The insights of contrary opinion apply to any type of investment, and any reasonably intelligent person can put them to work. But the greatest beauty of contrary thinking is that it never goes out of date. It's a philosophy you can take with you for a lifetime. Growth-stock fads may come and go. Gold may skyrocket, or crash and lie dormant for years. Depressions, inflations, wars, revolutions, elections and the like may transform the economic and political landscape. Yet, through it all, contrary thinking will keep you a step ahead of the crowd.

I'm not so naive as to suppose that all the contrary indicators discussed in this book will continue to send off reliable signals into the distant future. In fact, if too many people begin to pay attention to any particular indicator (such as the CBOE put-call ratio or the *Time* magazine cover theme), it will probably lose some of its effectiveness. (The markets always do whatever is necessary to frustrate the greatest number of investors!) As a result, contrary investors will be impelled from time to time to develop new barometers of crowd sentiment.

But you needn't worry that someday contrary thinking will cease to be profitable, allegedly because everyone will have become a contrarian. Human nature changes little, if at all, over the centuries. As long as the herd instinct is with us, people will tend to follow the leader—especially when the leader seems to know what the future holds. Groupthink is alive and well in today's society. If you doubt it, remember Cabbage Patch.

By reading, watching and listening critically, you'll begin to sense when a crowd is forming—when public opinion about economic or investment issues is becoming lopsided. "I know insanity when I see it" was how a California high tech executive described the price at which his company's stock went public a couple of years ago. (He shrewdly dumped huge blocks of shares near the 1983 peak.) You'll react the same way at important market turning points.

When calm, dispassionate analysis suggests to you that the market has gone crazy, you're probably right! *Don't* wait for others to reach the same conclusion. *Don't* wait to "see how it turns out." Run for the exits if the market is boiling with euphoria; back up the truck and buy if the market is frozen with panic.

The late Bernard Baruch, who lost millions but nevertheless survived the 1929 crash with most of his fortune, devised a brilliant two-part formula that a sane (but perplexed) investor can call to mind whenever the market seems to have gone daft. In the depths of the depression, Baruch wrote a new foreword for the 1932 edition of Charles Mackay's *Extraordinary Popular Delusions*. He said:

> *I have always thought that if, in the lamentable era of the "New Economics," culminating in 1929, even in the very presence of dizzily spiralling prices, we had all continuously repeated, "two and two still make four," much of the evil might have been averted. Similarly, even in the general moment of gloom in which this foreword is written, when many begin to wonder if declines will never halt, the appropriate abracadabra may be: "They always did."*

The next time some market pundit announces the dawning of a new era after prices have already soared, remind yourself that "two and two still make four"—that value still counts, and trees don't grow to the sky. By the same token, when the market is collapsing week after week and it seems that the declines will never end, reassure yourself: "They always did." There's always a bottom *somewhere*. If you learn to think about the markets with your head instead of your heart, you may yet overtake Bernard Baruch. Perhaps even J. Paul Getty.

Resources

The following books and newsletters are "cobweb sweepers" for the mind. While not all of the authors or publishers would formally label themselves contrarians, their independent-minded approach will help you develop a contrarian attitude toward the markets and life in general.

Books

• *America's Great Depression* by Murray N. Rothbard (Kansas City, Mo.: Sheed & Ward, 1975, $20 hardback*). An eye-opening economic history of the depression that lays the blame for the crash at the Federal Reserve's doorstep. Excellent discussion of the causes of the business cycle.

• *The Art of Contrary Thinking* by Humphrey Neill (Caldwell, Ida.: The Caxton Printers, 1980, $4.95 paperback+). Neill coined the term "contrary opinion" and first applied it to the investment markets. A work of genius.

• *The Bible.* The Old Testament prophets, such as Moses, Elijah, and Isaiah, furnish superb examples of men standing alone against the crowd. In the New Testament, Paul and, of course, Jesus are the most prominent contrarians. Christ's dictum in Matthew 7:13-14 is a gem of contrary thinking: "Go through the narrow gate. The gate is wide, and the way is broad, that leads to destruction, and many are going that way. But the gate is small, and the way is narrow, that leads to life, and only a few are finding it" (Beck, translator).

• *Contrary Opinion: How to Use It for Profit in Trading Commodity Futures* by R. Earl Hadady (Pasadena, Calif.: Hadady

*Available from the Ludwig von Mises Institute, 851 Burlway Rd., Burlingame, CA 94010. Postage $2.75 extra.

+ Available from Fraser Publishing, P.O. Box 494, Burlington, VT 05402. Postage $2 extra.

Publications, 1983, $37.50). The first systematic attempt to apply contrary thinking to futures trading.

• *The Crowd* by Gustave Le Bon (New York: Viking Press, $8.95 paperback). Classic study of the mass mind, written in the 1890s. You'll see the 1988 presidential campaign on every page.

• *Extraordinary Popular Delusions and the Madness of Crowds* by Charles Mackay (New York: Farrar, Straus & Giroux, $12.95 paperback). Cited at length in Chapter 2, this book chronicles such famous financial manias as the Dutch tulip craze, the South Sea Bubble and the Mississippi Company.

• *High Finance on a Low Budget* by Mark and JoAnn Skousen (Alexandria, Va.: KCI Communications Inc., 1987, $19.95). How to get off the borrow-and-spend treadmill and enjoy true financial security. Develops many of the themes in the Skousens' book, *Never Say Budget!* (now out of print).

• *Human Action* by Ludwig von Mises (Chicago: Henry Regnery Co., 1966, $49 hardback*). The greatest economic treatise of our time, by the greatest of free-market thinkers. Chapter 20 of Mises' book explains all you'll ever need to know about how inflationary government policies case and perpetuate the boom-bust cycle.

• *The Mystery of Banking* by Murray N. Rothbard (New York: Richardson & Snyder, 1983, $10 paperback+). Why today's fractional-reserve banking system is inherently unstable and inflationary.

• *Walden* by Henry David Thoreau (numerous editions). Life in the woods with America's foremost individualist.

Newsletters

• *Richard E. Band's Contrary Investing Letter* (7811

*Available from the Ludwig von Mises Institute, 851 Burlway Rd., Burlingame, CA 94010. Postage $2.75 extra.

+Available from Fraser Publishing, P.O. Box 494, Burlington, VT 05402. Postage $2 extra.

Montrose Rd., Potomac, MD 20854, $139 per year). Richard E. Band, editor. The only newsletter for contrarians that covers all major markets, from stocks and bonds to precious metals and real estate.

• *Analysis & Outlook* (P.O. Box 1167, Port Townsend, WA 98368, $78). R.W. Bradford, editor and publisher, is one of the few coin dealers who will advise you not only to buy rare coins but also to *sell* them.

• *Bank Credit Analyst* (3463 Peel St., Montreal, Que. H3A 1W7, $565). Edited by Dr. Anthony Boeckh, this is the Mercedes-Benz of independent advisory services. Boeckh and his colleagues began in late 1986 to warn of the danger of a stock market crash.

• *The Bullish Consensus* (P.O. Box 90490, Pasadena, CA 91109, $395). Edited by Earl Hadady. Weekly sentiment index for commodity futures (daily index also available via telephone hot-line), plus occasional commentary on economic issues.

• *The Contrary Investor* (P.O. Box 494, Burlington, VT 05402, $85). James L. Fraser, editor. Philosophical and humorous. Concentrates mostly on the stock market, but offers commentary on economic, social and political trends as well.

• *Deliberations* (P.O. Box 182, Adelaide St. Sta., Toronto, Ont. M5C 2J1, $215). Editor Ian McAvity combines technical analysis, fundamental analysis and contrary opinion to arrive at his views of the stock market, bonds, precious metals and currencies. Outstanding charts.

• *Elliott Wave Theorist* (P.O. Box 1618, Gainesville, GA 30503, $233). Robert Prechter, editor of this technically oriented letter, has made headlines with many of his controversial market forecasts. Whatever you may think of the Elliott Wave, his analysis of investor psychology is brilliant.

• *Growth Stock Outlook* (P.O. Box 9911, Chevy Chase, MD 20815, $175). Charles Allmon, editor. Only newsletter on growth stocks that has survived bull and bear markets for more than two decades.

• *Investors Intelligence* (P.O. 2046, New Rochelle, NY 10801,

$124). Michael Burke, editor. Publishes the original stock market sentiment index. News on insider trading, extensive quotations from a broad cross-section of market advisories.

• *Kondratieff Wave Analyst* (P.O. Box 977, Crystal Lake, IL 60014, $125). Donald D. Hoppe, editor. Hoppe is a skilled contrarian who has called many important market turns in stocks, bonds and metals. Especially recommended for history buffs; Hoppe frequently draws parallels with manias and crashes of the past.

• *Personal Finance* (1101 King St., Suite 400, Alexandria, VA 22314, $118 per year). The nation's largest investment newsletter. Articles by two dozen contributing editors in different areas of expertise. Strong contrarian flavor.

• *The Professional Tape Reader* (P.O. Box 2407, Hollywood, FL 33022, $275). Stan Weinstein, editor. Focuses on the stock market. Monitors a wide range of sentiment and momentum indicators.

Notes

Chapter 1

1. *Manchester Union Leader* (N.H.), Dec. 2, 1983.

Chapter 2

1. Ludwig von Mises, *Human Action* (Chicago: Henry Regnery Co., 1966). See especially chap. 20. For an easier introduction to the business cycle, see Murray N. Rothbard, *America's Great Depression* (Kansas City, Mo.: Sheed & Ward, 1975), chap. 1.

2. Charles Mackay, *Extraordinary Popular Delusions and the Madness of Crowds* (New York: L.C. Page & Co., 1932), p. 89. (Paperback edition still in print; see resources list, p. 244.)

3. Ibid., p. 94.

4. Ibid.

5. Ibid., p. 95.

6. Ibid., p. 94.

7. Ibid., p. 95.

8. Ibid.

9. Ibid., p.14.

10. Ibid., p. 19.

11. Ibid., p. 24.

12. Ibid., p. 50.

13. Ibid., p.52.

14. Ibid., p. 55.

15. Ibid., pp. 55-56.

16. *Growth Stock Outlook,* Oct. 15, 1983, p. 1.

17. John Kenneth Galbraith, *The Great Crash,* (Boston: Houghton Mifflin, 3rd ed., 1972), p. 15.

18. Ibid., p. 82, quoting from Frederick Lewis Allen, *Only Yesterday* (New York: Harper & Bros., 1931).

19. Ibid., p. 75.

20. Ibid., p. 31.

Chapter 3

1. Bruce Herschensohn, *The Gods of Antenna* (New Rochelle, N.Y.: Arlington House, 1975). Don Kowet kept up the drumfire against CBS in *A Matter of Honor* (New York: Macmillan, 1984), which detailed the network's unfair treatment of Gen. William Westmoreland, former commander of U.S. forces in Vietnam. A small encyclopedia could be written about the biases of current CBS News anchorman Dan Rather.

2. *Barron's,* Mar. 7, 1983.

3. *Fortune,* October 26, 1987.

4. *Barron's*, Jan. 5, 1987.

5. *The Wall Street Journal,* Oct. 4, 1974.

6. Ibid., Sept. 30, 1974.

7. Ibid., Dec. 6, 1974.

8. Ibid. Aug. 13, 1982.

9. Ibid.

10. *The New York Times,* Aug. 15, 1982.

11. *The Wall Street Journal,* Nov. 21, 1980.

12. Ibid., June 20, 1983.

13. Ibid.

14. Ibid., June 23, 1983.

15. Ibid., Jan. 17, 1980.

16. Ibid.

17. Ibid., Jan. 18, 1980.

18. *Western Mining News,* June 25, 1982.

19. *Barron's,* July 9, 1984.

20. Ibid., July 30, 1984.

Chapter 4

1. R. Earl Hadady, *Contrary Opinion: How to Use It for Profit in Trading Commodity Futures* (Pasadena, Calif.: Hadady Publications, 1983), p. 41.

2. Ibid., p. 42.

Chapter 5

1. Stocks purchased by chief executive officers do best; stocks sold by directors do worst. Kenneth Nunn et al., "Are Some Insiders More Inside Than Others?" *Journal of Portfolio Management,* Spring 1983.

Chapter 7

1. *The Wall Street Journal,* Dec. 7, 1987.

2. David Dreman, *Contrarian Investment Strategy* (New York: Random House, 1979; updated as *The New Contrarian Investment Strategy* in 1982).

3. Ibid., p. 245.

4. A book that offers guidance on how to recognize value in a bankrupt company is William J. Grace Jr., *The Phoenix Approach* (New York: Bantam Books, 1984).

5. Lowell Miller, *The Perfect Investment* (New York: E.P. Dutton, 1983). Currently available as a McGraw-Hill paperback.

Chapter 8

1. *Investor's Daily,* Oct. 4, 1988.

2. *The Wall Street Journal,* Oct. 14, 1988.

3. *Barron's,* Aug. 10, 1987.

4. *The Wall Street Journal,* Aug. 25, 1987.

Chapter 9

1. *The New York Times,* March 10, 1980.

2. *The Wall Street Journal,* Oct. 1, 1987.

3. Ibid., Oct. 15, 1987.

4. Ibid., May 9, 1988.

5. Between 1978 and 1987, according to Altman, high-yield ("junk") bonds produced an average total return of 13.2 percent a year, after adjusting for defaults, whereas long-term government bonds returned only 11.3 percent. See Altman's article, "Analyzing Risks and Returns in the High-Yield Bond Market," *American Association of Individual Investors Journal,* Feb. 1988.

Chapter 10

1. See *Stocks, Bonds, Bills and Inflation: 1988 Yearbook* (Chicago: Ibbotson Associates, 1988), p. 190.

Chapter 11

1. An excellent reference for readers who wish to study gold's long-term record as an inflation hedge is Prof. Roy Jastram's book, *The Golden Constant* (New York: John Wiley & Sons, 1977).

2. *The New York Times,* Apr. 28, 1987.

3. *The Wall Street Journal,* Apr. 7, 1987.

4. Though somewhat out of date, the best book ever written on investing in real estate—distressed or not—is probably William Nickerson, *How I*

Turned $1,000 into $3,000,000 in Real Estate in My Spare Time (New York: Simon & Schuster, 1980).

Chapter 12

1. The options exchanges publish a number of helpful booklets for budding speculators. For information on stock options, contact the Options Clearing Corp. (200 S. Wacker Dr., Chicago, IL 60606, 312-322-6200); bonds, the Chicago Board of Trade (La Salle at Jackson, Chicago, IL 60604, 312-435-3558); gold and silver, the Commodity Exchange Inc. (4 World Trade Center, New York, NY 10048, 212-938-2900); foreign currencies, the Philadelphia Stock Exchange (1900 Market St., Philadelphia, PA 19103, 215-496-5000).

2. A minor consolation when you're writing puts is that the price of the underlying asset (Sears stock, for instance) can never go below zero. Hence, your risk as a put writier is, in a sense, limited.

3. For a detailed discussion of options strategies, see Max G. Ansbacher, *The New Options Market* (New York: Walker & Co., 1987).

Chapter 13

1. A comprehensive reference on no-load funds is Sheldon Jacobs' annual *Handbook for No-Load Fund Investors,* available from The No-Load Fund Investor Inc. (P.O. Box 283, Hastings-on-Hudson, NY 10706). This book lists 10-year performance records for more than 500 funds, together with addresses, phone numbers, minimum investment, shareholder services (such as IRAs and telephone-redemption privileges) and a brief description of each fund's policies and objectives.

2. Mark and JoAnn Skousen, *Never Say Budget!* (Merrifield, Va.: Mark Skousen Books, 1983), Chapter 5.

Epilogue

1. Humphrey Neill, *The Art of Contrary Thinking* (Caldwell, Ida.: The Caxton Printers, 1980), p. 10.

2. Ibid., p. 3.

Index

A

Adam computer, 17
Aden sisters, 46
Advance-decline line, 144
Advanced Micro Devices, 92
Advisors, investment, 57, 71-72,
    224-225
Advisory sentiment, 60, 99
Aging population, 154
Allmon, Charles, 117, 122, 248
Alpha Strategy (Pugsley), 55
Altman, Edward, 162
American Eagle (gold coin), 189
American Gold News, 183
American Solar King, 18
America's Great Depression
    (Rothbard), 245
Amsterdam Stock Exchange, 22
Analysis & Outlook (newsletter), 247
Annuities, deferred, 234
Apple Computer, 2, 18, 39
Art of Contrary Thinking, The
    (Neill), 245
Asset-allocation strategy, 105-110
Associated Press, 148
Astute Investor, The (newsletter), 99
Atlantic, The (magazine), 138
Austrian school of economics, 19
Austrian 100 Coronas, 189
Avon Products, 47

B

Baby Boom generation, 154, 157
Babson, Roger W., 14, 75
Babson Enterprise, 107
Baker, James, 131
Bank Credit Analyst, The, 60-61, 247
Bank of England, 29
Bank liquidity, 137
Bard, L.R., 116

Barron's, 40, 45, 54, 70, 84, 85, 88,
    102, 143, 161, 164, 192
Baruch, Bernard, 21, 243-244
Batra, Ravi, 138
Bear markets, 9, 64-66, 92, 121,
    184; of 1973-74, 47
Bearish Sentiment Index, 58-59
Beatles; Beatlemania, 11, 240
Beckman, Robert C., 129
Bell, Alexander Graham, 2
Bell bonds, 148
Benham Certified Metals, 190
Benham Gold Index Trust, 193
Beyond Our Means (Malabre), 138
Bible, The, 245
Blanchard, James U. & Co., 189
Blanchard Precious Metals Fund,
    193
Bliss, A.T., 18
Blood in the Streets (Davidson), 138
Blunt, John, 29
Boeckh, Anthony, 247
Bolar Pharmaceutical, 116
Bonds, 67, 70, 148-149, 159, 169,
    171-172, 208, closed-end funds,
    164-166; corporate, 158-159, 162;
    futures, 161; junk, 161-164; long-
    term, 7; Treasury, 148, 158, 160,
    162, 165-166; U.S. savings, 167,
    179-181; yields, 149, 159, 227;
    zero coupon, 167-168, 228
Book value, company, 174
Boom and bust cycles, 18-21, 34-35
Bork nomination, 131
Bradford, R.W., 201, 247
Bretton Woods agreement, 194
Browne, Harry, 223
Bull markets, 9, 61, 64-66, 92, 121,
    184-185
Bullish Consensus (newsletter), 63-
    66, 71, 143, 161, 217, 247

Bullish Consensus poll, 63-65, 69, 186, 213, 217
Burke, Michael, 62, 248
Burnham Pacific Properties, 178
Bush, George, 139
Business Week, 39-41, 149, 185, 195

C

Cabbage Patch dolls, 12
Callahan Mining, 193
Call-put ratios, 87-90, 186, 213, 216
Capital Insights Inc., 209
Capital Preservation Fund, 180
Carolina Power & Light, 177
Carter, Jimmy; Carter administration, 138, 148, 169
Casey, Douglas, 44, 55
Cavelti, Peter, 193
Census Bureau, 155
Central Fund of Canada, 190-192
Certificates of Deposit (CDs), 132-133, 179
Charts, Chartists (see Technical Analysis)
Chevron, 119
Chicago Board of Trade; Options exchange, 88, 213
Chidester, William T., 117
Chrysler, 117, 122, 124
Citibank, 190
Citicorp, 126
Closed-end investment companies, 31
Coeur d'Alene Mines, 193
Cohen, Abraham W., 58
Coin dealers, 189
Coleco Industries, 17
Collectibles, 200-202
Columbia Special, 107
Comdisco, 18
Comex gold options, 213
Comex gold put-call ratio, 185, 188
Coming Currency Collapse, The, 55
Commodities, 63-67, 216-222, 227
Commodities futures, 216-219
Commonwealth Edison, 177
Companies, bankrupt, 122; dis-tressed, 122; dull, 117-119
Computer industry, 2
Computers, personal, 2, 183
Computer trading (program trading), 130
Consumer installment debt, 135
Consumer Price Index, 185
Conti, prince de, 25
ContiCommodity, 51-52
Continental Illinois Bank, 169, 224
Contrarian Investment Strategy (Dreman), 118
Contrary indicators, 80, 243
Contrary Investing (Band: first edition), 113
Contrary investors, contrarian thinking, 3-4, 8-10, 13-15, 42, 44-45, 52, 62, 67-71, 71, 79, 127-128, 142, 191, 205-206, 213, 222, 239-244
Contrary Investor, The (newsletter), 247
Contrary Opinion (Hadady), 245
Control Data, 92
Coolidge, Calvin, 32
Cornfeld, Bernie, 28
Corporate insiders, 80, 87, 124-127
Corporate interest expense, 151-152
Crash of 1929, 15, 18, 30
Crash of 1987, 33, 50, 71, 95, 126, 129-133, 136, 138-143, 151, 159, 161, 178, 204, 226
Credit expansion, 21
Crisis Investing (Casey), 55
Cromwell, Oliver, 171
Cronkite, Walter, 37
Crowd, The (Le Bon), 246
Crowd mentality, 3, 11-14, 42, 54, 242
Currencies, foreign, 194-197
Current Income Shares, 165

D

Davidson, James Dale, 138
Debt crisis, national, 134-135, 141
Deflation, 183, 232
Deliberations (newsletter), 247

Depression, Great, 30
Dessauer, John, 54
Digital Equipment, 126
Dines, James, 45-46, 113
Discount rate, 140
Diversification, 95, 232
Dividend yield, 103-106, 173, 210
Dollar, 40, 42, 43, 132, 137, 150,
    195-197
Dollar-cost averaging, 109
Dominion Resources, 176
Dow Jones Industrial Average, 6,
    30, 48-49, 75, 102, 114, 125, 129,
    142, 174
Dow Jones Utility Average, 40
Dreman, David, 118, 120-121, 128
Drexel Burnham Lambert, 50-51, 63
Dreyfus New Leaders, 107
DuPont, 126
Dutch guilder, 194
Dutch tulip mania, 21-24

E

Economy, U.S., 33, 142
E.F. Hutton & Co., 49
Einstein, Albert, 240
Elijah as a contrary thinker, 245
Eliot, T.S., 48
Elliott Wave Theorist (newsletter),
    16, 247
English, John Wesley, 200
European Common Market, 137
Evergreen Total Return, 108
Expense ratio, 96-97
Expert opinions
*Extraordinary Popular Delusions
    and the Madness of Crowds*
    (Mackay), 21, 244, 246
Exxon, 119

F

Family Dollar Stores, 116
Farmland, 198
Federal budget (deficit), 135,
    139-140, 152, 156
Federal deposit insurance agencies,
    136

Federal Reserve banks, board and
    system, 6, 30, 32-33, 131-134,
    137-138, 140, 144, 149-150, 166,
    169, 184, 194, 207, 245
Federal Reserve Bank of Cleveland,
    150
Federal Reserve Bank of Richmond,
    166
Fidelity High Income Fund, 164
Fidelity Select American Gold, 193
Financial World, 40
First Australia Prime Income Fund,
    165
First RepublicBank, 169
Fisher, Irving, 31
Forbes (magazine), 76, 121
Ford Motor Company, 120-121
Fort Dearborn Income Securities,
    165
Fortune (magazine), 39, 41-43, 195,
    224
Frank, Al, 117
Fraser, James L., 247
Fundamental analysis, 15
Futures Charts, 219
Futures contracts, 130-131

G

Gas and oil, 41
General Electric, 92
General Motors, 92, 126, 131
German mark, 194
Getty, J. Paul, 1, 48, 244
Getty Oil Company, 1, 3
Global Yield Fund, 165
GNMA certificates, 178
Goethe, Johann Wolfgang von, 239
Gold, 45-46, 50-54, 64-65, 70, 75,
    185-191, 218-220, 221, 227
Gold standard, 147
Goldinger, Jay, 209
Gramm-Rudman Law, 139, 156
Grant, W.T., 122
Granville, Joe, 44
Great Depression of 1990, The
    (Batra), 138

Great Lakes Chemical, 116
Green's Commodity Market Comments (newsletter), 204
Gross National Product (GNP), 140
Growth Fund Guide (newsletter), 104
Growth funds, 107-108
Growth Stock Outlook (newsletter), 117, 248
Guardian Life's *Value Guard II*, 234
Guardian Mutual, 108

H

Hadady, R. Earl, 63, 161, 213, 217, 245, 247
Hamilton, Alexander, 132
Hamilton, William P., 32
Harley, Robert, 26
Hasty Pudding Club, 11
Hayes, Rutherford B., 2
Hecla Mining, 193
Heine, Heinrich, 17
High Finance on a Low Budget (Skousen), 246
Holt, T.J., 210
Home Shopping Network, 211
Hoover, Herbert, 20
Hoppe, Donald J., 247
Housing starts, 140, 199
How to Be Rich (Getty), 1
How to Survive and Prosper During the Coming Bad Years (Ruff), 55
Hulbert Financial Digest, 117
Human Action (Mises), 246
Hutton, E.F. & Co.
Hysteria and unanimity, 44

I

Iacocca, Lee, 124
Ibbotson Associates of Chicago, 111
IBM, 2, 39, 92
INA Investment Securities, 165
Income investing, 147-148
Independence Square Income Securities, 165
Index of leading indicators, 140

Individual Retirement Account (IRA), 233-234
Inflation, 19-21, 23, 25, 29, 32, 62, 132, 137, 148-149, 159, 169, 171, 181, 183-185, 194-195, 202
Insider Indicator, 83
Insider trading, 80-84, 99, 124-127, 211
Insiders, The (newsletter), 84
Insiders Chronicle (newsletter), 84
Insider Transactions Report (newsletter), 84
Interest paid on debt, 153
Interest rates, 19, 62, 132-133, 148, 150-154, 159, 168, 169, 181, 208, 232, 236
International Cash Portfolios, 197
Interpublic Group, 116
Investor psychology, 8-10
Investor sentiment, 145, 188
Investor's Daily, 140
Investors Intelligence (newsletter), 58-63, 71, 91, 143, 248
IRA (see Individual Retirement Account)
Isaiah as a contrarian, 245

J

Jacobs, Sheldon, 95
Japanese yen, 194
Jenner, William, 240
Jesus as contrarian, 245
Jobs, Steven, 2
J.W. English Real Estate Inc., 200

K

Kansas City Power and Light, 177
Kelly Services, 116
Kentucky Utilities, 176
Kerschner, Edward, 109
Kipling, Rudyard, 233
Kondratieff Wave Analyst (newsletter), 247
Krugerrands, 52, 54

L

Laidlaw-Coggeshall Inc., 47
Law, John, 24
Lawson Products, 116
Le Bon, Gustave, 246
Legg Mason Special, 108
Legg Mason Wood Walker, 39
Leverage, 30, 135, 152-153, 203,
    208, 211-212
Leveraged buyouts, 140
Lexington Goldfund, 193
Liberty Coin Service, 189, 201
Liquidity, 179
Lockheed, 126
Louis XIV, 24
Ludwig von Mises Institute, 245-246
Luther, Martin, 240

M

M1 money supply, 134
Mackay, Charles, 21-22, 25, 28, 244,
    246
Malabre, Alfred L. Jr., 138
Maple Leaf (gold coin), 189
Margin, stocks and bonds, 30, 135,
    203-204, 207-209
Marine Midland Bank, 47
Market Laboratory (Barron's), 84-
    86, 102
Market Vane (newsletter), 63
Market timing, 76-80, 91-92
Markets, boom-bust cycle, 18-21;
    breadth, 144; cycle, 145;
    corrections, 10, 13; momentum,
    219, 221; mood, 8, 15, 57, 144;
    psychology, 5, 8-10, 16; timing,
    107, 121; trend, 53, 68, 79, 217;
    turning points, 55, 241
Mass media, 37, 92
Matthew, The Gospel According to,
    111, 245
Maugham, W. Somerset, 57
McAvity, Ian, 247
Measurex Corp., 116
Member-short ratio, 84, 86-87
Merrill Lynch, 63, 120-121

Miller, Adolph C., 30
Miller, Lowell, 123-124
Mining stocks, 41, 187-189
Mises, Ludwig von, 19
Mississippi Company, The, 21, 24
Mobil, 119
Molex Inc., 116
Money-supply growth, 140, 144
Money (magazine), 41
Money and credit supply, 32
Money market deposit accounts
    (MMDAs),
Money market funds and accounts,
    179-181, 226
Montgomery, Paul Macrae, 39
Mortgages, 234-236
Moses as contrarian, 245
Mutual funds, 79, 90-110, 232
Mutual Shares (mutual fund), 105,
    108, 123
Mystery of Banking, The (Rothbard),
    23, 246

N

National Association of Real Estate
    Investment Trusts, 178
National debt (U.S.), 134-138
National Debt, The (Malkin), 138
National Securities Corp., 194
Neill, Humphrey, 11, 67, 239, 246
Never Say Budget! (Skousen), 233,
    246
New England Electric, 177
New Plan Realty Trust, 179
New York Commodity Exchange
    (Comex), 51
New York State Electric and Gas,
    177
New York Stock Exchange (NYSE),
    49-50, 76, 96, 118-119, 126,
    129-130
New York Times, The, 38, 42, 49,
    160, 186, 195
Newsweek, 39, 54
Newton, Isaac, 17

Nixon, Richard M.; Nixon adminis-
tration, 138, 150, 169, 194
Nordson Corp., 116
Norman, Montagu, 30
Nuclear power industry, utilities,
176
Nurock, Robert, 99
NYSE (see New York Stock
Exchange)

O

Office buildings, 198
Options, 87-90, 99, 204, 211-216,
214-216
Orange & Rockland Utilities, 176
Osborne Computer, 211

P

Pacific Gas and Electric, 177
PacifiCorp, 176
Paine Webber Asset Allocation
Fund, 109-110
Panic of '89, The (Erdman), 138
Paul as contrarian, 245
Payroll deduction plans, 233
P/E ratio (see Price-Earnings ratio)
Penn Central, 122
Pennington, Edward and Leanna, 12
People (magazine), 41
Perfect Investment, The (Miller), 123
Personal Finance (newsletter), 40,
45, 124, 133, 160, 201, 218
Personal Portfolio Manager, 117
Peterson, Peter G., 138
Pogue, Jerry, 194
Polaroid, 47
Polls, polling, 57
*Poor's Weekly Business and
Investment Letter*, 32
Pradilla, Charles, 109
Prechter, Robert R., Jr., 45, 247
Precious metals, 77 (see also Gold
and Silver)
Price-dividend ratio, 105-106, 110
Price-earnings (P/E) ratio, 102-104,
118, 120, 210
Prudent Speculator, The, 117

Pugsley, John A., 55
Purchasing-power parity (PPP), 196-
197
Putnam, George III, 123

Q

Quality ratio, 162-163

R

Radio Corp.; RCA, 30
Rare coins, 227
Reagan, Ronald, Reagan
administration, 20, 132, 184, 198
Real estate, 77, 197-200, 227, 234-
236; California real estate
speculators, 22; investment
trusts (REITs), 177-179, 198;
limited partnerships, 200
Recession, 33, 141-142, 162, 198
Rees-Moog, 138
Reynolds Securities, 48
Risk and return, 225-227
Risk profile, 228-231
RJR Nabisco, 140
Rogers, Will, 37
Roosevelt, Franklin D., 147
Rose & Co., 168
Rothbard, Murray N., 23, 32, 245
Rouleau, Walter, 104-105
Royal Trust Bank (Austria), 197
Royal Trust Company, 197
Ruff, Howard, 55
Rukeyser, Louis, 99

S

Sage, Russel, 2
Saint-Gaudens, 201
Sam Sloat Coins, 189
Savings and spending habits, 232-
234
SCEcorp, 177
Schultz, Harry, 54
Scudder Gold Fund, 193
Securities and Exchange
Commission (SEC), 28
Selling climax, 48
Shakespeare, William, 75

Shearson Lehamn Bros., 63
Short selling, 76-77, 209-211, 220
Silver, silver market, 50-53, 190-
192, 226-227
Skousen, Mark and JoAnn, 233, 246
Smith, Jerome, 55
Social Security, 156-158, 232
Socrates, 240
Solon the Athenian, 183
Sosnoff, Martin, 111
South African kaffirs, 192
South Sea Bubble, 21, 26-29
Southern Company, 177
Speculation, speculators, 22, 26, 32,
87, 88, 124, 135, 187, 203-212,
214-215, 221-222
Stahl, Charles, 204
Standard & Poor's 500, 100-104,
112, 118-119, 168, 172, 178
State Mutual Securities, 165
Stearns, Bear, 160
Stochastic oscillator, 219
Stocks, 111, 172-173; bank, 120;
blue chips, 114-115; cyclical, 120-
121; distressed, 122-124; funds,
61, 77, 101; growth, 116; low P/E,
121; small, 107, 111-115; yields,
227
Stock market, 6
Stock market timing, 107
Swiss bank account, 227
Swiss franc, 194
Sysco Corp., 116

T

T. Rowe Price Equity Income, 108
T. Rowe Price High Yield Fund, 164
T. Rowe Price New Horizons Fund,
112-113
Tampa Electric, 173
Tandy Corp., 92
Technical analysis, 15-16, 44, 72,
206
Technical Market Index, 99
Texaco, 119
Texas Utilities, 173
Thoreau, Henry David, 246

Time (magazine), 39, 54, 232, 236
Toronto Stock Exchange, 41
Toys "R" Us, 122
Treasury (U.S.), 157, 184
Treasury bills, 210, 216, 228
Treasury bonds (see Bonds)
Turnaround Letter, 122
Twentieth Century Growth (mutual
fund), 106

U

United Dominion Realty Trust, 179
USA Today, 149
USLIFE Income Fund, 165
U.S.-Candian free trade pact, 137
U.S. News and World Report, 144
U.S. stamps, 227
U.S. Steel, 92
Utilities, stocks, 40, 123, 173-177

V

Value Line Inc., 87
Value Line Composite Index, 114
Value Line Corporate Stock Index
Value Line Investment Survey, 115,
119
Vanguard Municipal Bond Fund,
164
Vanguard Specialized Portfolios—
Precious Metals, 193
Vanguard Treasury Bond Portfolio,
166
Vestaur Securities, 165
Volcker, Paul, 33, 138, 194

W

Walden (Thoreau), 246
Wall Street analysts, 15
Wall Street Journal, The, 4, 32, 38,
42, 47-51, 54, 88, 113, 142-143,
148, 160-162, 186, 192, 196
Wall Street Week (TV), 48, 99
Wall Street Week Index, 99-101, 110
Walpole, Robert, 27
Wang Laboratories, 93
Warrants, 124
Washington, George, 195

Washington Post, The, 195
Waterfall decline, 48
Weingarten Realty, 179
Westergaard, John, 113
Western Mining News, 51
Westinghouse, 126
Wisconsin Public Service, 176
Windsor Fund, 108

Worthington Industries, 116
Wright, Jim, 183

Y

Yield comparisons table, 162
Yield curve, 133, 209
Yuppies, 142, 154-155